CHICKEN SOUP FOR THE
HORSE LOVER'S SOUL

CHICKEN SOUP FOR THE HORSE LOVER'S SOUL

Inspirational Stories About Horses and the People Who Love Them

Jack Canfield
Mark Victor Hansen
Marty Becker, DVM
Gary Seidler
Peter Vegso
Theresa Peluso

Health Communications, Inc.
Deerfield Beach, Florida

www.hcibooks.com
www.chickensoup.com

We would like to acknowledge the many publishers and individuals who granted us permission to reprint the cited material. (Note: The stories that were written by Jack Canfield, Mark Victor Hansen, Marty Becker, Gary Seidler, Peter Vegso or Theresa Peluso are not included in this listing.)

The Racking Horse. Reprinted by permission of Rhonda Reese. ©1999 Rhonda Reese.

A Rocky Rescue. Reprinted by permission of Diane M. Ciarloni. ©2002 Diane M. Ciarloni.

Cowboy Heart. Reprinted by permission of Roger Dean Kiser. ©2002 Roger Dean Kiser.

Shadow. Reprinted by permission of T.C. Wadsworth. ©1999 T.C. Wadsworth.

Old Twist. Reprinted by permission of Tom Maupin. ©2002 Tom Maupin.

A Silent Bond. Reprinted by permission of Tiernan McKay. ©2003 Tiernan McKay.

Daddy Always Said "Yes" to Horses. Reprinted by permission of Teresa Becker. ©2002 Teresa Becker.

(Continued on page 412)

Library of Congress Cataloging-in-Publication Data

Chicken soup for the horse lover's soul : inspirational stories about horses and the people who love them / Jack Canfield . . . [et al.].
    p. cm.
ISBN-13: 978-0-7573-0098-1 (tp)
ISBN-10: 0-7573-0098-7 (tp)
    1. Horses—Anecdotes. 2. Horse owners—Anecdotes. 3. Human-animal relationships—Anecdotes. I. Canfield, Jack, 1944–

SF301.C47 2003
636.1—dc21

2003056627

Publisher: Health Communications, Inc.
          3201 S.W. 15th Street
          Deerfield Beach, FL 33442-8190

R-11-06

Cover design by Andrea Perrine Brower
Inside formatting by Lawna Patterson Oldfield

We dedicate this book to the
legions of people who have loved
and cared for God's most noble
and beautiful creature: the horse.

This book is also dedicated to
Anne, Melinda and Hayley Vegso.

To those whose passion for horses
never falters including:
Farm Manager, Chuck Patton,
Trainers: Ben Cecil, Barry Croft, Phil Gleaves,
Duane Knipe and Bill Mott, and to all of
the exercise riders, grooms and jockeys who care.

Contents

3. THESE AMAZING ANIMALS

4. HORSES AS HEALERS

Acknowledgments

We began working on this book in 2002, the Chinese "Year of the Horse." A culture with thousands of years of experience certainly can't be ignored and we took the inspiration to heart. Actually accomplishing the task of publishing this book, while enjoying our families and juggling demanding careers, requires the support and resilience of many people.

Our spouses: Inga, Patty, Teresa, Lana, Anne and Brian. None of it matters without you. Our children, Christopher, Travis, Riley, Oran, Kyle, Elisabeth, Melanie, Mikkel, Lex, Mandy, Oliver, Robert, Melinda and Hayley—we do it all *for you.*

The talented, enthusiastic staff, free-lancers and interns who support each one of us at Chicken Soup for the Soul Enterprises, Self Esteem Seminars, Mark Victor Hansen and Associates, Pet Complex, P.A., and Health Communications. You are the people who keep the wheels turning smoothly every day without fail, and we know it!

Our volunteer readers, who took time from busy schedules and hectic lives, to read and evaluate stories in the preliminary manuscript. Their feedback helped us select the stories you are about to enjoy and their comments assisted us in making each story the best it could be: Lynn Allen, Judy Askins, Nancy Autio, Teresa Becker, Kathy Brennan-Thompson, D'ette Corona, James Davis, Sandy Dolan, Rachel Doyle, Dorothy and Gene Drucker, Randee Feldman, Paola Fernandez, Barbara Kerr, Jeanette Larson, Barbara

Lomonaco, Heather McNamara, Kerri Meritt, Colleen Moulton, Sarah Newman, Linda Patton, Tom Persechino, Diana Pulice, Melody Rogers-Kelly, Crystal Ruzicka, Brianne Schwabauer, Portia Stewart, Laura and Naomi Sullwold, Susan Tobias, Mindy Valcarcel, Danene Van Hecker, Casie Welcker, Jeanie Winstrom.

We received nearly 2,000 stories for consideration in this book. That would not have been possible without the people who reached out to their communities and made them aware of the project, from individual folks speaking to each other in chat rooms and newsgroups, to the associations and media that serve this industry so effectively. Although a complete list would exhaust available space, we do want to recognize a few: Tom Persechino from the American Quarter Horse Association and *America's Horse* magazine, Ron Fuller, DVM, and the Ohio Quarter Horse Association, Carol Holden and Sam Huff, John Mooney, President of the Maryland-Virginia Racing Circuit, Inc., Betsy Parker of *Thoroughbred Times*, Eric Wing and his folks at the National Thoroughbred Racing Association, Kristin Ingwell and Lenny Shulman at *The Blood-Horse* magazine, the members of the American Horse Publishers group, JoAnn Guidry and *Florida Horse* magazine, the *Back Country Horsemen of America* magazine, Portia Stewart at *Veterinary Economics*, Debie Ginsburg and The California Thoroughbred Owners and Breeders Association, Boots Reynolds and *Western Horseman* magazine.

Many people have helped us along the way, and we are certain to have neglected to mention everyone by name, however it in no way diminishes our appreciation for their support.

And lastly, *but most importantly,* thank you to everyone who submitted a story. The response was wonderful and the competition keen. You shared cherished memories, relived sad moments, celebrated great partnerships and honored treasured friends. We deeply appreciate your letting us into your lives and we regret that everyone's story could not be represented here. We hope what was chosen for publication conveys what was in your heart and in some way also tells *your* story.

Introduction

As our ancestors sat cross-legged around fires in caves for warmth and protection, the rhythmic pounding of wild horses' hooves broke the silence. The thundering sound echoed across time and space.

Primitive cave art in Lascaux, France and classic stories of horses carrying Roman legions, Spanish invaders, and Native Americans to war contrast with modern images of horses racing across our television sets carrying the Lone Ranger, Roy Rogers and Ben Cartwright. Mounted horse racing was popular in the Greek Olympics almost 700 years before Christ. Today, tapes of 4-H shows are re-played in living rooms and photo finishes are simulcast at racetracks around the country.

Mourned by warriors, immortalized by Hollywood and cherished by little girls, the special relationship between mankind and horses not only exists historically, it still flourishes today. The magic of the relationship between horse and human lies not in its strength and longevity; it lies in the mystery of how two different species can be drawn so closely to one another.

Watch as a little girl, only a hock high, holds an apple in her hand as this massive animal takes it gingerly into its mouth. So delicate she is, in contrast to the horse's massive size and strength. The eternal instinct to flee is subdued as a rider climbs onto a horse's back; a position this prey animal should find threatening, yet there is no fear, only a mutual shared trust.

In a marvelously symbiotic relationship, horses give humans speed, stamina and strength, while we provide them with a steady food supply and protection from predators.

We have shared a destiny for thousands of years as the horse's role in our lives has changed from utilitarian to one of emotion and pleasure. Within the past hundred years, horses were as much a part of our daily lives as our cars and tractors are today. Long before airplanes and cell phones, the horse had become integral to our very existence and ability to communicate, as it not only moved faster and farther than almost any animal, it could and would carry a human upon its back. For early man, the experience of riding was as close to flying as he could possibly get.

Horses manifest an extraordinary sense of fun, frivolity and joy. Good old-fashioned "horse play" is an essential part of a horse's daily life; something we humans would do well to mimic. Many of us come home from work feeling like a human piñata—beaten but not quite broken—slip on our boots and head for the barn where we bury our heads in our horses and take in their aroma. Sharing time with a horse elevates senses, expands awareness and amplifies this thing called life.

Horse lovers scrimp on groceries so our horses can eat the best. We won't go to the doctor if we're flat on our back in bed, yet we call the vet if our horse has the equivalent of a cold. This dedication and commitment is rewarded by a soft nicker, a gentle ruff of breath, the quiet reassurance of a neck to cradle, a flawless dressage move, a fluid jump, a record-breaking time around the barrels or a blue ribbon from the county fair. That's all a horse lover needs.

For all their strength, horses can touch with amazing gentleness. For all their speed, they can gloriously harness their "stay apparatus" and stand three legged for hours in the sun. For their size as the largest domesticated animal, they allow waiflike riders to control them with simple pressure of a leg. It is in these amazing contradictions that we find ourselves lost in the mystery of the bond between our two species.

Saying good-bye to one of these magnificent animals causes us to reflect on this partnership. While we find it brimming with warm memories, we grieve for their loss as we would for any other family member. These themes of extreme sadness and joy were shared in many of the stories we considered for this book.

The stories in *Chicken Soup for the Horse Lover's Soul* were selected to give you a richer, deeper understanding of the bond between humans and horses. You will find stories so moving that they will test the limits of your tear ducts while others will have you laughing out loud or running to give your horse a hug and a treat. Other stories shine an illuminating light on the horse's unique versatility, intelligence and intuitiveness; or their strength, stamina and athletic prowess. You will welcome new foals and say good-bye to others. But, when all is said and done, that mysterious spell cast upon little boys and girls by ponies and stories like *Black Beauty* still cannot be explained. The mystery isn't meant to be solved, but enjoyed.

Ranchhands to city slickers, rodeo queens to seniors who never lost their love for horses, will see themselves saddling up in the stories of *Chicken Soup for the Horse Lover's Soul*. As you read, no doubt you'll be reacquainted with old friends, recall sad and happy experiences, or decide to delight someone with a gift that they will beam upon receiving.

Happy tales and happy trails.

1

A SPECIAL BOND

Somewhere in time's Own Space
  There must be some sweet pastured place
  Where creeks sing on and tall trees grow
  Some Paradise where horses go,
  For by the love that guides my pen
  I know great horses live again.

Stanley Harrison

The Racking Horse

A horse is worth more than riches.

Spanish Proverb

The first time Bart told me about his horse Dude, I knew their bond had been something special. But I never suspected that Dude would deliver a wonderful gift to me.

Growing up on a 100-year-old family farm in Tennessee, Bart loved all animals. But Dude, the chestnut-colored Quarter Horse that Bart received when he turned nine, became his favorite. Years later when Bart's father sold Dude, Bart grieved in secret.

Even before I met and married Bart, I knew all about grieving in secret, too. Because of my dad's job, our family relocated every year. Deep inside, I wished we could stay in one place where I could develop lasting friendships. But I never said anything to my parents. I didn't want to hurt them. Yet sometimes I wondered if even God could keep track of us the way we moved from place to place.

One summer evening in 1987, as Bart and I glided on our front-porch swing, my husband suddenly blurted out, "Did I ever tell you that Dude won the World Racking Horse Championship?"

"Rocking horse championship?" I asked.

"Racking," Bart corrected, smiling gently. "It's a kind of dancing that horses do. Takes lots of training. You use four reins to guide the horse. It's pretty hard." Bart gazed at the pasture. "Dude was the greatest racking horse ever."

"Then why'd you let your dad sell him?" I probed.

"I didn't know he was even thinking about it," Bart explained. "When I was seventeen, I started a short construction job down in Florida. I guess Dad figured I wouldn't be riding anymore, so he sold Dude without even asking me. Running a horse farm means you buy and sell horses all the time, and that's what Dad did.

"I've always wondered if that horse missed me as much as I've missed him. I've never had the heart to try to find him. I couldn't stand knowing if something bad . . ." Bart's voice trailed off.

After that, few nights passed without Bart mentioning Dude. My heart ached for him. I didn't know what to do. Then one afternoon while I walked through the pasture, a strange thought came to me. In my heart, a quiet voice said, "Lori, find Dude for Bart."

How absurd! I thought. I knew nothing about horses, certainly not how to find and buy one. That was Bart's department.

The harder I tried to dismiss the thought, the stronger it grew. I did not dare mention it to anyone except God. Each day I asked him to guide me.

On a Saturday morning three weeks after the first "find Dude" notion, a new meter reader, Mr. Parker, stopped by while I was working in the garden. We struck up a friendly conversation. When he mentioned he'd once bought a horse from Bart's dad, I interrupted.

"You remember the horse's name?" I asked.

"Sure do," Mr. Parker said. "Dude. Paid $2,500 for him."

I wiped the dirt from my hands and jumped up, barely catching my breath.

"Do you know what happened to him?" I asked.

"Yep. I sold him for a good profit."

"Where's Dude now?" I asked. "I need to find him."

"That'd be impossible," Mr. Parker explained. "I sold that horse years ago. He might even be dead by now."

"But could you . . . would you . . . be willing to try to help me find him?" After I explained the situation, Mr. Parker stared at me for several seconds. Finally, he agreed to join the search for Dude, promising not to say anything to Bart.

Each Friday for almost a year, I phoned Mr. Parker to see if his sleuthing had turned up anything. Each week his answer was the same: "Sorry, nothing yet."

One Friday I called Mr. Parker with another idea. "Could you at least find one of Dude's babies for me?"

"Don't think so," he chuckled. "Dude was a gelding."

"That's fine," I said. "I'll take a gelding baby."

"You really *do* need help." Mr. Parker explained that geldings are unable to reproduce. Then he seemed to double his efforts to help. Several weeks later, he phoned me on a Monday.

"I found him," he shouted. "I found Dude!"

"Where?" I said, wanting to jump through the phone.

"On a farm in Georgia," Mr. Parker said. "A family bought Dude for their teenage son. But they can't do anything with the horse. In fact, they think Dude's crazy. Maybe dangerous. Bet you could get him back real easy."

Mr. Parker was right. I called the family in Rising Fawn, Georgia, and made arrangements to buy Dude for $300. I struggled to keep my secret until the weekend. On Friday, I met Bart at the front door after work.

"Will you go for a ride with me?" I asked in my most persuasive voice. "I have a surprise for you."

"Honey," Bart protested, "I'm tired."

"Please, Bart. I've packed a picnic supper. It'll be worth the ride, I promise."

Bart got into the Jeep. As I drove, my heart beat so fast that I thought it would burst as I chatted about family matters.

"Where are we going?" Bart asked after thirty minutes.

"Just a bit farther," I said.

Bart sighed. "Honey, I love you. But I can't believe I let you drag me off."

I didn't defend myself. I'd waited too long to ruin things now. However, by the time I steered off the main highway onto a gravel road, Bart was so annoyed that he wasn't speaking to me. When I turned from the gravel road to a dirt trail, Bart glared.

"We're here," I said, stopping in front of the third fence post.

"Here where? Lori, have you lost your mind?" Bart barked.

"Stop yelling," I said. "Whistle."

"What?" Bart shouted.

"Whistle," I repeated. "Like you used to . . . for Dude. Just whistle. You'll understand in a minute."

"Well . . . I. . . . This is crazy," Bart sputtered as he got out of the Jeep.

To humor me, Bart whistled. Nothing happened.

"Oh, God," I whispered. "Don't let this be a mistake."

"Do it again," I prodded.

Bart whistled once more, and we heard a sound in the distance. What was it? I could barely breathe.

Bart whistled again. Suddenly over the horizon, a horse came at a gallop. Before I could speak, Bart leaped over the fence.

"Dude!" he yelled, running toward his beloved friend. I watched the blurs of horse and husband meet as if they were performing in one of those slow-motion reunion scenes on television. Bart hopped up on his pal, stroking his mane and patting his neck.

Immediately, a sandy-haired, tobacco-chewing teenage boy and his huffing parents crested the hill.

"Mister, what are you doing?" the boy yelled. "That horse is crazy. Can't nobody do nothing with him."

"No," Bart boomed. "He's not crazy. He's Dude."

To everyone's amazement, at Bart's soft command to the unbridled horse, Dude threw his head high and began racking. As the horse pranced through the pasture, no one spoke. When Dude finished dancing for joy, Bart slid off him.

"I want Dude home," he said.

"I know," I replied with tears in my eyes. "All the arrangements have been made. We can come back and get him."

"Nope," Bart insisted. "He's coming home tonight."

I phoned my in-laws and soon they arrived with a horse trailer. We paid for Dude and headed home.

Bart spent the night in the barn. I knew he and Dude had a lot of catching up to do. As I looked out of the bedroom window, the moon cast a warm glow over the farm. I smiled, knowing that my husband and I now had a wonderful story to tell our future children and grandchildren.

"Thank you, Lord," I whispered. Then the truth hit me. I'd searched longer for Dude than I'd ever lived in one place. God had used the process of finding my husband's beloved horse to renew my trust in the friend who sticks closer than a brother.

"Thank you, Lord," I whispered again as I fell asleep. "Thank you for never losing track of Dude—or me."

Lori Bledsoe as told to Rhonda Reese

A Rocky Rescue

The Lord was ever present in Mama's daily life. So it was natural for her to invoke his assistance for any task that proved difficult—from the piddling ones that hardly seemed to require divine intervention to those that were knottier and more difficult to resolve. I can remember being no more than seven or eight years old and watching her as she pitted all the strength of her five-foot-tall body into popping the lid from a jar of canned green beans. It wouldn't budge.

Mom stopped and sighed. Then holding the stubborn jar in her left hand, she raised her eyes heavenward and said, "Lord, I'd like to feed these beans to my family for dinner, but I need your help in getting this lid off. Thank you, Lord."

Her tone was reverential and totally respectful, but the little prayer was delivered in an attitude of one friend talking to another. Matter of fact. Affectionate. But, most importantly, confident of receiving an answer.

Mom lowered her eyes and put her right hand on the lid. She gave a twist and off it came, so easily that it appeared oiled.

I can remember being impressed, even as a youngster, by Mom's faith. I believed in her and I believed in God, but for whatever reasons, I just couldn't muster up that closeness to him that she enjoyed. There were times when I wondered how in the world she could talk so much to someone she'd never seen. I asked her about it once, and she told me she had seen him. Of course, she went on to explain that she saw him in the flowers and trees and stars and in a host of his other creations. That was fine, but it wasn't what I had in mind.

Mom didn't read the Bible a lot, but curiously she managed to find various passages relating to horses. You see, I was a horse nut and I had my very own big, black, wonderful Tennessee Walker. His name was Bob's Merry Legs and he was far more than just a horse. He was a friend. He listened to all of the secret things that welled up inside my heart. The broad white blaze on his face caught my tears. His ears moved back and forth as he strained to catch every syllable that I uttered to him. Mom knew that if there was any way to reach me with God, it was through horses.

So she read to me passages from Job, with the Lord speaking of the horse's might and majesty. She told me how Jesus would come back one day and he'd be riding a big white horse as all of his saints rode horses behind him. I could envision the scene. It made my heart beat faster and my pulse race with excitement. I imagined an even grander cavalcade, with angels on horses, their robes flowing downward over the animals strong withers and backward across their muscled rumps. Then when I went outside with Bob, I pictured him in heaven and thought Jesus might be proud to ride him.

Every morning that there was school, I got out of bed, dressed, ate breakfast and went outside to visit with Bob before catching the yellow bus that I rode for a total of three hours each day. One morning I went through my routine and then headed for the barn, snatching some sugar cubes as I passed the kitchen counter. I went out the back door, whistling and calling for my friend. His routine was as predictable as mine. He would hear my whistle and call, look out the barn door and then come romping into the paddock to whinny and hang his head over the fence. This particular morning, however, something was wrong. There was no Bob. I panicked.

"Bob?" I called again. I opened the paddock gate and went into the barn. He wasn't there. I went back to the paddock and from the angle of the barn doorway, I spotted the problem. There was a section of fence down and Bob obviously had wandered off. I was frightened.

I ran back to the house and told Mom that I wouldn't be going to school—a rather presumptuous announcement for a ten-year-old fifth-grader.

"What are you talking about?" she asked.

"Bob's missing."

She didn't repeat what I'd said. Mom was like that. In a crisis, she always had an immediate grasp of the situation.

"I'll go get Daddy," she responded. "You wait here."

I could hardly stand still. My best friend was out there somewhere. I knew it would take Mom only a few minutes to drive to the field where Daddy was working in the cotton. That's where I was raised: on a 100-acre cotton farm that was crisscrossed with dozens of dirt roads. Bob and I knew all of them.

It seemed like forever, but no more than ten minutes could have passed when Daddy pulled into the backyard in his truck with Mom behind in her car.

Mom got out. Daddy didn't. He yelled for me to get in the truck. I did and he started driving.

We covered those dirt roads, but there was no Bob. Daddy was trying not to show it, but I knew he was getting worried. Suddenly, he said, "I'm going across the main dirt road to Mr. Rogers' place." There was something about the way he said it that made my skin prickle. I can still remember the feeling.

We crossed the main road and headed toward a huge gravel pit. Daddy stopped a safe distance from the rim and we got out. We looked down and there, appearing very small, was Bob. I immediately started to cry as if my heart had broken.

Knowing that tears wouldn't help Bob, I wiped my eyes, hiccupped three or four times, edged closer to the rim of the gravel pit and looked down. I could see that Bob's right rear foot was cocked off the ground so that it was bearing no weight—a sure sign that it was injured. There was no use asking or even wondering how or why he'd gotten into the pit. The only concern was getting him out.

We lived in a tiny, rural community. There were no such things as rescue helicopters or even much in the way of emergency assistance. Daddy began walking around the rim and I followed. He came to a spot where the wall of the pit gradually sloped and a sort of trail led to the bottom. Bob, who wasn't wearing shoes, had left hoofprints in the dirt that was still soft from a rain three days before.

Daddy and I looked at one another.

"I have to go down and get him," I said.

"No way," Daddy responded. "You'll get hurt, your mother will kill me and I have no idea what else will happen. But I do know that you're not going down there."

I wiped away the last of the tears and looked Daddy straight in the eye. "Then how will we get him?"

"I'll go," Daddy answered.

"He won't follow you, and you know it," I said. "I'll be fine. I can scoot down and, then coming back up, I'll have Bob to hold on to. He won't let me fall." Suddenly, I knew I was speaking the truth. Bob was my best friend and that meant I was the one to rescue him. And I was his best friend, which meant he'd do all he could to keep me from harm.

Nevertheless, Daddy was torn.

"There's no choice, Daddy."

He knew I was right.

"We don't have a lead rope," he said.

"We don't need one. Bob's wearing a halter. Besides, I know he'll follow me without a rope or a halter."

Daddy knelt down and double-tied my tennis shoes, shortening the laces and tightening the knot. He got up and stood back. I knew that was his way of giving me his permission. I sat down at the top of the trail and started scooting, kicking rocks as I went.

I don't know how long it took me to reach Bob. I remember it seemed to take hours to scoot all the way to the bottom of the gravel pit and I shredded my jeans in the process.

When I was three-quarters of the way down, Bob hobbled in my direction and started whinnying. I thought of Mama. I knew what she would do.

"Lord," I breathed, "I know I have no business doing this, but my friend needs help. I know you like horses or you wouldn't have them in your Bible. I don't know if I can do this, Lord, so I'd sure appreciate it if you'd give me a hand. Thank you." I didn't realize it then, but I must surely have sounded just like Mama.

I reached the bottom and turned around to wave at Daddy. I immediately wished I hadn't because it made me think of the climb we'd need to make to get out of the pit. I reached up and patted Bob on the neck.

"You silly, silly horse," I crooned. "Why'd you ever get out and why in the world did you come here?" He looked at me as if to apologize for causing so much trouble.

"Okay," I said, "I know your foot hurts, but you don't have a choice—just like I didn't have one. I'll help you, but you'll have to help me, too." I took hold of his halter with one hand and put my other hand on the side of his neck to help steady me. We were ready when I suddenly halted.

"Lord," I said matter-of-factly, "we're going to need all the help you can give us. I'm just a kid and I'm scared. I know Bob's scared, too. Just please don't let us fall, Lord. Just let me and my friend get to the top. Thank you, Lord."

I was about to start forward when I stopped again. "Lord," I said, "if you were thinking about sending any angels down here today, it would sure be good if you could send some to go all around us. Maybe they could let us just sort of lean on them. Thanks again."

This time we started up, each step placed slowly and

carefully, Bob maneuvering his bulk along the narrow trail as small rocks scattered from under his feet. I plastered myself as close to him as possible. Every time I extended one foot forward, I said, "Please, Lord, don't let us fall." I don't know how many times I repeated those words as I slipped and fell to my knees perhaps dozens of times. Bob stopped with each slip. I stopped anytime he seemed to favor his hurt foot.

Eventually, we made it to the top, two best friends holding on to one another. I learned that day what it meant to take risks for a friend and, just as importantly, I learned what kind of relationship I could have with someone I'd never seen. Mama was right . . . as usual. And today, when I can't wrestle the lid from a jar, I simply stop and say, "Lord, I need some help to do this." It never fails, the lid slips off so easily it appears to be oiled.

Diane M. Ciarloni

Cowboy Heart

*It is not enough for a man to know how to ride;
he must know how to fall.*

Mexican Proverb

"Silt, Colorado!" hollered the Greyhound bus driver as he pulled off to the side of the road.

I grabbed my small bag and climbed off the bus. At the edge of the road was a large man who was standing beside an old army jeep.

"Are you Roger Kiser?" he asked me.

"Yes, sir," I replied.

"My name is Owen Boulton. I own the Rainbow K Ranch," he said as he stuck out his hand to shake mine.

I had been sent to Colorado by the juvenile judge in Florida so that I could work on a ranch. It was a program that had been set up to help troubled teenagers.

Within a week of my arrival at the Rainbow K, I had been turned into a full-fledged cowboy. I had been assigned a large horse, named Brownie, and had been given a full outfit of Western wear, as well as a list of never-ending duties, which started at around 4 A.M. each day.

Things went rather well for the first couple of months. We

worked from 4 A.M. until 6 P.M., seven days a week. We bailed hay, branded cattle, collected chicken eggs, mended fences and shoveled manure.

The best part was my horse, Brownie. I guess she had been given that name because she was brown in color. In addition to my other daily chores, I fed her, bathed her and brushed her.

Every morning when I came out to collect the eggs from the chicken coop, Brownie was waiting for me by the gate. I would walk over and pat her on her side. She would toss her head backward and make a strange sound as if she were blowing through her lips. Slobber would fly everywhere.

"I bet you sure could whistle loud if you had some hands," I would tell her. She would stomp her feet and turn around in a circle.

There were not very many things on the face of this earth that I loved when I was a young boy. But that horse was one thing that I would have died for.

After we ranchhands had eaten breakfast one morning, I was told to go with several of the older men to repair fences up on the northern range. We loaded the jeep with fencing materials and tools and off we went. It was almost 7 P.M. when we got back to the ranch.

As we drove up to the barn, I saw about twenty ranchhands all sitting around in a circle. I got out of the jeep and walked toward the crowd.

"What's going on?" I asked.

"It's your horse, Brownie. She's dead," said one of the men.

Slowly I walked up to where Brownie was lying in the corral. I bent down and patted her on her side. It took everything I had to keep from crying in front of all those men.

All at once, the corral gate opened and Mr. Boulton came riding in on an old tractor. He began scooping out a large hole right next to Brownie.

"What's he gonna do?" I yelled out.

"We always bury the horses right where they drop," said one of the ranchhands.

I stood to the side while he dug the hole for Brownie, wiping the tears from my eyes as they rolled down my cheeks. I will never forget that feeling of sadness for as long as I live.

When the large hole had been dug, the men all stood back so that Brownie could be moved into it. Mr. Boulton lowered the tractor's big scoop and moved toward Brownie.

"PLEASE, MR. OWEN, SIR! Please don't move Brownie with that tractor bucket. You'll cut her and mess her up!" I yelled as I ran out in front of the tractor, waiving my hands and arms.

"Look here, boy," said Mr. Boulton. "We have no choice but to do this when a horse dies. She is just too heavy to move by hand."

"I'll get her in the hole. I swear I will, Mr. Owen, sir," I screamed as loud as I could. I ran over to Brownie and I pushed on her head as hard as I could, but she barely moved. I pushed and pushed, but her body was just too heavy. Nothing I tried to do would move her any closer to the hole. Finally, I stopped pushing. I crumbled there in the dirt, with my head resting against Brownie's side.

"Please don't use that bucket scoop on Brownie," I pleaded over and over.

One at a time, the ranchhands began to get down off their horses. Each positioned himself around the large brown horse and together they began to push and pull with all their might. Inch by inch, Brownie moved toward the large hole in the ground. All at once, she began to slide downhill. I raised her head as best I could, so that her face would not be scarred. The next thing I knew, I was being pulled down into the hole.

Suddenly, everything went totally silent. I just sat there at the bottom of the hole with Brownie's head resting on my lap. Dust and dirt settling all around me.

Slowly, I got to my feet and I placed her head flat on the ground. Then I positioned each of her legs so they were straight. I removed my Western shirt and I placed it over her face so that dirt would not get into her eyes. I stood there crying as my best friend was being covered with earth.

Most of that night I stayed in the barn, cleaning Brownie's stall. I cried until I could cry no more. I guess I was just too embarrassed to go back to the bunkhouse with the rest of the ranchhands.

Early the next morning, I walked back to the bunkhouse to shower and change clothes before going out to collect the chicken eggs. As I entered the small wooden house, I noticed that the ranchhands were up and getting dressed. There on my bunk was eight dollars and some change. On a match-book cover was written, "Buy yourself a new Western shirt."

When I looked up, all the men were smiling at me. One of them said, "You may be a city boy, R.D. [that's what they always called me], but you definitely have the heart that it takes to be a real honest-to-goodness cowboy."

I wiped my swollen red eyes and I smiled real proud-like.

Roger Dean Kiser

A Good Horse Is Hard to Find

Shadow

It started to snow outside, and hoping for a bit of diversion from the typical Minnesota winter weather, we decided to go to a horse sale in town, We watched with interest as the fancy horses with shiny coats came parading in. Some had glitter on their hips or festive red and green ribbons in their manes because it was just before Christmas. There were horses of all colors, shapes and sizes, and everyone was in a bidding frenzy,

Lots of people were going to get expensive horses for Christmas it seemed. Some of the animals had experience working cows and some had experience in the show ring. Others could earn their keep by pulling a sleigh. Eager to own the finest prospects, a number of people in the crowd were bidding hundreds and even thousands of dollars.

"Here's a four-year-old sorrel mare, 15.3-hands high, with forty-two halter points," the auctioneer bellowed. "Her bloodlines include Sonny Dee Bar, Tender Six and Zanzabar Joe. Do I hear five thousand, five thousand one, five two?"

I was fascinated by the spectacle. Every magnificent horse that came through had a story and bloodline that the auctioneer read. The crowd would "ooh" and "aah" in response and then the bidding war would begin. A couple over here, then a man over there and a lady in front of me all bid on the same horse, until he was "going, going, gone!" Then the next horse entered and the process started all over again, taking at most, ten to fifteen minutes per horse. Fifty to sixty horses were sold that day.

Eventually, they got to the last one, a skinny little black pony. The crowd roared with laughter. The pony was led in by a fifteen-year-old boy, who sat on her and then jumped up and down on her back, proclaiming, "She's broke to ride." She had big brown eyes under a long forelock that was full of dried manure and weed seeds.

"She's going to take some time to clean up," the auctioneer stated. "And she needs a few groceries to fatten her up."

Then, looking around, he asked, "Anybody know the story on this one?"

One of the helpers whispered something into his ear and he announced, "The owner forgot about this one out in the pasture and now he wants to get rid of her. She is not registered. There's no pedigree that we know of. Okay, who will give me three hundred for the old mare?"

The crowd was still laughing.

"How about two? Okay, one! Will anybody give me fifty bucks for her?"

The crowd continued to snicker at the lonely, forgotten little pony.

"Okay, get her out of here!" he told the boy who led her in.

So she turned her head as if to say good-bye then hung her head and walked out. The boy put her back in her stall and proceeded to help the new owners with their horses. One by one, the horses clip-clopped, by her stall to meet their new families. The lonely little black mare just hung her head.

Every time a person walked by, her ears would perk up and she would raise her head in anticipation that maybe, just maybe, someone wanted her. But then there would be only more snickers and the sound of fading footsteps. Finally, she would drop her head. The pony turned around so she didn't have to watch the other horses parade by.

It broke our hearts to watch this. We just looked at each other and nodded. Randy went one way and I went the other. We found the auctioneer and said, "Will you take ten dollars?"

He looked at us, puzzled, "For what?" he asked.

"The little black mare," we said excitedly.

"SOLD!" he said with a shake of his head and a smirk.

Without access to a proper horse trailer, we loaded her into the bed of my Toyota pickup, and to a chorus of titters and guffaws, headed for home.

For the last two years of her life, Shadow had the neighborhood kids begging to ride her, brush her or just be by her side, dreaming of the adventures tomorrow would bring for the both of them. We laugh when we remember the faces of those folks at the auction and the sight of the dirty old pony in the bed of our pickup. But the joy and the laughter we had sharing life with Shadow far exceeded the laughter at the sale barn that night.

T.C. Wadsworth

Old Twist

The majestic eye peered through the opening in the stall door. It was a gaze that reflected years of success and experience as a champion reining horse. It also conveyed gentleness and wisdom. It belonged to an old Quarter Horse named Twist. Now past thirty years old, he had spent the last few years relegated to the rank of dependable trail companion for his owner. But inside the rough, aged exterior, the heart of a true winner still beat with the same spirit to be part of a rider's life. This spirit had not faded even as younger horses arrived at the barn and took up more and more of Twist's owner's time. Little did I know the effect that the old champion's spirit would have on my daughter.

A few years before, my daughter Stacy had had a bad experience with a runaway horse. She was just eight at the time, and a terrifying fall accompanied the disaster. Although she broke no bones, her confidence, love for horses and the desire to learn to ride were shattered. No matter how her mother and I tried, we had no success in healing the damage caused on that fateful day. But as I stood there and saw Stacy look into the eye of the old fellow in the stall, I knew this was going to be the beginning of a special relationship.

Fortunately, Stacy's accident had not diminished her love for animals in general, and this small opening was all that Twist needed to establish a special bond. Stacy was now thirteen years old, which is a critical age for all young ladies to handle. It is a time when special bonds are not easy to form, but so crucial to possess. Would Twist be able to wipe away Stacy's reluctance to get back into a saddle after five years? It was as if Twist recognized the challenge and the importance of victory. It wasn't a blue ribbon, trophy or award that was at stake, but the heart of a child, and what a special medal of victory he then would possess.

In the days and weeks that followed, my daughter began to express daily interest in coming to the barn with me and my wife. We were careful not to interfere. We did not dare disrupt the magic of the old man at work. Though she said she was there to see the barn cats, Stacy would seek out Twist. She took the initiative to spend time with him, feeding, brushing, combing and stroking him from head to hoof, all the while talking to him about her life.

Though age had taken away some of the tone of the old Quarter Horse's muscles, it had not lessened his ability to strike the stance of a champion as he stood quietly while she groomed him.

Then one day as my wife was readying one of our horses for a ride, Twist's owner noticed the old guy's eager expression and desire to be included, too. So the owner asked Stacy if she wanted to get Twist ready and take him out for a ride. In response, Stacy looked once again into the old man's eye. I can't say that he winked at her, but it was that moment their two spirits met and completed the bond that had been forming over a couple of months. Continuing to look deep into his eyes, Stacy didn't speak, she only nodded yes.

Moments later, I stood there as they rode off together, Stacy winning renewed confidence and desire, and Twist winning his medal of a child's heart. I had not seen his head held higher or his walk more regal than in that first minute.

As this first ride turned into many more, Twist took very good care of his young friend and slowly replaced her fear with confidence. I nearly cried the day I looked across the field and caught sight of Stacy and Twist cantering back to the barn. Her long hair was pulled back and flowing in the breeze in a way that seemed to mimick the appearance of the old man's tail. He had won. He had beaten fear, removing years of bad memories and replacing them with moments of happiness that are etched forever not only in my daughter's heart but mine as well. I know I always will be grateful for what Twist did for my family. I will forever remember the time I looked deep into the eyes of this champion and saw the love of a child looking back at me.

Tom Maupin

A Silent Bond

Never thank yourself; always thank the horses for the happiness and joy we experience through them.

Hans H.E. Isenbart

Apparently, my trainer found the fuzzy chestnut named Tic Tac giving pony rides someplace in Texas. I always had a problem believing that this fiery steed could have come from such humble beginnings. Of course, he was no fiery steed, but I was ten years old at the time, filled with high hopes for my riding career, and no successful rider was without a feisty mount, right? Tic Tac would be mine.

The first time I rode the 15.3-hand Morgan–Quarter Horse cross, he reared up so high that I heard the Lone Ranger's theme song play in my head. Maybe we should have named him Silver. Of course, that would not have fit him at all. My mother, watching my lesson from the edge of the ring, was mortified as she saw us suspended in midair. I, on the other hand, was thrilled with Tic Tac's obvious energy and spirit.

My trainer at the time had a remarkable ability to instill within me an immense amount of confidence. Every time I watched her ride, I sat in awe, hoping to be just like her. She made me believe that I could ride anything, anywhere, anytime. Over the years, this overconfidence often has resulted in catastrophic spills, broken bones and countless bruises, but it also has given me the courage to get back on.

I rode many horses in the barn in exchange for helping to muck stalls, clean tack and bring in the horses from the pasture. I grew to love the work and relished the smell of manure and sawdust as every horse-crazy girl does. Although I appreciated the chance to ride other horses, Tic Tac was always my favorite. I was terribly upset when other people rode him during their lessons and I secretly hoped that he would pull another vertical rear and scare them into riding another horse the next time. But he never did. Everyone fell in love with him, just as I had.

We never knew Tic Tac's birthday, so I let him share mine. Each November 9 I brought out a bag of birthday treats and set them by his stall. Then after a bareback gallop in the pasture, I sat with him for hours as he ate his grass, apples and carrots and I sipped Dr Pepper. I never talked to him, the way that many people chat with their horses. I hardly ever said a word, because I never felt I had to.

Tic Tac taught me many lessons that have served me well over my twenty-plus years in the saddle. One slippery day after a Texas rainstorm, I pointed him toward a tiny pile of branches on the ground. As his front feet began to leave the earth, he slammed on the brakes, startling me. Tic Tac never stopped at a fence. A little disappointed in him, I dug my heels into his side and coaxed him over the jump. He hesitated and then carefully popped over it. But the footing on the landing side was too soggy to support his legs, and they slipped out from under him. Both of us went tumbling into the mud. As I sat in the muck, looking up at Tic Tac, who had safely made it back to his feet, I noticed a stream of blood oozing down his soft muzzle. I immediately felt a flood of guilt for having urged him to jump when he knew better. Taking him back to the barn to tend to his still-bleeding scrape, I silently vowed never to question his instincts again. Lesson learned: When you've built trust with a horse, respect it.

On March 9, 1988, I began my daily walk to the barn. I was early and the horses were still turned out. Because the geldings were always in the rear pasture, I headed in that direction and looked for Tic Tac's halter on the fence, but it wasn't there. Scanning the grounds, I couldn't find him anywhere. I felt deflated because I thought that someone must be riding him. Returning to the barn, I found a friend who looked at me with sad eyes, and explained that Tic Tac had been taken to the veterinary clinic.

It must be colic, I thought. He had had several bouts of colic in those two years, but never before was it serious enough for him to have to travel to the clinic in Katy, Texas.

The next few hours were a blur. I remember my mom returning to the barn about an hour after she dropped me off. Someone must have called her to comfort me. I was numb as I sat in the driveway, waiting to see the trailer pull up, but eerily knowing that when it did, it would be empty.

While I waited for the rusty two-horse to rattle in, at least twenty different barn mates came to sit with me at various times. I have no recollection of what they said to me or even who they were. The words and the faces blended together and all I could do was stare down the road and recall every second of the past two years that I'd spent with Tic Tac.

After hours of waiting, the phone rang, and eventually someone handed it to me. I told my hand not to reach for the phone and I urged my legs to run, but they ignored me. Slowly, I placed the phone to my ear and began to walk toward Tic Tac's stall. On the other end, a tearful trainer and best friend told me what I already knew. Tic Tac was gone.

By the time she was able to force out the words, I was in his stall and could see an imprint in the shavings where he had been lying, probably trying to roll to ease his belly pains. My legs gave way and I collapsed, trying to relieve the pain that suddenly covered my entire body like a second skin.

At that time, I thought I'd never leave his stall because it was the only connection I had to him. I walked over to the feed bin and traced every line, hoping to feel the soft muzzle that was once scraped by my ignorance. I ran my hand through his water trough, begging to hear the muffled sound of his gentle gulps.

Eventually, my mom eased me from the ground and took me home. The house was silent and oddly still. My entire world seemed changed. My siblings and friends didn't know how to act around me. On one hand, they knew I was terribly sad and they felt bad for me, but on the other, they probably thought I was nuts because he was just a horse.

Since then, I've been on countless other horses and have had greater success in the show ring than I ever could have had with Tic Tac. Nevertheless, that special bond never has been and never will be duplicated. I'm reminded of this each time I find myself talking to a horse.

Every March 9 between 1988 and 1995, I couldn't bring myself to dry my tears and face the world. I wouldn't go to school. I wouldn't go to work. I wouldn't even go to the barn. My parents understood and never forced the issue. They let me sit in my room, holding a picture of Tic Tac. Sometimes, I reminisced about all of our wonderful times together. Other times, I relived that painful day of loss.

A couple of years ago, I decided not to be a slave to March 9. Instead of grieving, I spent that day in silent celebration of a remarkable relationship with a fuzzy chestnut with a crooked blaze. I don't regret those years I spent mourning that day. After all, never before had I experienced such an incredible sense of loss and abandonment, all of it made worse by the fact that I never said good-bye. But then again, I never said a word to Tic Tac because I never had to.

Tiernan McKay

Daddy Always Said
"Yes" to Horses

He has galloped through young girls' dreams, added richness to grown women's lives, and served men in war and strife.

Toni Robinson

The only "no" I ever heard from my dad Jim turned out to be "no problem." From the time I was a little girl to the time that my dad died, he called me Baby Teresa. Most everyone said he spoiled me and I could only nod my head or smile in agreement.

Every girl's dream is to have a horse. My daddy agreed.

When I was just three years old, I got my first horse. It was a beautiful Palomino rocking horse made of plastic. Cradled in a metal frame and suspended by giant springs, he was my pride and joy, and I could maneuver that horse like a jockey going down the homestretch. I loved my plastic Palomino, but soon he wasn't good enough.

I didn't want to be limited by earthly bounds. I wanted a swinging horse that was suspended in the air. My daddy agreed.

He took the rocking horse from the frame and suspended it

with ropes from a ceiling beam in our basement. Not knowing that the attachment was only temporary, I ran and leaped onto the horse's back just like they did in those old Western movies. But unlike the cowboys in the movies, I didn't ride off into the sunset. I was carried off to the emergency room in my father's arms. When I had landed on the Palomino's plastic saddle, the ropes had pulled loose from the ceiling and I crashed face first onto the concrete floor. When I woke up in the emergency room, I had a concussion, two black eyes and a bruised ego.

When I returned home, the horse was gone, clandestinely put out to pasture, I learned years later, at a friend's house.

When I was ten years old, my next horse was the real deal: a certified hay-munching, apple-eating, horse-apple-producing Arabian cross. Just four years old, Sandarrow was a mighty mite. He'd been advertised in the local paper as gentle and calm. He was the first horse we ever looked at. I wanted him the moment I laid eyes on him. My daddy agreed.

Sandarrow was light yellow, almost white, with a short strong neck. Stocky, strong and surging with unrestrained power, he certainly was not gentle and calm. He was more of a rodeo horse than a kid's horse. Nothing scared Sandarrow or restrained him for long. Halters? He'd break them. Barbed-wire fences? He'd walk right through them. When I took him to the local county fair for 4-H, he climbed the six-foot wooden stall door as if he were a monkey with hooves, and then he strode out into the alleyway, wearing a silly horse grin. He hightailed it out of the fairgrounds, through town and into the countryside, racing around meadows, taunting my daddy to catch him.

This was the early 1960s, before safety helmets, protective clothing, rider safety training and the other precautions we take for granted today. Sandarrow preferred to ride bareback: that is, with no rider at all. To achieve his goal, he would often rub me off on fences, run under low-hanging branches, buck like a bronco or speed off like a Formula One racer.

One day when I was eleven, I decided to have a quick ride before a dance recital, so I jumped on Sandarrow without bothering to put on my shoes or his saddle. He ran down the hill by our house, weaving like an equine bobsled, through the trees and toward the garden where my daddy was working. I don't think I touched Sandarrow's back the whole way down the hill.

When we got to the garden fence, Sandarrow started bucking. I could see my dad's eyes bulging with fear as I bounced up and down on his back as if I were jumping on a trampoline. Finally, Sandarrow spun and off I flew, landing flat on my back.

With the wind knocked out of me and dazed from a concussion, I couldn't move from where I'd landed. Sandarrow stomped on my right foot, breaking nearly every bone. Then, my daddy said, he kicked with both feet, narrowly missing my head.

Terrified, my daddy scooped me up in his arms and ran with me back to our house, which was a short distance down the hill. My daddy was a small man and I was almost as large as he was. But I remember how strong he felt, how fast he moved and how he kept looking down into my tear-filled eyes, reassuring me, "You'll be okay, Baby Teresa. Daddy has you." He wanted to get rid of Sandarrow after the accident, but I begged to keep him. Daddy agreed.

The rest of the summer, I still rode Sandarrow. This time however, I wore a cowboy boot on one foot and a cast on the other.

Before I knew it, Daddy's girl had grown up and I was longing to acquire a new horse to keep at the Pi Phi sorority house at the University of Idaho. Actually, what I was interested in now was horsepower. I wanted a car of my own and had my eye on a vintage Chevy Corvette that a boyfriend in the military service was offering to me because he was going on assignment overseas. I could see my friends and myself cruising the mountain roads of the Palouse in that car, Daddy disagreed.

Oh, he did get me a Chevy, though, a compact Chevy Vega, which, because it used oil like crazy, couldn't pass a gas station. Still, my father, a logger by trade, babied the car almost as much as he babied me and kept it running for nearly ten years.

My daddy was always very active and enjoyed robust health until he was eighty-one. That year, Mother Nature, snuck up on him and started pulling him down. First, he lost the vision in his right eye, then he had a heart attack from which he recovered. But then he was hamstrung by terminal lung cancer. From the time a diagnosis was made, he lived only a month. But during that time, we pulled out old photo albums and looked at pictures of the rocking horse and my black eyes, Sandarrow and Baby Teresa's baby blue car.

After my father passed away, I went into his room alone to soak up the essence of this diminutive man who was a giant to me. I smelled his Levi's and fingered the suspenders that were still attached. I held his watch and the glasses that were on the dresser. Inside the dresser, I found a cloth bag containing all of my baby teeth. Apparently, the tooth fairy and my daddy were good friends.

Finally, I sat on the edge of the bed he'd slept in for more than sixty of his eighty years and I looked at his nightstand. There was a Beetle Bailey alarm clock, a 1920s-era art deco lamp and a worn, faded, diorama about the size of a deck of cards.

I moved in close. This was a Minnie Mouse diorama that my daddy had bought me at Disneyland when I was only six years old. It featured Minnie riding a horse into the sunset. Unbeknownst to me, Daddy had customized it, putting a lock of my hair on Minnie's head and a picture of me in the painted sky behind her. My mother Valdie later told me that for more than forty years, this horse sat by my father's head and every night he would pat the top of the diorama and say, "Good night, Baby Teresa."

Tears burst forth as I called out to God to take good care of this man who never said no to a girl who wanted a horse. He agreed.

Teresa Becker

Syd and Roanie

The wind of heaven is that which blows between a horse's ears.

Arabian Proverb

Syd Parkin is fifty-nine years old and still regrets standing only five feet, three inches tall. Not because he is too short, but rather because he is too tall to be a jockey. On the one-year anniversary of surviving a life-threatening aneurysm, Syd rode to the top of a mountain ridge, where he and his horse Roanie had a very special bonding experience. He credits Roanie for teaching him to appreciate all the little miracles and blessings each day has to offer. Syd put it this way: "Even on your worst day, if you look hard enough, you can find one good thing. For instance, I almost died, but I got two great things: Roanie and a second chance at life."

They were partners for five years and spent time together every day. Then one afternoon, while on a simple trail ride, some unknowing teenagers on rental horses came charging up behind them. They startled Roanie while crossing a cement road and in a split second Syd's and Roanie's lives were forever changed. Roanie slipped, fell down hard, doing the splits, and shattered his pelvis.

Syd and several veterinarians did everything in their power to rehabilitate his faithful partner. Despite all of their efforts over an agonizing ten months, Syd had to face the heartbreaking reality that Roanie would never recover. He was advised to put him down. Syd confided to me: "I just can't do it yet. I don't know if it's really the right thing to do." I told him to trust his own judgment. "You'll know when it's time." Syd responded, "I just wish Roanie could give me a sign so I'd know."

I asked for and was granted a moment alone with Roanie. His strong animal instinct to survive was palpably low. I spoke softly, "How ya doin', Roanie boy? Not too good, huh? I know you've been fighting real hard. You look tired boy. Your dad loves you so much. I think maybe you're hanging on because you're feeling how hard it is for him to let you go. Roanie, he just needs a sign from you that it's okay. I promise I'll help look after your dad. So if you can, please let him know it's okay to let you go."

I fought back tears that fell anyway. As I looked deeply into his big, soft, soulful eyes, I got a strong sense that Roanie had understood every word I'd said.

I returned to Syd and asked if there was anything else that I could do. He replied, "No. I'm calling the vet tomorrow to make the appointment." He broke down saying, "I just can't be there when he goes down. I won't be able to take seeing him hit the ground." I promised Syd that I would be there and that I would be looking into Roanie's eyes so that he would go while looking into a familiar, loving face. Syd nodded okay, but this provided little comfort. "If I were a *real* man, a *real* cowboy, I could do it." I told him not to be so hard on himself. "Not being able to watch doesn't mean you're less of a man. On the contrary, it means you're a kind, loving, sensitive man who loves his horse too much to witness something too painful to see."

He thanked me for my offer and said he'd take me up on it. All night I wondered if I'd be able to keep my promise. It's difficult to explain what I felt, except to say that as impossible as being there was going to be, it would be even more impossible not to be there.

I called Syd the next day, and he told me that the veterinarian was coming to put Roanie down. "But it's okay. When I went to see him this morning, Roanie gave me a sign. Now I know it's the right thing to do." The appointment was set for eleven o'clock the next morning. I arrived at ten-thirty to discover that Syd had spent the entire night in Roanie's stall. He had written him a three-page letter and read it to him. Neither of them got much sleep. Syd was doing his best and to his credit, he mustered up enough strength to help me put out orange parking cones to reserve the spot closest to Roanie's stall for the veterinarian and for the truck that eventually would be hauling Roanie away.

The hauling truck arrived first. It was clean and white with a shiny sterile-looking metal bed. My eyes quickly looked away for all too soon, I would witness the precious cargo its coldness would hold. The stable was hushed with unusual stillness and a reverent quiet. I believe the other horses knew what was going on. The veterinarian arrived on time. Syd apologized: "I've never done this before, so you're going to have to talk me through this. Do I just bring him out here by the truck?" The veterinarian nodded yes. I put my hand on Syd's shoulder, trying to transfer all the love and support I could as we walked slowly but deliberately to Roanie's stall. "Breathe," I said as a reminder to Syd and myself. Roanie was munching on a feast of his favorite treats that Syd had prepared for him. Syd slowly undid Roanie's halter from the pipe corral. As Roanie sweetly lifted his head to cooperate, as he had done a thousand times before, I was never more impressed with a man's courage—nor strength of heart—as I watched Syd tenderly slip that halter on Roanie's face for what was so painfully the last time. Every action, every word he spoke echoed under the enormous weight of *"this is the last time."*

Syd stood beside his friend and stroked him with a loving touch. "You're a good boy. I love you, Roanie boy." He then lifted Roanie's mane, put his face against the horse's neck and inhaled several times, rubbing his nose back and forth, savoring and taking in every molecule of what he called the greatest smell on earth. "Just one more," he said with tears streaming down his face. As long as I live, I will never forget the way he smelled that horse's neck. Then Syd looked into Roanie's eyes and said, "Good-bye boy. I love you, Roanie. Thanks for being my friend."

As Syd led the horse out of his stall, again I placed my hand on his shoulder and said, "You will smell him again, you know. He will come to visit you in his spirit form and you will feel him around you." Syd nodded. In previous weeks we had discussed the idea that our spirit or life energy never dies, that it leaves our earthly body, but lives on. I told him how my mother's spirit comes to me in the form of hummingbirds, how I have sensed my Aunt Nancy's presence in butterflies, and that Roanie would find a similar way to visit him.

However, in this harsh moment of earthly mortality, Syd had to do the impossible. He led his beloved partner to the hauling truck. It was the longest, most difficult fifty feet they ever walked. The veterinarian gave Roanie a strong sedative. Roanie started to get wobbly. Syd said his final good-byes. Afraid that Roanie might stumble and fall, I pleaded, "Syd, go. Please. Go now." I don't know how, but he managed to find the strength to leave and he headed for the bridge where I was to meet him when it was all over. But now it was time for me to fulfill my promise.

The sedative was doing its job. The veterinarian administered the fatal injection. I stood my post and held Roanie's gaze. As he slowly descended and gently lay on the ground, his breath blowing hard through his soft pink nostrils, I went down with him, never taking my eyes off of his.

"It's okay boy. You did good. You are so loved. So loved." I stroked his face. He lay very still and although he did not appear to be breathing, I asked, "He's not gone yet, is he?" The veterinarian felt for his pulse. "No, not yet," he responded. Still stroking his face, with my heart breaking, I mustered up as much humor as I could. "Now listen, Roanie, when you get to heaven, I want you to trot right up to Trigger and bite him on the butt. You tell him he wasn't the only star. You were just as loved." What more could I say to my noble friend?

"Roanie, your dad is standing on the bridge," I continued. "He loves you so much. If you can, please boy, let him feel you. Let him feel your spirit as you pass. Good-bye, boy. I love you, Roanie." I kissed his face and looked to the veterinarian. "He's gone now, isn't he?" After checking for a pulse, he solemnly nodded yes. I kissed Roanie one last time, stood up, collected myself, then cut a small lock of hair from his mane, which Syd had requested, and a lock from his tail. I removed Roanie's halter and lead rope for what was truly the last time. One last soft pat on his face. "Okay," I said. "Thank you."

I stood as if on guard as they hoisted Roanie into the truck. As soon as they were out of sight, I headed for the bridge that Syd, Roanie, my horse Annie and I had ridden across so many times before. As I approached him, I prayed for any words that might offer him some measure of comfort. We just grabbed each other and hugged. I started to cry. Syd said, "It's okay." I looked at him. "Really, I'm okay. The whole time I was waiting, the wind was blowing strong on my back. Then suddenly, I felt this warm gush of wind blow into my face. It was Roanie. I felt him go through me. He was telling me he was all right."

Syd and I walked the rest of the way across the bridge, telling Roanie stories, thus beginning our path of grieving and healing. I am happy to say that since then, Syd has gotten another horse Bodie. My horse Annie and I were honored to go along on their maiden ride together. We rode to the same mountain ridge where Syd had had his life-changing bonding moment with Roanie. As we stopped to admire the beautiful valley below, bathed in the pinkish gold light of the setting sun, a hummingbird suddenly appeared, stopped directly in front of us and hovered there for about ten seconds. We shared a knowing smile. "Syd, I believe we just had a visit!" Syd responded simply: "Yup, just another one of those small miracles you can see every day if you look for them."

Judy Pioli Askins

A Horse with Heart

With a coat the color of smooth beach sand, and a silky mane and tail of the richest ebony, T.J. stood more than 16 hands tall. His heart was unbelievably full of love and loyalty. His kind eyes and soft breath were always a comfort. He understood me. He never uttered a word of disappointment on the many occasions that I'd seek the solace of his sleek neck and strong shoulders. He never failed to carry my burdens away.

Even as a three-year-old, he was a joy to ride. Whether we were galloping bareback across Mr. White's wheat fields in the middle of the night or schooling extensively in the ring, he always seemed to enjoy himself. His ears flicked forward with his nicker of anticipation of our ride as I entered the barn that damp day in April.

"Ready to go out and play, boy?" I questioned him even though I knew he was more than ready to go. The gleam in the depths of his eyes affirmed my assumption.

"I have been waiting for you all day," he seemed to say.

I brought out my brushes and began to curry his coat and massage his favorite spots. At a spot just in front of his withers, I circled with extra pressure while he craned his neck forward in sheer delight "Oh, yeah . . . right there . . . feels so good!" he seemed to communicate to me and I smiled at his pleasure. After knocking the dirt off of him with a brush, I wrapped his legs in navy blue polo wraps to support them and pushed my comfy saddle up onto his broad back. I shimmied into my chaps and stuffed my hair into my helmet. I was just as excited as he was for this ride because today was the first day with no rain in more than a week. I helped him slip his noble head into the bridle and I fastened the buckles. Then we walked out of the barn toward the driest spot on the farm.

As he walked to warm up, I watched the sun tease us by peeking out from behind the clouds and then scooting out of sight again as if afraid of its reflection in the puddles. I urged T.J. into a trot with a tiny bit of pressure from my lower legs. I was so proud of how responsive he was that day, moving out for me and then collecting as I asked him. We worked in some circles and figure eights. We practiced his transitions, which were as smooth as butter. T.J. had come a long way from being a "spaghetti noodle" two-year-old to the balanced horse that he was that day. The footing felt good enough for a canter, and neither of us could resist it. His canter was wonderfully fluid as he stretched across the ground. Again, we worked a few circles and figure eights at the canter, this time with simple lead changes in the middle. As a change from the routine workout, I decided to try a couple flying lead changes with him. We'd worked on them before and T.J. knew how to do them. We proceeded across the pasture on his left lead, keeping a balanced straight line all the way to the corner. When we were almost to the corner, I simply shifted my weight to ask for the opposite lead. I felt T.J. shift his body with me as he executed the maneuver, but something was not right. Where was his left hind leg? I could not feel it beneath us where it was supposed to be.

When T.J. had used his left hind leg to thrust over to the right lead, he had pushed off on a slick spot of mud. His hind end slipped out from underneath him and we unceremoniously headed for the ground. With my legs still astride him, we landed in motion. Lying on his side, T.J. was sliding swiftly toward a six-inch-square post in the three-rail board fence. Because I was still on his back, pinched between his side and the ground, I watched in agony as I waited to be smashed between his back and the fence post. In what seemed like slow motion, I glanced at my horse. I thought about how horrible it would be if I could never gallop bareback across the wheat fields with him again. I thought about how much I loved him.

In the space of a heartbeat, T.J. bunched every muscle in his body and flipped over me so that now he was the one sliding into the fence, legs first. His massive body slammed into the fence with enough force to level the six- by-six post. Immediately after he hit the fence, I slid into him. All that I could hear was both of us breathing, trying to suck air into our lungs while we sorted out what just had happened. Slowly, I pulled myself to my feet on rubbery legs. I reached down and stroked his coat as I stepped around him to survey the damage.

"Easy, boy. You're okay." I tried to soothe him even though he was much calmer than I was. T.J. just lay still while I untangled the splintered boards from between his legs. I dragged the broken post out of his way and urged him to try to stand up. He pulled his front legs over, stretched them out in front of his chest and pushed his neck out for balance as he struggled to rise from the ground. After a quick glance to see that all four legs were still intact, I swung my arms around his neck in a fierce hug. A few minutes passed and, through my tears, I stroked his face and kissed him.

We stood there for a while, just taking everything in. Then gingerly, we walked back to the barn so that I could take a closer look at him. T.J. walked away from that fence with a couple scrapes on his legs and belly, but without major injuries that required veterinary attention.

I was only bruised and a little sore, which was pain that I was grateful to bear, considering how devastating that day could have been. I still do not know exactly how T.J. was able to roll over me in the air without touching me. I do not need to know. I do know that he willingly chose to sacrifice himself for me that day. He loved me that much. His heart was full of love and loyalty. He showed me his love every day. He showed me the depth of his devotion that damp April day, and I will never forget it.

Jerri Simmons-Fletcher

Sleeping Baby

"Kori! Kori! Has anyone seen Kori?" my sister Suzi asked, running into the kitchen. Kori was my fourteen-month-old niece. She recently had learned to walk, go up and down stairs and push open doors.

"Oh, have you checked upstairs?" I asked, not bothering to look up from my favorite cartoon.

"Of course I have! I've checked everywhere!"

My mother and little sister Trudy entered the kitchen.

"She's not in the bedrooms," my mother said, concerned.

"Maybe she's fallen asleep somewhere," I said.

My mother began barking orders. "Jennilyn, you check the closets. I'll check the yard and the swings. Suzi, you check with the neighbors. Trudy, go to the barn and see if she's with Grandpa."

Everyone began a frantic search. Frequent shouts of "She's not in here!" resounded throughout the house.

Soon Suzi returned from the neighbors. "They haven't seen her!" she gasped, catching her breath.

Grandpa strode swiftly through the back door. "She's not in the barn. I've checked the stables and around the pond."

"The pond!" A look of horror filled my sister's face.

"She's not in the pond. The water's crystal clear today. I promise she's not there." Gently, he hugged Suzi. "We'll find her."

"I'll go check the attic again," Suzi sniffled, holding back tears.

"And we'll all go check around the fields," commanded my father.

I looked at my watch. Nearly an hour had gone by. The sun was high in the sky and the warm summer breeze shifted the tall grass in the field. *That looks like a good place for a baby to get lost,* I thought as I parted the knee-high grass under my feet. I could see Trudy searching on the far side of the field. Behind her, our three horses were grazing.

Suddenly, Trudy was running toward me and shouting, "I found her! I found her!"

I ran into the house. "Trudy found her! Trudy found her!"

"Where? Is she okay?" my sister cried, bounding down the stairs from the attic.

"She's in the field!" I hollered.

Just as we were racing out the door, Trudy raced in.

"The horses are protecting her. She's okay. Get Dad," cried Trudy. "The horses won't let me in."

Excitedly, we all raced to the field. The horses were still on the far side, standing guard. As we drew closer, we could see the horses, head to tail, forming a tight circle. Lady Star whinnied as we approached.

In the center of the circle, Kori was sleeping peacefully on a bed of grass.

Jennilyn McKinnon

A Gift of Gold

A pony is a childhood dream. A horse is an adult treasure.

Rebecca Carroll

Some moments feel like magic. It is as if I can hear and feel the presence of my daughter Emily while taking my summer-evening riding lessons. While I am preparing to ride in my first horse show, I am experiencing something I will hold dear to my heart for a long time. These magical moments give me hope, joy and a calm inner peace because next week it will have been three years since I lost my daughter in a tragic car accident.

Emily was nine years old when she fell in love with an old bay mare. I watched the tender relationship between a young girl and her first horse blossom. Emily's love for her horse consumed her life and after she'd taken a few riding lessons, I knew she was hooked. I was immediately designated Horse Show Mom.

I spent many chilly winter evenings and lots of sweltering summer days watching Emily ride in lessons and school for shows. My little girl progressed from looking slightly scared and frustrated to looking confident and self-assured. In the process, I learned enough equine terminology so I could talk the talk. But the hardest thing to learn was how to act cool and calm when my little darlin' fell off her horse!

Our days were busy, preparing for shows. There was always work to be done: cleaning tack, washing and grooming the horse and finding the right chaps to match Emily's show clothes. There were weekly trips to the dry cleaners, as well as submitting entry forms and writing checks—lots of them. My role as Horse Show Mom was hard work, but very rewarding. Little did I know that the memories of those moments would need to last me for a lifetime.

After much anticipation and many sleepless nights, the long-awaited events arrived. Show days were fun, exciting and exhausting for all of us. In the show ring, there is a partnership of two, but behind the scenes, three often work together—the horse, the rider and the Horse Show Mom—to present the perfect package. Painting hooves, polishing boots and French-braiding Emily's hair were only a few of my duties. I will always remember telling my little equestrian to "Sit up and smile!"

Ah, the years flew by, and Emily grew tall. To keep up with the stiff competition she needed to upgrade to a larger and fancier horse. After we spent many months searching for the perfect match, Parker came into our lives. He was kind and forgiving, and sturdy and strong, and soon he became our treasured friend. The three of us became an integral part of the "family" at our barn. We had many good times together, laughing, crying and experiencing many fabulous and frantic moments.

When Emily turned seventeen, she announced that she was not going to show her horse anymore. She wanted to spend more time with her high school basketball team than with her dappled-gray gelding.

I was heartbroken at the news. "What about Parker? What about your friends at the barn? What about your trainer?" I couldn't believe it was over and I guess what I was really saying was "What about me?"

I had to settle for visiting the barn with carrots for some of my old equine friends and watching other kids practice for horse shows. But I still yearned for those early-morning moments, hearing the horses nicker in anticipation of what was to come and watching them march up the ramp of the horse trailer.

Well, many years have passed and my memories are sweet. Somehow, I feel close to Emily while spending time with horses. At times, the memories are bittersweet and tears spill from my eyes. Other times, I can smile and laugh. And at age fifty, I find that those memories now are getting me ready to ride in my first horse show. Now it is my turn to execute the proper leg, hand and body position to sit the jog and to pick up the correct lead for the lope.

My Paint gelding Murphy is a beautiful and talented animal. He moves with great ease in a solid way. He is definitely a "been there, done that" kind of guy. And somehow I think he knows he is a cherished friend who is helping me heal a broken heart.

As the sun sets, a cool breeze touches my face. I cluck for the jog and Murphy's transitions appear effortless. I sit tall in the saddle, my eyes up, my heels down and my hands light. I am doing something that I had watched my daughter do endless times. But this time, I am on board the horse, gently gliding around the arena as though I have done it a million times.

We trot figure eights over some poles in the center of the ring with a loose rein and graceful, rhythmic motion. For a novice, it is not an easy task, riding patterns over obstacles and keeping the pace forward and even. It takes a considerable amount of concentration and skill. Yet, with a steady cadence, we perform the task easily. Murphy and I approach the center pole in a straight line (almost every time) and are able to change directions subtly without a second thought as we cross the obstacle.

Well, this time I am "a top," and the sweetness of Emily's silent messages ring through my being. As if she is perched on my shoulder, not two of us, but three softly glide around the ring, and I hear her comments surround me like silken scarves wrapped around my soul.

It is possible that these moments mean more to me than any judge's scorecard might show. I am sure my handsome steed knows that he is part of this celebrated blessing. Preparing for competition gives me goals and something to look forward to. But the sound of Emily's quiet voice in my mind as the sun sets and the breeze touches my face is more precious than a world of blue ribbons or any prize I might earn in the show ring. It is a gift of gold that will forever glisten in my heart.

"Relax Mom. Just feel the motion and listen with your body. Keep the pace even, for he knows his job. Be soft with your hands and he will take good care of you.

"And, oh yeah, Mom. Sit up and smile!"

Robin Roberts

Chance of a Lifetime

Think, when we talk of horses, that you see them
Printing their proud hooves in the receiving earth;
For 'tis your thoughts that now must deck our kings.

William Shakespeare

It was a blistering hot day in June, when a man came to my small horse farm in Missouri, asking for some goat's milk. He needed it for his teenage nephew's new Quarter Horse filly because she was deathly ill. The man said two veterinarians had examined the foal and concluded that it would cost thousands of dollars to save her. His nephew didn't have that kind of money and planned to shoot the foal instead. The uncle told the teenager, "Give me twenty-four hours to try to save her." I gave him all the goat's milk I had and offered to help in any way I could. The man said, "You know, this filly just might end up here with you!" I thought he was joking. He wasn't.

The next day, a truck pulled into my driveway with the three-week–old foal lying on the flatbed, being held by the man's daughter. The man gently lifted the bright red filly off the truck and laid her on the grass. A makeshift pen was set up around her. It was under a shady tree, just outside my back door, so I could easily check on her every hour, day and night.

I have multiple sclerosis, which has gotten steadily worse, and I wasn't looking for a new project when this foal arrived on my doorstep. In fact, just before she got here, my husband Dave and I had decided to sell half of our horses, along with all of our goats and most of our farm birds. I wanted to lessen my work load. Still, I gladly accepted when the man asked me to help save this filly. He emphasized there was no money to pay for any more vet bills. He added, "Nobody expects her to make it through the next day or two." I took that as my cue to prove everyone wrong.

After the man left, I checked over every inch of the poor creature's tiny, frail body. She was in horrible shape, with fever sores in her mouth and pressure sores all over one side of her body. Her joints were grotesquely swollen and disfigured by a bacterial infection called neonatal septicemia. She looked like a skeleton, barely covered with skin and clumps of hair. She had a high fever, due to the life-threatening bacteria circulating in her bloodstream. She couldn't stand up or even lift her head. Her helpless brown eyes were sunken from dehydration, yet there was a twinkle in those eyes that captured my heart. I loved her from the moment I first saw her.

I didn't own her, but I'd become responsible for her. In those first few hours, I put together a basic medical kit and treated her wounds. She was desperate for nourishment. I searched the Internet and found that goat's milk is the next best thing to mare's milk for feeding a foal. So, I milked my goats, put the milk in a bottle with a foal nipple on it and just squirted what I could into the filly's mouth. She got some of it, but not enough. Finally, out of desperation, at four in the morning, I brought my goat Megan over to the filly. I held Megan's teat to the foal's mouth and she took to it immediately! She wasn't strong enough to hold her head up, but with my help, she was able to nurse directly from Megan. She drank until she couldn't hold anymore. My first hurdle was overcome.

By the next day, my efforts to feed the filly every half-hour were paying off. She seemed better. By the third day, she was able to sit up by herself. I kept reminding myself that she wasn't mine, but it did no good. I felt like she belonged to me much more than she belonged to the teenage boy who didn't care whether she lived or died. Her will to live was strong and she deserved to be given a name. I decided to call her Megan's Chance in honor of Megan, the old white nanny goat who had supplied milk, companionship and the chance for this little angel to live. Chance became her nickname.

Megan would groom Chance just as if she were her own baby. It was amazing and touching to watch an old goat mothering a young filly. Megan would lie down on the grass next to Chance and the two of them would pass the time in quiet contentment. The other animals on the farm also sought to comfort her. The geese and one of my chickens adopted her and stayed next to her most of the time. Our dog, a Yorkie–Pom mix named Pookey, would go up to Chance as she was lying on the ground and whisper into her ear. That seemed to bring a smile to Chance's face.

As the days wore on, the bond strengthened between Chance and me. She'd whinny when she heard me coming to see her. Just the sound of my footsteps lit a spark in her. Secretly, it warmed my heart to know that she didn't whinny to anyone else. I was her special mama, and she was my special child. It took awhile for me to realize that Chance would enrich not only my life, but also the lives of many people around the world.

I frequent several equine message boards on the Internet where horse lovers and owners get together to visit and trade thoughts on dealing with horse problems. When I first asked for advice about Chance, I had no idea that word of her troubles would spread the way it did. E-mails came flooding in to me from people who offered suggestions and words of support and who asked to see photos of her. I started a daily on-line diary on my Web site, where people could read the latest news about Chance and her struggle to live. I posted new pictures of her almost every day.

All over the world, people were falling in love with this determined little soul. The on-line horse-loving community watched with great interest as Chance and I experienced our ups and downs from day to day. Thousands shared my joy when Chance began gaining weight and sat up by herself for the first time. People were thrilled as her mouth ulcers and pressure sores healed. And when her fever shot back up and her joints began to swell again, I didn't cry alone.

There were days when the two of us were extremely tired, yet we kept up the fight. As we would rest together in the grass, I would tell Chance, "You have to keep trying. So many people are hoping and praying and sending their love." Chance would put her head in my lap as I'd hold her, stroke her and kiss her muzzle. Her lovely eyes were still saying, "I'm not giving up yet, Mama. I'm just resting."

As news of Chance's brave struggle spread over the Internet, people wrote to me saying they were doing acts of kindness in her honor. Some helped animals and others helped people needing assistance. More and more lives were indirectly touched by Chance and her courage. I felt so proud that I was able to share this wonderful little spark and watch it grow exponentially. We were all part of a miracle that was spreading.

Chance's health experienced lots of ups and downs as summer dragged on. Overall, she failed to improve as much as I'd hoped. I knew she needed to see a veterinarian, so I contacted the man who'd brought her to me and asked that his nephew give her to me officially. He did. At last, Chance was legally mine.

We went to the veterinarian and were told that most foals with this illness die. Only when it's caught at the very beginning is there any hope of recovery. The bacteria were out of control, destroying Chance's joints as well as one of her eyes. The veterinarian said that her vital organs eventually would be attacked. It was only a matter of time before

Chance would have to be put to sleep.

My goal now became simple. I wanted to help Chance experience the joys of being a horse as much as possible before her time was up. Against all odds, she was soon trying to stand up. The first time she stood, with her body contorted and her legs twisted, I laughed and cried with joy. Then she took her first steps: another milestone! She started to walk more. Several times a day, I would help her to stand and then balance her, as she would stroll all over the yard.

Chance seemed determined to see what the world had to offer her. She was carefully supervised as she met other horses on my farm. She nickered almost uncontrollably the first time she saw them. She quivered with excitement. We were watching yet another miracle in this filly's life. And through all of this, my health was holding up, which was also miraculous.

Suddenly, at two and a half months old, Chance seemed to grow tired of the fight. She had tasted green grass, enjoyed painless days and made many friends in the other animals and people who often came to visit her. Chance knew what unconditional love felt like and her very existence had spread love and hope throughout the world. Now God seemed to be letting her know it was almost time to come back home to him.

Chance no longer had a desire to get up and was content to pass the hours and days with her head in my lap. She must have felt my sadness because she would lift her head, time and time again, and nuzzle my face, asking for kisses and hugs. Somehow though, her eyes let me know that it was okay to let her go.

One Wednesday morning, I made a difficult phone call asking the veterinarian to end Chance's life the following Saturday. Then I went out and talked with Chance about it, telling her how selfish I was feeling and that I just wasn't ready to let God have her back yet. But as I was sitting there, a bird landed on the fence post just three feet from us. I turned to get a better look, expecting it to fly away, but it continued to sit there, looking at us. Then I heard the sound of flapping wings getting louder and louder. I looked up to see a flock of geese circling overhead. There was no honking, just the noise of dozens of wings. I sobbed and said out loud, "Okay God, you can have your angel back. Just please make sure she, too, gets strong beautiful wings."

Saturday morning at the veterinarian's office, Chance laid her head in my lap, as she'd done so many times before. She closed her eyes, stretched hard and sighed with contentment. The sedation went into her body, she fell asleep in my arms, and the air was sucked from my lungs as Chance took her last breath. At that moment, I knew she'd awakened in heaven.

Three days after we had laid Chance to rest under the trees at our pond, I went to visit her grave. On the dirt right above her body was a beautiful perfect feather. God kept his promise. Chance had gotten her wings.

Denise Bell-Evans

Throwing My Loop

There are times when you can trust a horse, times when you can't, and times when you have to.

Anonymous

Old ranchers often say that a man is allotted one special horse in his lifetime. I have had mine. She was a chocolate bay mare with an irregularly shaped star on her forehead. Her name was Susie and she was my friend and partner a long time ago. She taught me a most valuable lesson—one that changed my life.

I loved Susie the first time I saw her. She was standing in a pasture with a large number of mean old Brahma bulls. She had an ugly scar running from her right knee to just above the hoof. The man who owned her said he didn't know what caused the injury, but he doubted she would ever be able to run much. I thought he was wrong. I was sixteen years old and she was just two. I knew it was only a matter of time until we were pretty famous as roping partners.

The old fellow let me pay for her a little at a time. After umpiring an infinite number of Little League games, life-guarding at the local pool and mowing yards, I finally was able to make Susie mine. Actually, to say that she was mine is not quite right. I never really owned Susie. We just joined up. Like so many important things in our lives, maybe it was always meant to be.

My dad and uncles taught us a few things. More importantly, they got us help from some old calf ropers who knew what they were doing in terms of training a roping horse. Susie and I practiced long hours and after a couple of years, we were fairly competitive at small rodeos.

She was always calm in the box and had really good speed. She would spring out of there like a fighter jet, running real low and hard, and put me right where I needed to be every single time. It was effortless to rope on her. Once I threw my loop, this filly would stop in her tracks as if she'd hit a brick wall. She worked the rope really well and if everything went right, we were tough.

For instance, if Susie and I drew a lightweight calf that ran real slow with his head sticking up like a chicken, man, I was good! I could just throw my loop on him, flank him and, as long as he didn't fuss or kick, I could wrap him up, and we would take home the money. Yep, it was easy if everything went perfectly.

Problem was, everything didn't always go perfectly.

I handled this imperfection of life primarily by doing two things: I whined a lot and blamed everybody on earth but myself and old Susie. I couldn't blame Susie because she was as good a roping horse as a man could want. She always did her part.

Mostly, in my view, my parents and teachers caused the problems. When I was little, my mom and dad were really nice folks. Momma made up my bed, took out the trash and cared for everything and everybody. Teachers were nice, too, when I was in the first, second and third grade. We just had to do a little coloring in books, eat lunch and dessert, then take a nap. I had a good life as a little kid.

Then I turned into a teenager, and everybody seemed to change on me overnight. Suddenly, my mom was waking me up every morning, saying things like, "You need to get up and make up your bed, water the horses, take out the trash, mow the yard and help out around here." Frankly, I was shocked. I tried to explain to her that I simply did not do these sorts of things. Then my dad would come home and take her side every time.

Even worse, though, were my teachers. One day we're taking naps and eating chocolate cake, and the next thing you know, we're diagraming sentences and doing word problems in arithmetic.

Yep, things were rough.

That was when my downhill slide began. My parents and teachers were on me all the time, wanting me to work and learn something new every single day, but I didn't. None of it was my fault, of course. In my view, how on earth was I supposed to learn anything if I got all the bad teachers? Then these teachers would put Cs, Ds and Fs on my report card, and my parents would start yelling all over again.

Unfortunately, things got worse. My Cs, Ds and Fs from middle school and high school turned into thirteen Fs in college. I never passed a course, but it wasn't my fault. Once again, I'd gotten all the bad teachers. A counselor even diagnosed my problem. He gave me a test that found I had a below-average IQ. Whew, was I relieved! Now I had the perfect excuse not to ever try.

Things went downhill even more, and with my parents, teachers and coaches on me all the time, I came up with a plan that only a twenty-year-old could think of. Because I was pretty good with a rope and I had the world's best roping horse, I knew that old Susie and I could make it out there on the road. All we needed was a little luck.

My dad tried to explain to me that if I wasn't winning at every small rodeo now, it wasn't likely that I was going to win at the big ones. He tried to get me to see how my lack of ability was going to become even more apparent when Susie and I were up against heavier cattle. And he pointed out other problems of life on the road. But what did he know?

After all, he was old. He was forty, for goodness sake.

So I loaded up Susie in a little one-horse trailer and we hit the open highway. We were two young kids off to rope a dream. I was going down the road singing, "Old Susie was long and lean, a roping machine and her eyes were green," and all I could see in my rearview mirror was a dusty little Texas town that I no longer needed.

It all started off great. We won a little here and there. But there is nothing like life and the open road to teach a fella what's important. I learned many things on that road.

I learned that my daddy kept a good roof over our heads. Growing up under a roof that didn't leak never seemed very special until it wasn't there. I learned that no one in America was interested in whether I ate. Certainly no one would cook my food for free, but I remembered that my momma had always done exactly that. I also learned that the cattle were heavier than I had ever seen and the cowboys were better than I ever imagined and then that little town in Texas didn't seem so dusty after all.

On a cool night in Colorado, Susie and I were up in a roping event. We hadn't eaten on Thursday or Friday. We had drawn a small calf and desperately needed to win some money so we could eat. I knew we would be okay because old Susie would put me right there, and because I was good with a rope, we would be fine.

I backed her into the box, and she was as calm as she always was. I called for the calf, and just like a fighter jet, she took off. Even though she had to be hungry, she was giving me all she had. She put me right there like she always did. I leaned just a bit and knew that supper was only ten or eleven seconds away as I let my loop fly.

And I missed him. Just completely missed him.

That was bad, but things would get worse. I had to stand by a waste barrel that night and wait for a family to throw away half-eaten food so I could feed my friend. As I watched my partner reduced to eating garbage because of me, I tried so hard to think of someone to blame, but there was no one there but me. I had done this to my friend.

The longer I stood there, the more painful the experience became. I suddenly understood that my parents and teachers had not been trying to do anything but help me. They had done all that they could do to prevent my ending up at a place like this, but I wouldn't listen. Now I realized that if I couldn't take care of my horse, it was very unlikely I could provide for a spouse or a child. My horse had always done her part. I had never done mine.

The great English theologian C.S. Lewis once said, "Every conversion begins with a blessed defeat." That night was my defeat. I made a resolution to be different.

There are others who have had a similar experience. Long ago, a physician named Luke wrote about someone who must have been a lot like me. His dad tried to help him, too, but like me, this young man wouldn't listen. He spent all his money and ended up just like me, broke, hungry and full of regret.

Now, I'm certainly no preacher, but that doesn't mean cowboys can't learn from the Bible. This fellow that Luke wrote about was wasting his life until he realized that he needed his family, friends, and teachers—all the people who are sent to help us. The Bible says this young man "came to himself" and the prodigal son then knew that it was time to go home and live a different life.

And I came home, too. I have sinned many times since, but not academically. Even with my below-average IQ, I never made another B, C, D or F in school. I don't tell you this story to boast, but rather to give you what Emily Dickinson called "that feathered thing": hope.

It's just a matter of using the gifts that you have been given, applying yourself and living by that old cowboy line "When you get bucked off, get up and get back on!" In short, do your part. I learned that lesson from a very special horse. Her name was Susie and she was long and lean and a roping machine.

We have a horse farm now and some evenings at dusk, I walk in the pasture. I look at the pretty green hills behind my barn, and sometimes the breeze rustles gently and the hay meadow sways softly as if it's one living thing. And just for a minute, I can still smell Susie. I can feel her under me, running hard with her head low, giving me everything she had.

I also remember a man is allotted one special horse in his life. Fortunately, I've had mine.

Michael Johnson

Nerf Spurs. © *Cartoon copyright by Mark Parisi, printed with permission.*

2

HORSES AS TEACHERS

The educated horse is a thinking horse, and it seems that he understands that every now and then something happens that he must chalk up as a mistake and be done with it.

Dennis Murphy in Practical Horseman

The Language of Horses

Above all, a horse should never be chastised out of foul mood or anger, but always with complete dispassion.

François Robichon de la Guérinière

As a very young boy, I was sure that horses had a language and if I could speak that language, I could train them in a new and entirely different way. So it was at the age of eight that I set a life goal for myself to be able to communicate fluently with horses.

We lived on a horse facility in Salinas, California, at the time, and I spent every waking hour trying to communicate with the untamed, domesticated horses.

The summer I was thirteen, I went to Nevada for three weeks for a job. I had been hired to help capture wild mustangs. This was the first opportunity I'd had to work with totally wild horses. Determined to make the best use of my time, I rose early each day and rode a long way into the desert, where I used binoculars to study the habits of the mustang herds that lived there.

I was utterly spellbound by these horses. I would sit for hours and hours, watching those beautiful animals as they ran, grazed and played in the wide spaces of the desert.

What astonished me most was how the wild horses communicated with each other. They rarely used sounds; instead, they used a complex language of motion. The position of their bodies, and the speed and direction of their travel were the key elements of their language. And by varying the degree of rigidity or relaxation in the eyes, ears, neck, head and the position of the spine, a horse could signal anything he needed to communicate.

As I watched I thought: *Could this convince a wild horse to let me get close enough to touch him without him running away?*

So that I could easily spot him, I picked a horse with unique markings, and tried to herd him away from the others. For many days, I tried every way I could think of to get near him. But he always sensed me and he was off before I was even close. One day, I got lucky and came up behind him in a small canyon. At last, I had his full attention. Then, using only my body to convey the signals I'd seen the horses use with each other, I persuaded the wary stallion to stand still. He studied me silently as I moved closer and closer. He was watchful but he wasn't afraid. Barely breathing, I took the step that brought me within an arm's reach of him. I avoided his eyes as I stretched my hand toward him and laid it softly on his neck. It lasted only a few seconds, but it was enough. I watched him gallop away, my chest exploding with joy. I had communicated with a horse!

My desire to learn to communicate with horses became a deep inner passion that I fiercely hid from the rest of the world. Unwilling to share with anyone what was most important to me, I was usually alone, except for the horses. The only thing that mattered to me was my life's dream.

Every summer, I returned to Nevada for three weeks to work, continuing my research in the desert. Four years later, when I was seventeen, I progressed so far that I not only touched a wild mustang, I saddled, bridled and rode one without once using any pain or intimidation to do so. Proudly, I rode the wild horse back to the ranch. The ranchhands who saw me ride in called me a liar when I told them what I'd done. They insisted the horse I rode must once have been a domesticated horse who had run away and ended up with the mustangs. Deeply hurt, I realized the futility of my dreams. With no one to believe in me, it was *my* spirit that was broken.

I eventually got over the humiliation of being ridiculed and decided to continue my training methods, but I vowed I would never again tell anyone what I did.

And so I became a horse trainer. I used my experiences with every horse I worked with to learn more and more about the language of horses. It was a slow but satisfying education.

Once, when I was about twenty-five, a family hired me to tackle a problem mare. She was a beautiful horse, intelligent and extremely talented. But during her training, a previous owner had inadvertently mishandled her and she had developed a serious problem. She wouldn't stop. She would blast away like a rocket and refuse to be halted, crashing through fences and slipping and sliding as she made dangerously sharp turns. She was diabolically treacherous. A short time earlier, the mare had almost killed her owner's daughter. The family was going on vacation and they asked me to sell the horse for them for whatever I could get for her. They had heard I was good with difficult horses and they knew that in order to sell her, someone would have to be able to bring her to a stop from a run. No one else was willing to try.

This mare was the most dangerous horse I had ever seen, but I used everything I had absorbed over the years to help her. Moving slowly and keeping my communication with her to just the basics, I earned her trust. Building on that trust, I continued to communicate with her, and soon her resistance melted. Our progress was swift and remarkable from that point on. It had seemed impossible, but within a few days, she was transformed.

While the owners were still away, I showed the mare in a

competition and she took first place. I brought her prize, a very expensive saddle, to the home of her owners. I wrote them a note, explaining that she had improved enough to win this saddle and under the circumstances, I felt that they should reconsider selling her. I pinned the note to the saddle and left it in the dining room for them to find upon their return.

They were ecstatic about the change in their horse and were thrilled to be able to keep her. This mare went on to become a world-class champion. Her owners found a new willingness in her and a sweet temperament that made her presence in their family even more precious than her value as a show horse.

Many times over the next thirty years, using the simple tools of gentleness, respect and communication, I managed to turn troubled horses around and experienced the satisfaction of seeing them return to loving families.

Today, the lonely work I began in the high deserts of Nevada so many years ago is full of recognition and satisfaction. I have achieved goals beyond the simple desires of a young boy of eight, but I still find myself watching quietly, this time inspired by others as they follow my path, as they work and learn, as they become fluent in the language of horses.

Monty Roberts with Carol Kline

Riding the Edge

Competitive riding should be classical riding at its best.

Charles de Kunffy

During the summer of 1961, most of us at Rock Creek Stables traveled from Louisville to county horse shows throughout Kentucky. I was only twelve, but my parents and our trainer Jim had high ambitions.

The year before, they had purchased Bubbling Fancy after she won the Five-Gaited Pony Championship in Lexington. Dad planned a display wall for the trophies he knew we were going to win. Jim laid plans to ready us for the World's Grand Championship.

Instead, they watched for two years while I struggled to handle this high-stepping, spirited chestnut Saddlebred. Jim just scratched his chin and drawled, "Yup, she's a lotta horse." I was a skinny, four-foot, ten-inch tall girl with nerves of steel when it came to horses and no stomach whatsoever for riding in front of crowds.

I had my own ambitions. In addition to wanting to overcome fears about showing, I yearned even more to find the connection with Fancy that I had with Sugar, my trail horse.

When Sugar and I galloped across the open meadows, we were one body, one heart, racing melded and timeless against the wind. Fancy and I might hit moments where Jim shouted "Right thar!" but we were still disconnected, striving out-of-sync toward a good performance.

Jim pushed hard against my fears, entering us in a show every week. When we arrived in Harrodsburg, Kentucky, in late July, there weren't many shows left before the World's Championship in August.

At the Harrodsburg show, the barns teemed with activity: trainers unloading horses, grooms dragging bales of hay, harnesses being slapped on skittish roadsters, high-strung Saddlebreds whinnying their excitement. Smells of fresh popcorn and hot dogs wafted above the scent of tanbark, leather and horses.

Mom and I stepped into the makeshift tack room, where she helped me dress. My jacket, jodhpurs, boots and derby hat all matched. Their deep chocolate brown color showed off my long hair and Fancy's coat. The contrast was like wheat against dark earth.

Meanwhile, a groom brushed Fancy until she glistened. On went her show bridle and cutback saddle. Another groom knelt to fasten white leather cuffs around her front hooves to protect them from being kicked by her rear feet during a high-speed rack, the most thrilling of her five gaits.

Then they led Fancy, snorting and prancing, out of her dark stall. Jim bent over, knit his hands together for me to step into and boosted me onto her back.

We warmed up in the practice ring, working three of our five gaits—walk, trot and slow gait—leaving out the canter and rack, saving Fancy for the show ring. Fancy quivered with excitement and chomped on her bits. When Jim cracked his bull whip into the air, we bounded forward, her legs now tightly coiled springs.

"Right thar!"

But tension flooded my body as I glimpsed High Parader nearby. A small bay pony, he was winning a lot of shows that summer. High Parader was more cute than beautiful, but he rarely made a mistake. This was the first time our paths had crossed.

A loudspeaker blared, "Five-gaited ponies you're up!" Following Jim's strategy, I held Fancy back. Everyone else trotted in a bunched cluster up the dirt path into the show ring. The ring attendant moved to close the gates. Then we burst up the ramp and into the ring at full trot, Fancy's tail streaming high and long behind us. It worked: The crowd gasped; the judge turned to see what had captured their delight. Posting low in the saddle, hands steady on the reins, I smiled, but my anxiety spiked with the attention.

Intent on trotting fast, I pushed Fancy right to the edge, that point where she wanted to break gaits into a gallop. I picked my spot among the twelve horses in the ring—a clear position by the outer rail, where the judge could see Fancy's gorgeous form against the white wood fence.

Four times High Parader and his rider tried to pass us in front of the judge so that he would see only them. Each time, I had to act quickly to rein in Fancy but not so harshly that she would break her stride. Then I turned her short to cross the ring to a new spot. It was tricky because I wanted her pushing that edge, stepping high and fast into that tight margin where any sudden change increased the risk of breaking into another gait and losing points.

The class progressed, first in one direction, then we turned to repeat our gaits in the opposite direction.

As soon as we reversed direction, it happened. Fancy broke into a gallop. I hadn't felt it coming. I reined her in quickly until she trotted again. We were on the back side. Did the judge see us? I struggled to refocus.

Eventually, we reached the climax of the class, the call for the last, but most exciting, gait.

"Rack on!" the announcer shouted. The grandstands roared.

High Parader pounded close behind us. I gave Fancy the slightest signal through the rein. She accelerated into a rack.

Suddenly it clicked. We hit that sweet spot I longed for and we were one single creature united in motion. This time I let her energy loose, let her explode down the straightaway in a fast, high-strutting rack that launched the crowd to its feet. This time I could sense even the slightest change in her step, and before she could break stride into a gallop, I'd flick one hand, subtly signaling her on the side where she was about to step. Because I did it at precisely the right moment, this steadied her in her brilliant, flowing rack. Riding at the edge was scary. I had the feeling that I was just this side of totally out of control. A misstep here not only could break our stride, it could hurl me into a rolling crash amid dirt and flying hooves. But Jim had taught me that the edge, if we could hold it, was where we looked dazzling, so the edge was where I rode her. It was hair-raising and at the same time sheer joy, an infinite moment where nothing existed except this one pristine blur of motion that Fancy and I had become.

Suddenly, the class was over and the riders sent to one end of the ring to await the awards. We paced in the shadows, Fancy huffing hard under me. We had broken out of a trot for less than ten strides, but it had been a break just the same. Had we lost? Had High Parader fumbled, too? But he never did. His strength was a dull but dependable performance because he was never pressed to the dangerous yet exhilarating edge.

The loudspeaker called fifth place, fourth, third, second. . . . *Oh please, make it High Parader!*

"Second place, Number 186, Bubbling Fancy, Jane Douglass up."

Back at the barn, Mom and dad ran up as I dismounted.

"Second place is a great accomplishment, honey," said my dad, hugging me. "You should be proud!"

I shook my head.

Then I remembered the small carrot I had saved for Fancy. I touched her damp neck and held out the carrot. She surprised me with a nicker.

I smacked my forehead with recognition.

"Fancy! We did it!"

I didn't know about our prospects for the World's Championship in three weeks, but I did know this: I had forgotten to fear the cheering crowd because Fancy and I had found our connection.

Jane Douglass Rhodes

Big Brother Is Watching

A cowboy is a man with guts and a horse.

Will James

In the year after my father died, there was nothing I wanted more than a trophy. I was twelve and the hope of placing a trophy on my dresser woke me up in the middle of the night. All of my friends had trophies, from soccer and football, from raffle-ticket sales and BMX races and chess tournaments. One friend even had a trophy in the shape of deer antlers because he'd shot a thirteen-point buck. Any of those would have elated me. I believed they would have given me back something my father's absence had taken away. The problem was that I had no skills or talents that would yield a trophy.

My older brother Alan had shelves of trophies, too. He had some from Little League, but most came from horse shows. Before my father died, he had bought each of us a horse. Mine was a pinto pony that I named Colonel because of a white star on his shoulder. Alan's was a Quarter Horse, fourteen hands high, named Otis. Alan ran the barrels and did poleracing, and when he kicked Otis's sides and hollered for him to come on, they were nothing but run. Colonel always wanted to follow, and I could feel him gathering power and speed in his gallop, but I was afraid of falling, so I'd pull on the reins and we'd lag behind, able only to watch Alan ride.

After my father died, my mother rarely went to the stable where we boarded the horses. In fact, she really didn't go anywhere. She cut back on her hours at work and stopped going to play bridge. Mostly, she stayed in her room—in just a year it had become *her* room, not *their* room—watching infomercials, eating chocolate and chain-smoking. Alan ran a lot of errands for her and cooked our meals and paid our bills with money he made waiting tables.

This was also the year I started smoking. And I was spending time with the crowd at school that set fire to bathroom trash cans. I liked the feeling I got from being around everything I'd been told to stay away from. I might have been scared to let Colonel burst into a run beneath me, but I wasn't afraid to cut class and play video games at the mall. I liked that after I back-talked a history teacher, girls suddenly knew who I was. I liked the new heavy metal music I listened to and the way I'd learned to spit phlegm onto the ceiling. I appreciated the depths to which my grades dropped. I enjoyed hanging out with kids who, like me, had no trophies and who couldn't care less.

My brother didn't like this behavior, and when the worst of my report cards arrived in the mail, he rode with me into the pasture and interrogated me. To all of his questions—"What do you think you're doing? Who do you think you're fooling? Why are you throwing everything Mom and Dad worked for down the toilet?"—I answered: "I don't know." And the truth was, I didn't know. I was adrift, floating away from everything I'd known.

Alan started picking me up from school, denying me the opportunity to carouse with the smokers and bullies, and we drove to the stable to ride until night fell. Through all of this, I still loved riding and still found comfort in being around Colonel, but I hated being made to ride. After a week of forcing me to spend my afternoons exclusively with him, I took a self-righteous stand and told Alan that I refused to be chaperoned like this. I listed all the ways I thought he was treating me unfairly, and he let me work myself into a fury. When I'd exhausted all of my angles, Alan said, "I entered you in the horse show. It's in two weeks."

I was stunned, appalled and incredulous. I was thrilled, but I didn't let on. I huffed, "Why?"

He was cleaning Otis's hooves. Without looking at me, he said, "You want a trophy, right?"

The next week is a blur in my memory. Although I hated to admit he had such sway with my emotions, Alan's implied challenge completely refocused my attentions and my loyalties. Suddenly, I thought of nothing except strategies for running barrel events faster and methods to cut time off my pole races. I distanced myself from the smokers and bullies. When Alan picked me up after school, I asked him to drive faster to the stable. By week's end, Colonel and I had lit upon a new rhythm and we rode hard and fast, the way I'd always watch Alan ride. The night before the junior rodeo, I could already feel the trophy in my hands, the promising weight of its dignity. I could see my reflection in that golden angel's breasts.

Alan had entered me in four events, and in the first three, I floundered. My nerves sizzled in my knees and I made mistake after mistake, missing barrels I should have circled, steering Colonel to the left when we clearly should have gone right. I was on the verge of tears and in the full throes of anger. I was furious with Alan for subjecting me to my own shortcomings and with my mother for venturing back into the world to watch me fail. I was furious with my father for dying and furious with myself for being my pitiful self.

The last event was running poles and to everyone's surprise, I didn't do half bad. My time was nowhere near the fastest, but it seemed solid enough to secure me seventh place, the last place that would receive a trophy. Colonel and I watched the other riders. Before the last competitor, I was still in seventh. My mother smoked cigarette after cigarette, while Alan casually set out to find a port-o-potty. I asked how he could leave at a time like this—I couldn't stop smiling—but he just shrugged and said, "When you have to go, you have to go."

The last rider started off badly, missing a pole that would have to be circled before the run was over. The trophy was as good as mine. Then the rider hit his stride, and the second half of his run was flawless and breathtakingly swift. My heart stalled.

He'd finished two-tenths of a second faster than I had. He'd knocked me out of seventh place; he'd taken away my trophy.

But this is, as I've said, a story about my brother.

When he found me after the last rider he claimed not to have heard the judges announce the time that had beaten me out. He claimed that I'd heard incorrectly, that I was misremembering my own time. I thought he was making light of my situation, and I stormed off. How could I have not heard the right time, how could I have thought I'd ridden slower than I had?

When the announcement came during the awards ceremony, I was sitting under a mesquite tree, imagining ways to ingratiate myself back into the crowd of smokers and bullies, the kids who'd never wanted a trophy. I was only half-listening to the announcer, so when he called my name—and Colonel's—his voice didn't really register. It was a voice from a dream, the voice of a ghost. He said I was in seventh place, that I should come claim my trophy. He called my name again, like a question this time. "Donald Keyes, you out there?" None of this seemed real. For a split second, I thought the voice was my father's.

I can still remember running toward the corral as if my life depended on it. I can hear and feel my boots hitting the hard dirt of the arena, can hear the crowd laughing gently as they applaud. I can see Alan and my mother clapping, my mother wiping her eyes, my brother giving me a smug thumbs-up. I can remember wondering how I could have made the mistakes Alan had cited, hearing the wrong time, underestimating my own score. I can remember letting those mistakes go, releasing them with some of the pain that came from losing my father, some of the anger I had toward him for leaving us and some of the anger I had at myself for being so angry with him. It's strange how our minds work, how hope can become a stand-in for a father, the same way an older brother can. It's strange how our deepest wounds heal right before our eyes, yet we never notice this until the scars are gone.

I've always known that I didn't win that trophy, just as I've known that the reason the judge handed it to me had everything to do with Alan. I don't know where he went during that last rider's turn, but I suspect he ducked away to the judges' booth and somehow convinced them that awarding his little brother a trophy was maybe one of the most important things they would do in their lifetimes. Maybe he just presented my case—a young father who died suddenly, a mother who would never recover, the wrong crowd, the hours and hours of practice—or maybe he handed the judges twenty dollars, maybe a hundred. I imagine he did whatever he had to do, no matter what the cost. I imagine when he reads this—we haven't broached the subject for twenty years—he'll deny the allegations with typical stubbornness and dismiss them with kindly fraternal disinterest. He'll say I've always had a talent for making up stories, which is why I became a writer and university professor.

And I'll say, No. I became a writer and professor and a man, because he had faith in me. I'll say he knew what I needed when I didn't, that he reached out and cared for me when I was more trouble than I imagined. I'll say he taught me how to ride and how to live. And I'll say, Thank you. Again and again, my brother, thank you.

Don Keyes

God Bless Little Horse Lovin' Souls

Whenever you observe a horse closely, you feel as if a human being sitting inside were making fun of you.

Elias Canetti

Our nine-year-old daughter Lindsay was extremely excited about entering her young gelding in his first schooling show. After riding and taking lessons for several years, Lindsay had some show experience under her belt, but this was the first time she was going to enter with a horse of her very own. And because Snickers was only a three-year-old, it promised to be a big day for both of them.

We'd tried to instill in Lindsay the concept that winning ribbons isn't what showing should be all about. It was a tough message to get across because, heck, she's just a kid, and what child wouldn't want to come away from a show with proof of how well she had done? To help her understand this, we'd asked Lindsay to set a goal for herself, consisting of two specific accomplishments that she'd like to achieve with Snickers in the ring that day. That way, if she reached her goal, she'd be a winner regardless of how she placed in the class. After much thought, she came up with two ideas that were pretty straightforward: keep Snickers moving and don't let him cut the corners. Perfect!

About to enter the ring for her class, Lindsay was very excited. Snickers looked magnificent, groomed to within an inch of his life and braided to the hilt. Lindsay was equally well turned out, from her glossy black boots to the top of her velvet helmet. One look at her and it was obvious that she was bursting with pride.

I took a moment to remind her to focus on her goal and to just try her best. Because this was Snickers's first show, I told Lindsay not to expect too much from him, and how important it was that the experience be a positive one. She gave me a big smile and a thumbs-up and proceeded into the ring.

As it turned out, they did extremely well in the class. Snickers behaved like an old veteran, totally unfazed by it all. Lindsay kept him going forward nicely and she didn't let him cut the corners of the ring. Although they didn't place, she had accomplished her goal, and I was thrilled for them.

As I ran over to offer my heartfelt congratulations, I saw that Lindsay was bent over in the saddle with her arms wrapped around Snickers's neck, hugging and patting him. When she raised her head to look at me, I couldn't help but notice that her eyes were filled with tears.

"Sweetie, what's wrong?" I asked. "You guys were absolutely amazing!"

"Oh, Mom," she replied in a shaky voice. "Snickers did such a good job and I'm so proud of him."

Then, just before the tears really started to fall, she managed to add: "I understand all about the ribbons and stuff, but I'm afraid that Snickers is just too young not to be upset about it!"

Patricia Carter

Encounter with a Dangerous Spy

A horse gallops with his lungs, perseveres with his heart, and wins with his character.

Frederico Tesio

I confess. I do not like riding horses.

I would sooner run with the bulls of Pamplona than ride a horse. I would sooner bungee jump. I would sooner go over Niagara Falls in a barrel.

I am, to use the politically correct term, "equine challenged."

So you can imagine my reaction when Barbara Orr, an otherwise nice woman from Ojai, California, asked me if I wanted to try to ride an ill-tempered wild mustang named Tornado.

Actually, Barbara asked if I wanted to ride a mild-mannered, well-trained Thoroughbred named Spy. But, really, what's the difference? Neither has a seat belt.

"NO WAY!" I said, explaining that I had never ridden a horse in my life and now was no time to break my streak— or my leg.

Correction. Let me be more specific. I have never before ridden a live horse, which is not to say that I had never been on a bucking bronco. Twice, in fact, I had.

The first time was at age three when I rode one of those spring-suspended hobby horses. It was a dangerous toy: no seat belt. I got thrown over the front. Faulty stirrup, I think. And I lost my two top front teeth, I kid you not.

As they say, if you get thrown from a horse, you've got to get right back on. I did. Well, at age four. This time I got aboard a mean merry-go-round wild bronco named Cyclone as I recall. Or it should have been.

As the story was told to me after I regained consciousness —and after a trip to the emergency room—the carousel went around once, twice, three times, when my dad finally noticed that I was no longer on Cyclone. That's right, I got bucked off, thus becoming the only person in history to ever require a dozen stitches on the forehead due to a runaway merry-go-round horse.

I have worse luck with ponies than someone who loses the rent money at the track. Personally, I have forever since thought that horse sense means being smart enough not to get on a horse.

Trying to weasel out of falling off Spy, I confessed my equestrian mishaps to Barbara. After she stopped laughing and wiped the tears from her eyes, she said she would give me a free lesson.

Not usually one to look a gift horse in the mouth, I looked at the bit in Spy's mouth and said, "ARE YOU CRAZY? CAN YOU IMAGINE WHAT A REAL HORSE WOULD DO TO ME?"

"Chicken," said Orr.

"Darn right," I said.

"Fraidy cat," Ms. Orr-nery said.

Horse feathers. Dirty pool. I may be a chicken, but I am no fraidy cat. I gathered my courage up.

I got up on Spy.

Then I made my second mistake. I looked down. Vertigo. I suddenly realized where the phrase "On your high horse" originated. Horses are tall.

Spy, to be precise, stands 16.1, that's 16 hands (with a hand equaling four inches) plus one more inch. Or, if my math is correct, about eleven feet at the shoulders.

Barbara also told me that Spy, a beautiful gray Thoroughbred, weighs about 1,250 pounds, although I have to question that. I mean, really now, how did Barbara get Spy to stand still on the bathroom scale?

Anyway.

As if I weren't already shaking enough in my boots (okay, shaking in my Nikes) Barbara says: "On a 1,200-pound animal with a mind of its own, there is a potential for danger."

No duh! On a twenty-pound carousel horse with no mind of its own there is a potential for danger.

Barbara instructed me on how to make Spy turn. In addition to gently pulling the reins—left to go left and right to go right, simple even for a sportswriter—you simultaneously also squeeze with your right leg to go left and your left leg to go right.

I kept getting confused and would squeeze with my right leg while pulling the right rein. Poor Spy didn't know what to do, because, in effect, I was telling him to turn right and left at the same time.

"Don't kick him, squeeze him like a tube of toothpaste," Barbara further instructed me. Bad analogy. She obviously has not seen the mess I leave around the sink with the cap off.

Somehow, I figured out left means right and right means left and I got Spy to go where I wanted him to go. Or, if he didn't, I would just pretend I wanted to go where he took me.

Making a "cluck, cluck" sound gets a horse to walk. To go faster, you make a kissing sound and give a squeeze with your heels in his ribs.

I did the latter and had an instant flashback to when I was three because I almost got thrown from the saddle. Spy took off as if he'd seen a rattlesnake. Barbara called it "loping," but the truth of the matter is that Spy was galloping at Kentucky Derby speed—at least eighty miles an hour, I swear.

At this point, I think Barbara was impressed with my

natural ability because she said, and I quote, "I've never seen anyone ride a horse like you do."

The biggest problem I had was that I'd laugh out loud with delight at the fun I was having, and Spy would take my laugh as a "Whoa!" and stop.

In all, I rode for an hour and fifteen minutes. I would have gotten off sooner but I was having too much fun. Also, I forgot how to make Spy stop. Fortunately, Spy finally heard Barbara laughing at me and took it as a "Whoa!"

Despite the snickering, I had about as much fun as you can have with your clothes on. Toward the end, I was making Spy do figure eights and figure sevens and even some figure threes. I made him go fast, slow and even backward. I don't want to brag, but after seeing me, the birds started whistling the theme song to *Bonanza*.

Barbara was a miracle worker, but I learned a few things the hard way. One, a city slicker should never ride a horse for an hour and fifteen minutes the first time out because you won't be able to walk for three days afterward.

Two, I learned that you should always take your wallet out before riding a horse. All that bouncing around bent my credit cards so much that they don't work, even the ones that aren't maxed out over my limit.

Yes, I was a little sore. But, hey, no stitches were required. And I returned home with all my teeth, which, of course, explains why my smarty-pants wife did not believe me when I limped through the front door and proudly told her I had ridden a real horse.

Her exact words: "I don't believe you."

After she stopped cackling, she added: "So then, Hoss, how come you aren't missing any teeth? Where are your new stitches?"

By the way, Barbara Orr informed me, and with a little too much delight I might add, that Spy competes under the show name Just for Laughs. I think that is called painful irony.

Woody Woodburn

Between a Rock and a Hard Place

Between a Rock and a Hard Place. *Reprinted by permission of Boots Reynolds.* ©1987 *Boots Reynolds.*

Standing Ground

It was one of those frosty days when you can see your breath white and sparkling in front of you even though it's midday. The frost was feathered on the fence line and it sparkled on the horses' whiskers. I must have been eight or nine years old and feeling very big because I was to help Dad with the horses that day. Dad was telling me to stand in the downed fence line and turn the horses back if they came my way. We needed the bunch of them to go up the fence line and not through to the other pasture. There was only so much daylight to work with and Dad was always saying not to burn daylight.

I remember seeing them coming, the whole bunch of them running toward me, their heads and tails high as if they were having the best time making fresh tracks in the snow. I knew Dad was counting on me to hold them, but they were coming fast and they didn't look like they were going to turn just because I was standing there. I remember them passing in a rush as I felt myself shrinking up and feeling small and helpless. I hadn't moved, but I felt invisible.

Then came Dad, with a look of frustration on his face that I had seen before. Then I was filled with an awful feeling of shame and guilt. I was the cause of wasted hours and effort. We would have to go find the horses, get them back in and try again to send them up the line toward the barn. I was keenly aware of the ache of cold in my fingers and the fact that because of my failure we would be in the frosty air much longer. I wanted to blow away in the wind and become even smaller than I had felt as the band of horses and ponies rushed past me with such fun in their eyes.

I knew that Dad was annoyed and I felt the tears well up in my eyes as he came to the fence line. I stared at the ground. I had let him down and I didn't dare cry on top of it. He looked at me and said with clenched teeth and a level voice, "You have to hold your ground. If you think they are going to rush you, stand your ground and let them know you're there." I knew he would have yelled had it been my older brothers who had let the horses through and the knowledge only shamed me more. I didn't know how I was going to make myself bigger, but I knew we couldn't afford the time it would cost if there were a repeat of my performance.

By the time we had the horses back onto the right side of the fence line, they were really having fun, blowing and snorting as they crossed over the fence line and past my post once again. Now came the test. Dad looked at me with those clear blue eyes as if to say, "Hold 'em!" I had to keep them inside that fence. As they came toward me again, blowing and bucking, I could feel the sweat deep down inside my clothes and the scratchy frost on my collar. Fear started to creep up and stiffen my shoulders. I looked at them all in one glance. Midnight was leading the way, his shiny black coat glistening in contrast to the snow. Silver Bell, my little sorrel pony, was not far behind with her head thrown up and her eyes dancing. Dad was in the distance slowing to watch and wait. I locked my eyes on him and felt his words sink into my body: hold your ground. Hold my ground! I pulled my shoulders back and thought *I am big enough to hold my ground.* I felt frozen in place and I threw my arms wide and yelled "Ha! Ha!"

Midnight whirled, and I felt his breath as his feet threw

snow and mud against me, but I held my place and didn't give in to that sinking feeling that had made me feel so small the last time they came through. As he whirled, I saw the rest begin to turn up the fence line and I began to jump up and down and yell. I felt a tingle all the way down to my stiffened toes. I had held my ground! They had seen me and known that I was big enough to stand firm!

Dad waved me in behind them as they turned up the fence line and we followed them in. Dad didn't say anything about that morning to anyone, not even me. But the look on his face made me know that he was proud of me, and that was enough. That, and knowing that the horses had seen something different about me that second time around.

Starr Lee Cotton Heady

That Ol' Black Magic

The sight of that pony did something to me I've never quiet been able to explain. He was more than tremendous strength and speed and beauty of motion. He set me dreaming.

Walt Morey

I had one horse, a beautiful Tennessee Walker named Bob. He was all I needed and, if the truth be known, I didn't really need him all that much. Then, a few days following my fourteenth birthday, a neighbor friend told me about a black mare.

"She's really pretty," he said, "but she's wild. She's been running on about forty acres with a dozen or so mules. The guy who owns the land told me she's been there at least three or four years, which is why she's so wild. He also told me her owner hasn't paid board for her in eighteen months or more."

I was listening. I knew there was a point to this story and I also knew he hadn't made it yet. I was familiar with all of Robert's idiosyncrasies. He was seventeen with a flair for the dramatic.

"Anyway, Mr. Burns, he's the one who owns the place,

told me we can have her if we can catch her. Actually, I was thinking of you and not me since we already have more horses than we can feed or need."

"What do you mean *have her?*" I queried.

He shook his head. "I mean just what I said. We can have her. Free. For nothing. All we need to do is catch her."

"And just how wild is she?" I asked.

He grinned and then he laughed. "Pretty darned wild. Wanna' go look at her?"

The trip was short, and we caught Mr. Burns walking back to the barn with a couple of empty buckets. A black mare was standing in the middle of the mules gathered around some hay and a little grain in a corner of the field nearest the house.

I sat in Robert's truck with the window down, looking. The mare would be beautiful with some loving attention and care. As things were, her long mane and tail were matted with burrs. Her forelock was no better, standing straight out from her forehead in a compact burr column, making her look like a ragamuffin unicorn. Her feet were grown out to the point of being inhumane and, even from a distance, I could see that one eye was infected.

"It was probably a thistle," I said.

"What?" answered Robert.

"Her eye," I said. "The right one is infected. She probably poked a thistle in it.

"Just how would you propose to catch her?" I continued. "We sure couldn't walk up to her and slip on a halter and lead rope, especially if she stays bunched inside those mules. Do you know how hard those things kick? And they'll run right over you if they can't get in a good kick."

Robert chuckled. "Yeah, I know that, but here's what I was thinking. Mr. Burns already is feeding them in a corner. We ride over here on our horses and tie them to the fence, within easy smelling distance of the mules and the mare. We come over here the night before and string a second set of wire. We make it long enough to reach from one side of the corner to the other."

I rolled my eyes skyward. I already knew where he was headed, but I let him go on and assume the dramatic role of mastermind. It cost me nothing and it made him feel good. He went through his entire plan, ending with trapping the mules and the mare in the corner of the pasture and then releasing the mules, one or two at a time, while keeping the mare snared.

"And you really and truly think this will work?" I queried in dismay.

"Look," he said in an irritated tone, "this is a free horse. Free! She's not a spring chicken, but she's still plenty young enough to have a baby or two, and how many times have you said that's what you've always wanted?"

Yes, I thought, I definitely wanted this mare and, yes, I definitely would like to breed her. I smiled and shook my head in the affirmative. We got out of the truck and greeted Mr. Burns, filling him in on our plan. He was skeptical and made us promise to tell our parents and, further, make them promise not to sue him should anything happen to us. We agreed.

Suddenly, owning the mare became a reality. I pictured her in our barn. I mentally named her Black Magic because, obviously, she was black and, not so obviously, because it would be sheer magic when (not if) we caught her. I was even thinking about a chocolate-colored stallion named Soldier. Mr. Diggs, another neighbor, owned him. He'd be a perfect match for Black Magic. The mare was as good as mine and we hadn't made the first move toward trapping her.

The plan was in place and we began executing it the following evening. We twisted smooth wire around the gnarled, crusty tree branches that served as posts, checked in with Mr. Burns and then went home. The next day, we rode our horses back and arrived just as Mr. Burns was dumping the feed. We began working and we worked and we worked until darkness fell and Mr. Burns switched on all five of his big, outside floodlights.

We kept working until all of the mules were out and only the mare was in. She was upset, nervous, constantly moving, switching her ears back and forth and flaring her nostrils. She also was exhausted. Now what?

"If we leave," said Robert, "the mules will come back and aggravate her. I'm afraid she'll hurt herself trying to get out."

"Fine," I rebutted. "So what do we do with her?"

It was Mr. Burns who solved the knotty problem. "That corral over there is old, but it's sound and sturdy," he said. "It would put quite a bit of distance between the mare and the mules, and I don't think she could break out of it or hurt herself."

"But how do we get her over there?" I asked.

"Doing the same thing you've already done," he responded. "I have some hog wire in the barn. String it from either side of the corner to the corral gate. That'll make a sort of alley. Then herd her over there."

Thirty minutes later, the "walls" were up. The mare, who was covered in lather and wild-eyed, whirled around and looked at the gaping opening. She was confused. We kept our voices calm and started shooing her toward the alleyway leading to the corral. It was a frightening, rather torturous process, but it finally worked. Black Magic was actually in the corral.

The following day began weeks and weeks of hard work. We did everything possible to gentle the mare. Soothing voices. Special treats. Hours of sitting calmly and silently outside her corral gate. More hours standing motionless inside the gate.

Nothing worked. She refused the treats. She bolted as soon as we took one small step in her direction. She'd been in the corral for three weeks and, still, all we could see of her eyes were the whites. Worse, she was losing weight at a nearly alarming rate. She munched uninterestedly at the hay, and not even that if she saw anyone around.

"How could she get this wild?" I asked Mr. Burns.

"Don't know," he answered. "I guess God created some

animals to be wild and others he created to be part of a person's life. The wild ones have a different spirit. I've seen folks
try to force the first ones into the second group, and I can tell
you, the result is pitiful. You could call it broken. I hate to tell
you this, but I think this mare belongs to the first group."

Somewhere, deep inside my soul, I think I heard the truth
in Mr. Burns' voice, but I wasn't ready to give up. She had a
name. She was no longer just the black mare. She was Black
Magic. And she had a breeding to Soldier coming up and I
could already imagine see her long-legged baby running like
the wind across the pasture. I just needed to work harder.

And I did work harder, and Black Magic refused to
respond. There were moments, very fleeting moments, when
I caught a different look in her eyes. It was the faintest of all
possible hints that she would like to be a part of my life but,
unlike me, she'd accepted that it wasn't meant to be.

Now that I'm much, much older, I look back and smile. I
think of Black Magic and me like an ill-fated, star-crossed
pair of lovers. The attraction was there, but it would be fatal.
It was just a matter of who recognized it first. In this case, it
was Black Magic.

I knew what had to be done. Black Magic's coat had turned
dull. Her eyes were becoming sad and lackluster. She was a
different horse than the one we'd worked so hard to capture
two months earlier. It was time to turn her loose and, somewhere inside my fourteen-year-old soul, I knew it was more
than turning loose just one black horse. I knew it was also
turning loose my dreams and hopes. Although I didn't realize it then, it was also finding out that sometimes the best
way to show love is to turn something or someone loose. I
also learned that sometimes it's better not to capture something in the first place.

The hog-wire alleyway was still in place. I opened the corral gate and waited until Black Magic turned her head
toward the opening. She eyed it. She stood still and then
looked at me. She watched me and waited. All I did was nod
my head. I still don't know how, but she knew what I was

telling her. She didn't run. She just trotted down the alley-way and into the pasture where the mules had waited for her for the entire two months. She stopped once and looked back at me.

A kid can't possibly know what he is learning as life's equations fall into some sort of sequential order. And certainly no one ever knows what form the teachers will assume, since God sends all kinds. In this case, it was a black mare with burrs in her mane and tail, and outgrown feet. I learned about freedom and sacrifice. I learned about caring enough to let go, a lesson I've carried with me each time I've been faced with putting a beloved animal to sleep. I learned that sometimes people and animals enter our lives for only a short time, passing through the portals of our hearts just long enough to leave us with the results of an important lesson or the seeds of a life-changing idea.

Black Magic was a teacher. I never went to see her again. For whatever reason, it seemed that merely visiting her would break apart something very special. It was as if a piece of that hog wire was keeping us attached and, even though I'd learned about freedom, I didn't want to cut us apart forever.

I never did get a mare and I never did get a foal. But that was just as well because there was no room for them in the corner of my heart that was still occupied by the black mare and her imaginary chocolate-colored foal. Now, all these many, many years later, I can still feel the spell woven by that ol' Black Magic.

Diane M. Ciarloni

One Good Horse

A man on a horse is spiritually as well as physically bigger than a man on foot.

John Steinbeck

I was born the only son of a respected Montana cowboy. He was a man cut from the old cloth, quick with his fists when called upon, the last of the wild-horse runners. He was a good hand in the hills, a poker player and horse trader, more comfortable among men than women and children.

From my mother I inherited a slight, wiry frame and an artistic nature. From my father, I inherited expectations.

Because of my father's horse-trading, horses of all shapes, colors and dispositions passed through our corrals. If they were not too bad—no obvious pawing, kicking, biting or pitching of themselves over backward—I was expected to ride them.

The good horses sold quickly at a profit. The bad ones stayed longer.

My father was also a horse breeder. Later, his herd would show the good blood of foundation Texas-bred performance horses and AAA running stock. But it began with mustangs: jug-headed, blue roan mares and white-eyed stallions.

My father was also an opportunist. Whatever fad entered the horse world, he followed: Shetlands, Appaloosas, whatever the public wanted.

"I wish you would get some good horses on this place," I often heard my mother scold him.

But the barbs did not pierce his thick Irish hide. A "good" horse was any horse that made money.

At the age of ten, I was given my first horse to break. It was a blue roan we called Ribbon Tail, the product of a half-Shetland mare and a leopard Appaloosa stallion. He was to be my bar mitzvah, the horse that would make me a cowboy.

He was my nightmare.

Ribbon Tail had wood for brains and iron for will. He would respond not to love or discipline, training or torture. He was a barn-sour, stiff-necked, thick-hided curse to a little boy who dreamed the contradictory dreams of poetry, painting and pleasing his father.

Try as I might, I could not break the blue roan. I slept dreading the morning. I awoke with a sickness in my stomach and heart. I was raised being told, "A good cowboy made himself a hand on any horse he rode." It was the cowboy, I had been trained to believe, not the horse. So Ribbon Tail was not the failure. I was.

My sentence with the blue roan lasted two years. It was hard time. He humiliated me at brandings, roundups, anyplace where men and horses gathered.

And worse, I humiliated my father.

Finally, my father tried putting other boys on Ribbon Tail, fellows my age and older, boys more aggressive and fearless than I. But they failed, too. On any given day, no one was capable of making Ribbon Tail leave a corral.

When my mother finally talked my father into selling Ribbon Tail, I was relieved, but not ecstatic. By then, I was numb. My early love of horses was all but gone, and I considered myself a failure, a pariah of the plains.

It was a surprise then, when my father came home from

an auction a year later with a new horse for me. It was a yearling Paint stallion. Dad had been attracted by his splashy sorrel and white coloring.

"What is his breeding?" my mother asked.

"Dunno," Dad said. "No papers. He's probably a crop-out from a Quarter Horse herd."

I named the horse Gusto, and he changed my life.

I started Gusto when he was a two-year-old. He had a soft, kind eye and he liked people. The first time on him, I eased off a corral rail onto his bare back and rode him around the pen without a bridle. He reined naturally and was so smooth that I bragged to cowboy friends, "You can roll a cigarette on him at a gallop."

Gusto took to cows like he was part heeler, nipping calf tails on the long trail to our summer pasture. But mostly, he was a healer. With his gentle responsive ways, he closed the wounds in my soul that Ribbon Tail had left open and bleeding.

My father said nothing. Compliments were not his way. But anyone could see his chest swell with pride at the mention of Gusto.

Gusto was never to be a big horse. He stood under 15 hands and his back was a little too round. But he had a good hip, deep girth and more heart than one horse should carry. He would begin a hard day at a brisk walk, cover country and work cattle for hours in the heat and bring you home in the evening with the same rhythmic pace.

Gusto made anyone a hand. When we sorted pairs, he and I did most of the cutting. When it came to branding, he and I pulled the calves to the fire. When a big outside circle had to be ridden, either I rode Gusto or my father did.

He made us all forget the mean little roan we had called Ribbon Tail.

Gusto and I seemed inseparable, but graduation from high school and the blossoming of my creative side would finally put the miles and years between us.

I was riding a big circle the day the newspaper called. I

was eighteen and my writing career had started. I got off Gusto that day and I would never get on him the same again. I was leaving the ranch, moving from the tack room to the newsroom, my trail taking me to two different newspapers in Montana, free-lancing in California and New Mexico, and a stint with the information office of the Air Force.

With me gone, my younger sister Debbie claimed Gusto and began training him on barrels and poles. He thrived on competition, winning buckles, ribbons and trophies, and setting one indoor arena record.

When Debbie married, Gusto became my father's horse. With no children in the house, his companion on those long circles in the badlands was my mother, and sometimes she rode the Paint.

I was twenty-six years old when my father passed away and I returned to the ranch. Gusto was thirteen, his best years behind him, but I had come home to relearn cowboying. He served as coach for me and my wife, a city girl who learned to ride on his back. When my two children became old enough to set a saddle, Gusto took care of them.

The last time I seriously rode Gusto, he was nineteen. I could feel the arthritis stiffening his shoulders and the spring leaving his legs.

At the age of twenty-two, Gusto was retired. He still wintered at home, but his summers were spent across the road in the "rough section," in the company of mares and foals or yearlings.

"What are you going to do when Gusto dies?" a friend once asked me. "You are going to have to sell the ranch," he answered himself, stating in one sentence what a symbol Gusto had become.

He was always there, grazing the creek bottoms or standing on a high gumbo hill swatting flies. Strangers sometimes stopped and inquired about him. Some wanted to buy him. One fellow just stopped to say that Gusto was the prettiest horse he had ever seen.

But age was creeping up.

Always an easy keeper, Gusto began losing flesh. Always the king of the remuda, he was now on the bottom of the pecking order. New young horses treated him rudely, disrespectfully. He lay down often, rose slowly and painfully unhinged himself to walk.

One cold winter day after the morning feed, he lay down on the sun-warmed corral floor and went to sleep. He awoke hours later, after the other horses had long since left the corral. He seemed disoriented, almost panicky, as he struggled to his feet. He left the corral desperately, nickering as he walked, calling out like an old man who had fallen asleep on a park bench and awakened to find his family gone.

I kept putting off putting him down.

What will you do when Gusto dies? kept spinning in my head. And all the time, his arthritis worsened.

Finally, one November I knew I could not make Gusto endure another Montana winter. He was now twenty-six years old, which is old for a horse. I saddled my best horse, a registered Paint gelding, and rode out into the rough section. I found Gusto keeping company with a pregnant mare.

I dismounted, stroked Gusto's head, put my arms around his neck, and told him good-bye.

The next day, I left for a week-long elk-hunting trip. The grave had already been dug on a high cedar-topped ridge that overlooks the Sunday Creek valley. My son, now fourteen, rode out and brought Gusto in. My veterinarian put Gusto down.

When I knew it was done, I came home.

I have been ranching for twenty-three years now. I have endured some terrible droughts and harsh winters. Part of my heart has become tough and pragmatic. I know what has to be done and how to do it.

But another part of my heart is soft, vulnerable. It is the part that Gusto healed.

John L. Moore

Take a Deep Seat

Always smile when you are riding because it changes your intent.

James Shaw

When I decided to take riding lessons I had just turned fifty. I wasn't an athletic man. The chances of getting a broken neck on my first horse seemed pretty good. I wasn't in shape, and as it turns out, you don't just sit there. Nope. Not in English saddle, you don't.

"Get your heels down!" my instructor yelled. She was seventy if she was a day and she still had a figure so trim she dared to wear Lycra leggings under a gray sweatshirt and got away with it. I knew why later, when she went into the hayloft and started throwing huge bales around all by herself.

Her hair was coal black and her skin so smooth that teenage boys probably whistled at her in the mall. But when you got up close, you barely noticed a hardness to her that must have been a face lift and surely her hair was dyed, and you bet she had on plenty of makeup. Still, I didn't look as good as she did, and I doubted I'd live as long.

One day, they put me on a big gelding named Burt.

"You're looking sharp," Bev yelled at me. "You couldn't ride a boxcar with the doors shut, but you look good just sitting there."

"Why, Bev, that's the first compliment you ever gave me."

"Don't get used to it."

I could see her as a ballet teacher. I could see her with a long cane that she pounded on a dance floor as she moved her little swans around like puppets.

"Fascist!"

She laughed. Neither of us took the other too seriously. She knew I'd never be one of her fifteen-year-old equitation students, and I was just glad she was old enough to understand my jokes.

"Take a deep seat," she said.

I didn't know what that meant, and she was so busy yelling about my right foot turning out, that I forget to ask. Naturally, I did the wrong thing. I sat back on my tailbone as the horse trotted and I couldn't find the rhythm. I was supposed to rise up with the horse's outside leg and lower down with the inside. I was supposed to look good. Instead, I bounced around like one of those little monkeys they tie to a dog at the state fair.

"Stop that bouncing. Don't you sit around the corner. Darn you, post!"

I'd lost a stirrup by then. I was looking off to the side and trying to find it when I lost one rein. The obedient horse, good old Burt, went right where I'd pointed him—into a mammoth pile of sawdust.

Burt stood there up to his knees in the wood shavings they used to line the floors of the stalls and then he turned his head looking at me as if he was saying, "You dork!"

Bev just stared.

It was the kind of stare that required a witty response, so I said, "Oh yeah!" and I backed the horse out. I backed him an extra six steps just to show that I could.

"If there was a backward show, you'd win a blue ribbon." Bev ran a hand over her face. She did it again and then turned around. Her shoulders were shaking.

"Well, don't cry about it."

She turned around and tears were rolling down her face. She was about to bust a gut, laughing at me. "Oh good lord!" she said. "Have you ever seen anyone ride before?"

"Roy Rogers . . . Hopalong Cassidy."

"Not cowboys. English riders!"

I got down and she started complaining about that. "That's not how you dismount. I've told you before. Gimme those reins." Her fingers had started angling away from the palms. I could see arthritis in her future. And I knew about the show-ring accident that ended her career. I'd heard how she was dragged and that her back would never be the same.

"I'm going to do this once," she said. "You understand? I'm doing it because I like you, but you're an idiot." She took a halfhearted swipe at my head and said, "Boost me up."

She didn't weigh any more than my twelve-year-old daughter. I almost tossed her over the horse.

Bev squinted at me and shook her head again. "Now you watch."

What came next was a lesson in oneness. Bev moved with the horse so that the animal was free to trot as if he had no rider, no rider at all. Bev wasn't posting—going up and down with the horse—she was floating above him. She was allowing the horse total freedom and yet she was somehow totally in control.

I stood in the center of the arena and she rode around me. At first, she tried talking, explaining the intricacies of her movements. But quickly a look of bliss came upon her face and she forgot all about teaching.

As she floated above old Burt, I saw the years fade away until I was sure I saw a young woman still beautiful and still in the prime of her life.

Then her grin changed and I knew she was hurting.

She pulled the horse up in front of me. "Help me down," she said. "I'm old."

"Bev, you'll never be old as long as you live," I said. "I'm helping a goddess dismount."

"Yeah right. Don't think sucking up will get you any- where. You're going back on that horse and ride another hour."

"Yes ma'am."

"And when you're done, write me a check." She walked away with just the slightest of limps and I knew she'd prob- ably have a backache tonight.

"Thank you!"

She turned and flashed me a grin. "I haven't been on a horse in a long time," she said. "It was worth the pain pills I'll have to take tonight."

"It was worth it to me to see a truly glorious rider."

I think she blushed just a little. Then she stomped away, turning my lesson over to an eighteen-year-old girl whose smile would never be quite as big or as wonderful as Bev's was that day.

Gary Cadwallader

3

THESE AMAZING ANIMALS

The old mare watched the tractor work,
a thing of rubber and steel,
ready to follow the slightest wish
of the man who held the wheel.
She said to herself as it passed by,
you gave me an awful jolt,
but there's still one thing you can't do,
you cannot raise a colt.

George Rupp

Sgt. Reckless, a Mighty Marine

I figured they'd at least offer me a blindfold or maybe a cigarette. My commanding officer marched back and forth in front of me and I could hear the crowd outside growing restless.

"You know why you're in here, don't you? I'm saving your life. You've ruined hers. You've destroyed her reputation along with that of the baby."

"It's a foal, sir. It's a foal, not a baby horse," I replied meekly.

"I don't care what the technical term is. The fact remains you have ruined its life, its mother's reputation and, in all probability, made a laughingstock of the Marine Corps!" he growled. "Now, sit yourself down and think about the consequences of your actions while I go out there and see what I can do to straighten out this mess!"

So this was how it was going to end. I had survived the war only to face a firing squad stateside for telling the truth. I was only doing my job.

"Join the Marines and see the world!" the poster promised. Unfortunately, I missed the fine print that said I'd have to walk. It was 1953. The draft was still on for the Korean Conflict, so for me it was either get drafted or join the service of my choice. The Marines said they needed a few good men, but they would take me anyway. They were behind in their quota they said.

Boot camp—tent camp—Korea. That didn't take long. They were further behind than I thought. After losing half of our regimental staff to dysentery, they transferred me from cooking for the enlisted men to cooking for the officers up on the hill. They said they could keep a better eye on me and if just one officer got sick, they would transfer me to reconnaissance.

It was in recon that I first heard about the little horse Reckless. It seems a Lt. Pederson of the Recoilless Rifles Platoon, Anti-Tank Company, fifth Marine Regiment had bought her off the racetrack in Seoul, Korea, for $250. Reckless was bought for the sole purpose of serving as an artillery packhorse, and what a packhorse she became.

Those 75 mm rounds she carried weighed over twenty pounds apiece and, fully loaded, she could replace six men packing ammo up those steep hills to gun placements. This little sorrel, blaze-faced mare was quite a war-horse, quickly gaining the respect of the men of the entire fifth Marine Regiment. She stood only about 14 hands high, but she had the heart and soul of a true marine. Her stamina and determination were incredible.

During one battle, she carried more than 800 rounds to gun positions in front of enemy lines. The North Koreans must have been shocked to see her working her way through the war-ravaged brush, looking like some prehistoric, hump-backed monster covered with large scales. Her strange appearance resulted from the men placing flak jackets over her fully loaded packs to protect her from being hit by shrapnel from the shells exploding around her.

As it was, she was wounded twice. In one courageous battle called Outpost Vegas, this little mare made more than fifty trips to gun positions, carried more than 9,000 pounds of recoilless ammo and covered more than thirty miles. She was wounded on one of those trips, but she bravely finished her quest and thus was given the name Reckless by her squad. Her real name was Ah Chim Hai, which roughly translated meant "morning flame."

It's interesting to note that once the squad leader showed Reckless the locations of the gun placements, she would make the trips to the front lines and back by herself with no additional human guidance. For her heroic feats, Reckless received the Korean Service Medal with three battle stars, the United Nations Service Medal, the National Defense Service Medal and two Purple Hearts. She was a true marine heroine.

Whenever the fifth Marines pulled back from the front lines for some well-deserved R and R, Reckless was right there with them. She especially enjoyed snacking on the chocolate wafers and large crackers from the men's C rations. Being a true marine, she often washed these down with a mixed drink of Coca-Cola and beer.

During one of these relaxing moments, her squad remembered that Reckless had been a racehorse before becoming a war hero, and the men issued a challenge to Native Dancer, winner of the Preakiness and the Belmont, to a matched race. This would be her crowning glory!

Thank goodness the Vanderbilts didn't respond to the challenge because the results might have been very embarrassing. Reckless just didn't quite match up to the caliber of Native Dancer. But this was just a small setback for the marines, who saw this as more of a challenge than a defeat. They had even bigger and better plans for their little heroine.

When word was released to the press that Reckless would be coming to the United States to be stationed with the First Marine Division at Camp Pendleton, California, the governor issued a proclamation welcoming her to the state. She was invited to attend all kinds of functions befitting a dignitary of her status. Ed Sullivan even wanted her shipped back to New York City to be a special guest on his television show honoring the Marine Corps' birthday. Unfortunately, the ship transporting her to the United States got held up by a storm at sea and she missed the show.

Reckless was given a hero's welcome at Camp Pendleton

and promoted to the rank of sergeant. Her life became one parade after another. On these occasions, the fifth Marines would send someone to the base stables, where she had her own paddock and stall. They'd groom her and put on her blanket with all her medals and sergeant stripes and take her down to the parade grounds. She'd stand proudly beside the reviewing stand while the troops paraded by in full-dress uniform fit for the occasion. Then the warm California sun would take its toll. Her head would lower, her ears, eyelids and bottom lip would start to droop, she'd cock one hind foot and then start to snore. She was the only enlisted marine who could actually sleep through a parade and get away with it.

Now, unbeknownst to Reckless, some high-ranking public relations officers decided it would be a great idea to arrange a "marriage" between her and some famous Thoroughbred racehorse sire. The plan called for their offspring to be entered in and, no doubt, win the Kentucky Derby, thereby propelling Reckless and the Marine Corps even further into the limelight.

After the consummation of this marriage, Reckless was taken back to the base stable and turned out for daily frolics with the stable horses. At night, she was led back to her private stall and paddock, where she was queen of the stable and she knew it.

Before going any further, I must explain that in the armed forces, officers know everything. The enlisted men do not. That's just the military way, which means that most officers find it unnecessary to inform the enlisted ranks of their plans. This is exactly what happened with Reckless and her Derby-winning colt. We knew nothing about the officers' plans and most of the enlisted men would be discharged or transferred before the foal's birth.

It was at this time that Reckless and I crossed paths. After my "Korean vacation," I'd been transferred to special services and assigned to the base stable. One of my jobs was to help promote the annual Navy Relief Rodeo by being a trick roper and rodeo clown. Our base commander at the time was a strong supporter of the rodeo and through his efforts, we received some bucking horses and bulls for the sailors and marines to practice on.

One of the young bucking horses had gotten kicked in the chest and needed stitches. After a visit to the veterinarian, he was turned out with the stable horses so it would be easier to catch him when it came time to take out the stitches. The next morning when Reckless was turned out, the crew gathered to see her put this new guy in his place. To their surprise, they discovered, first, that he was a stallion, and second, that Reckless was in love. By the time they got her back to her paddock and the young stallion into a corral, Cupid had shot all his arrows.

"You can probably brush off most of those scuff marks and comb out her ruffed-up mane," I explained. "But I don't know how you're going to get that smirk off her face." We all agreed not to tell anybody about this and swore an oath of secrecy.

Apparently, the arranged marriage had failed, and no one had informed the powers that be to check her in twenty-eight days to see if the ink had dried on the license. All was forgotten until one day I looked up and saw a staff car and veterinarian's truck parked outside Reckless's paddock. After the vet had checked her over, the staff car pulled up to the office where I was and the officers unloaded with big smiles on their faces. One proudly announced that Reckless was going to have a baby.

It was at this point that I became very confused. Why were they so excited about her being in foal with a common bucking horse? I didn't know about the earlier marriage with the champion stallion, and they didn't know about her affair with the rodeo bronc. I was fully expecting to be blamed for her condition while quietly wondering who'd let the cat out of the bag. Instead, I was being ordered to make a big sign to put along the main base highway that ran by her paddock. They explained that they wanted everybody to be aware of the expected arrival and its gender once it got here.

The sign was to say, "It's a . . . ." and then the appropriate sign of "Boy" or "Girl" was to be put up when the foal was born. Also, whoever was on duty at the time of the blessed event was to call the special services officer immediately and he would notify the press.

Well, it seems the foal came about a month later than expected, and you can guess who was on duty the night it happened. Actually, it was about daylight when I looked out and saw her cleaning him off. So as instructed, I hung the "Boy" sign, made the phone call and started my morning chores. Suddenly, the driveway filled with staff cars and news media.

They were driving Reckless nuts. She was frantically trying to maneuver between the colt and the flashing cameras. I told the newspeople to step outside the paddock and I'd lead her past them so they could get the shots they wanted. The officers beamed with pride as the cameras clicked. When they were finished, I turned Reckless loose, and she scurried to the backside of her paddock with her wobbly legged offspring in tow.

While heading back to the barns, I heard one of the officers mention the Kentucky Derby. As I stopped to listen more closely, one of the reporters turned to me and asked in a very loud voice, "What is the name again of that famous sire that's the daddy of this colt?"

I proudly answered, "Well, sir, he ain't very famous, but he's one of our best bareback broncs. You know, a buckin' horse."

You could have cut the silence with a knife. My CO grabbed my arm and invited me immediately into the office for a "debriefing" while the other officers and the news media were left in a very disgruntled and confused state. During my meeting with the CO the entire story of the corps' plans for Reckless was brought to my attention. I learned all about the tremendous amount of time and energy devoted to developing a PR strategy to keep her name in the spotlight and to make her even more famous.

In just a few seconds, I had managed to dishonor the reputation of a war heroine and destroy a huge public relations campaign for the marines.

My enlistment was up shortly after Reckless had her colt. After recent research, I discovered that she fell in love two more times. None of those offspring were derby winners either. Reckless spent the rest of her life at Camp Pendleton in the lap of luxury. She passed away in the spring of 1968. It was a well-earned retirement for such a brave and courageous little mare. A monument was erected in her honor at the base stable where she still rules to this day.

Boots Reynolds

Sgt. Reckless

The Guiding Sight

"She's a card and she cracks me up every day. I ask her to give me some sweets, and she does, coming close to me and planting a kiss on the nose!"

(Dan Shaw of Ellsworth, Maine must be talking about his girl-friend, right? Well, maybe not.)

"When we go to the mall, my wife goes one way *(Wife! Uh-oh. Now we have trouble...)* and I go the other. I'll ask Cuddles to find the escalator. 'Now find the elevator, then find the elevator button.' She puts her nose near the button, so I know what to press."

(Aha! Cuddles must be a dog! That's it!)

"If she needs to go outside, she'll tap on the floor with her tiny hoof. If I don't answer right away, she'll tap and neigh. Then, if I still don't answer, she'll tap, neigh and cross her back legs."

(Neigh? Back legs? It can't be. But it is... a horse!)

Cuddles is the first official guide horse, assisting Shaw, who is blind, carefully down the aisles of his grocery store, across busy streets and even to his seat on an airplane. Cuddles is a miniature mare who stands approximately twenty-four inches tall at the base of the mane and could possibly live to the ripe old equine age of forty.

Miniatures were first imported to the United States in the

early 1900s as workhorses to take advantage of their small size and great strength in pulling ore carts in coal mines. Cuddles doesn't pull Shaw, but gently leads him where he can't see to go safely himself, even navigating New York City's top tourist sights. Cuddles is the first guide horse to go to the top of the Empire State Building, to the Statue of Liberty and down into the cavernous and noisy subway. She also toured the famous toy store, FAO Schwarz, no doubt to look over the stuffed horses on display.

Shaw, age forty-six, began losing his sight to retinitis pigmentosa—"It's in the genes," he says—when he was seventeen and couldn't imagine himself with a white cane or a guide dog. He'd experienced overwhelming grief from the previous loss of a pet dog. Then he heard about The Guide Horse Foundation in North Carolina. There, miniatures undergo eight months of training to deal with those normal things that occur in human life that might otherwise spook a horse. Police horses are trained the same way.

Cuddles responds to Shaw's more than twenty-five vocal commands, and she can see very well in almost complete darkness, something with which Dan is all too familiar. Yes, she frequently goes in his house to watch television with him and perform other more necessary duties. Litterbox trained, no, but the little horse does tap on Shaw's door with her tiny sneaker-clad hoof when Nature calls.

Shaw says Cuddles has allowed him "to feel free for the first time in twenty years." Now, he leads a full life, he says, which includes connecting with people and animals in ways he never would have imagined.

He recalls one notable moment, of many, from his New York City adventure. In front of the famed and elegant Plaza Hotel on the edge of Central Park, Shaw decided to take Cuddles for a ride in a carriage pulled by large draft horses.

"I let Cuddles pick out her own horse, so she walked up and down the sidewalk and sniffed each one, finally settling on her choice. I think the two kind of spoke to one another, the huge horse and the little one."

Their joint sojourns to Shaw's favorite nearby fishing hole are highlights of his leisure time: "It's about a mile and a half away, and I went with a person the first three times. You go down a paved road, down a dirt road, across a bridge and down a path. Now, I just say, 'Let's go fishing, Cuddles,' and off we go. She knows the way. When I get there, she eats grass while I fish. No, I haven't taught her to tap once for bass, twice for trout yet," laughs Shaw.

The two share remarkable communication, he believes. "She's so smart. If I'm in her corral and I'm walking toward something I shouldn't be, she'll block me. If I call, she'll come right to the gate."

Her keen intuition averted probable injury to Shaw in the summer of 2002, when they visited a local horse show. Shaw made an oral presentation about his buddy and they received a standing ovation. "We don't do tricks," he affirms. "Guide dogs don't do tricks."

He remembers that it was terribly windy as the two stood by a show corral and a huge canopy, the latter anchored by heavy metal pipes and other weights.

"Suddenly, out of nowhere, Cuddles yanked me to the side, about ten paces," recounts Shaw. The canopy came crashing down where the two had just stood, pipes and all. "If she pulls me, I always go with her," he says. "It's said that horses can sense danger before it happens. I believe it."

Shaw thinks his miniature maintains a unique perspective of him, the human. "She's accepted me as part of her herd. It's like when a horse goes blind in its herd. Another horse will take care of it. She's taking care of me."

Shaw wants to take care of Cuddles and he does. After attending a special school, he was able to continue his beloved craft of woodworking. He still makes birdhouses, arbors, furniture and buildings. He built a barn for Cuddles and her miniature barn mate, twenty-eight-inch tall Nevada. "I feel that because of what Cuddles does for me, the least I can do is let her be a horse," says Shaw. The structure features a television, a heated water bucket and other amenities befitting his best friend. He stresses that it's critically important to him that Cuddles have her "down time."

Shaw has accrued so many fun experiences that he's telling them in two books: *Dan Meets Cuddles,* and the second, *Adventures of Dan and Cuddles,* which was penned especially for second and third graders "who've seen us in *Weekly Reader* and *National Geographic for Kids,*" explains Shaw.

Shaw calls Cuddles "one awesome little deal. Whenever you think you know her, she always comes up and does something else. She's the little soldier when she gets dressed in the morning with her harness and boots. But when they come off, she's just the playful little horse."

Shaw feels a connection with another human–animal partnership saga: Morris Frank had the first Seeing Eye dog in America, a female named Buddy, and Frank subsequently helped establish the first school for such dogs in America. He wrote a book, *First Lady of the Seeing Eye,* made into a Disney TV movie in 1984. The film was entitled *Love Leads the Way.*

Its title is appropriate for Cuddles, says Shaw. The tiny horse is leading him lovingly and carefully through his life while paving the way for other visually impaired individuals to gain amazing insight, if not real sight, when they, too, acquire their own guide horses.

Stephanie Stephens

The Stallion and the Redwing

It was about the most beautiful sight on our southwestern Ohio farm: the stallion and the redwinged blackbird.

Day after day during early summer, the redwing perched in the highest branch of the three small trees—a hawthorn, a wild cherry and a crab apple—that grew in a clump along the back lane that led from the barn to the far pasture. Beneath these trees, none more than twenty feet tall, our dappled-gray Welsh stallion stood in the shade, idly switching his tail at the flies.

Often, for an hour or more at a time, the redwing sat there, alert, apparently on guard, as its mate went to and fro to her nest secured in several tall weeds in the uncut hayfield. It chattered constantly with a tick, tick, tick.

They certainly were aware of each other's presence, the horse and the bird. And all was at peace between them. Whether there was any communication is something I did not wonder about at the time. I know it was a stunningly beautiful picture, complete only when both of them were in it.

Late in the summer, the redwing and his family departed for the winter. According to a log I had kept, they would return the first week in March.

It was in October that the stallion, more than twenty years old, died. We buried him with grief and dignity, as befits a herd sire, in a deep grave along the fence that led south from the corncrib. The grave was exactly twelve steel fence posts from the gate. I counted them carefully and then recorded the location in my log so that we could find the grave in later years.

When the redwinged blackbirds had not returned to the farm by the first week of March, I became uneasy. As I went to the barn early on the seventh to do the chores, I wondered what might have happened. Then I heard it, far away, but unmistakably the tick, tick, tick of a redwing. Whether this was chirp, monologue or song, it was a welcome sound, like hearing from a dear old friend.

I went to the doors on the east side of the barn and pushed them open. I knew just where to look. The redwing would be sitting in the very top of one of the three small trees, facing the field where its mate later would build a nest.

I strained my eyes. I searched every branch and limb, which did not yet bear leaves. The redwing should be there. It wasn't. Yet, I could hear it. Tick, tick, tick.

After standing there puzzled for a full minute, I became convinced that the bird's voice must have been coming from some other direction. I went outside the barn and looked up at the towering silver maple next to the overhang. The bird sometimes spent time up there. But it was not there now. It was nowhere in sight.

I went beyond the corncrib. Then, more by chance than anything, I saw it. Down along another fence that stretched southward from the corncrib, the bird was perched atop a steel post. I could see it clearly. It was spreading its wings in the fashion of the species, calling out tick, tick, tick. Tick, tick, tick your-ee-ee-ee.

Yet it was all a little strange. I had never seen the bird in that spot before. And it was odd that it remained there, clinging in the stiff breeze to the very top of the fence post.

I waved my arm, but it did not frighten the redwing away. It continued its song.

As my eye measured the distance, something clicked in

my mind and I began counting the fence posts between the bird and me. One, two . . . seven, eight . . . ten, eleven, twelve. The redwing was sitting on the twelfth post—the one closest to the stallion's grave.

It took me a while to organize my thoughts. I counted again. Yes, the bird was on the twelfth post, as close to the stallion's grave as it could get.

I went to the house and checked back through my log. The redwings had left the farm a full two months before the stallion had died. How, then, could the bird know that the stallion was buried at a spot far from its usual perch? Had it come here to sing over the grave?

I might have dismissed it as mere coincidence. I might even have forgotten it, except for one fact: On the morning of March 5, the following spring, I heard the familiar sound of a redwinged blackbird. Tick, tick, tick. Without even thinking, I ran to the corner of the corncrib and gazed down along the fence row. There was the bird, not on the ninth post or the fifteenth post, but on top of the twelfth post.

It was singing over the stallion's grave just as it had the previous spring. It remained there for twenty or thirty minutes and then flew to the clump of three trees along the back lane. Never once, after that first day of its return, did I see it go back to the grave.

The redwing returned on March 3 the year after that and on March 8 the fourth year. It always alighted on the twelfth post the first day of its return before going anywhere else, and there it seemed to talk briefly to the stallion buried beneath the dense pasture grass.

This spring the redwing did not return. It is past April 1, and I know I shall not see it again. Like the stallion, it has undoubtedly lived out its life.

Although it is not here, I still see it in my mind's eye, in the clump of three small trees and atop the twelfth steel post. And I continue to ponder the relationship between the bird and the stallion. Does there develop an affinity, a kinship between nature's creatures that we, mere humans, cannot comprehend or explain? Does some understanding, some loyalty, exist that rivals or even transcends anything that exists among men?

Only the stallion and the redwing knew.

Gerald W. Young

A Change of Command

"Do you need some help?"

"No, I can do it myself," came Bill's grumbled reply.

I circled my restless young Paint and watched Sundance stand patiently as Bill fumbled with the saddle hitch.

The sorrel Quarter Horse was from excellent breeding stock, lean with good muscle tone. Only the graying hairs on his face hinted of his age, which was twenty-four. For fifteen of those years he'd belonged to me. The rider, like the horse, hid his years well. Silver hair peaked out around a black Stetson hat. The tanned face remained unlined despite years in the sun. And like the horse, the man was fit and trim. When working with the horses, his steel-blue eyes sparkled with a clarity otherwise missing those days and a smile touched his lips.

Slight arthritis had somewhat slowed the horse. Alzheimer's disease had slowed the man. With no family of his own, Bill had become a part of mine, and I worried about letting him continue to ride as I worried about when to take away the keys to his car.

Sundance and I remembered horse shows where he and Bill had competed in barrel-racing and pole-bending events. We remembered long leisurely trail rides and running flat-out across the prairie, pretending we were in the wilds of Montana instead of rural Illinois.

Sundance worked well for me, but had a special bond with Bill, a visible excitement when they rode together. Whenever Bill eased into the saddle and lightly touched the big gelding with the tips of his spurs, the horse pranced, eager to run, ready to perform. Only the gentle touch of a spur and Bill's hands on the reins told him it was time for action.

I hid the spurs a while back, and Bill didn't seem to notice. Horse and rider no longer ran the way they used to. Rides were kept to a walk and trot around the arena and out into the pasture. I kept an eye on them and worried.

I hesitated when Bill asked to ride one crisp October morning. The vacant look in his eyes had become more pronounced, and although I wanted him to be active for as long as he could be, I didn't want him hurt. I also couldn't say no.

Bill finally got the cinch tightened and climbed into the saddle. He settled himself with a big sigh. Sundance eased forward at a slow pace, and contentment softened the rider's face. Bill asked for a trot, and I watched the horse's reluctance.

"This horse is acting pretty . . . ," Bill searched for the words he wanted. "He seems pretty sluggish today."

I nodded. "Well, he's getting older and his joints are a little stiff in the morning. Be patient with him."

Bill grunted an undecipherable response when his commands remained unanswered. After several requests, the horse gently broke into a smooth jog trot.

Sundance concentrated on the ground ahead, carefully measuring his stride. I glimpsed Bill's hand ease toward the saddle horn once for balance.

Bill cued the horse to canter—whether by conscious intent or from years of riding, I wasn't quite sure. Sundance continued in his easy trot. When asked again for a canter, the gelding looked toward me, and I hoped I had conveyed my concern to the horse.

I pulled my Paint to a stop and watched, my heart skipping a beat now and then.

Bill touched the horse with his right heel and gave a voice command at the same time. "Canter, canter." Sundance hesitated, shook his head slightly and slowed to a walk.

With a sigh, Bill reached down and patted Sundance on his neck. "Okay, boy. We'll take it easy on you today."

I tried to swallow around the lump in my throat and smile in spite of the tears in my eyes. My heart settled its rhythm, and I felt at peace at what I'd witnessed between horse and rider. I no longer feared letting Bill ride. Where once Bill had been in command, the control had shifted to the horse. Sundance knew the man was different from the rider who had once urged flying lead changes through the poles, from the man who had ridden like the wind across the prairie. The horse I loved was protecting the friend we both loved.

Sandra Tatara

From One Mom to Another

For a hundred and fifty years, in the pasture of dead horses, roots of pine trees pushed through the pale curves of your ribs, yellow blossoms flourished above you in autumn, and in winter frost heaved your bones in the ground— old toilers, soil makers; O Roger, Mackerel, Riley, Ned, Nellie, Chester, Lady Ghost.

Donald Hall, "Names of Horses"

I will never be persuaded that animals don't understand tragedy and don't communicate with each other because I witnessed an extraordinary episode between Christie and Dixie, two Belgian mares who never appeared to even like each other, until Dixie turned to Christie in her last hours.

Dixie was scarred, scared, undernourished and wild-eyed when I first saw her. Her nose had been broken numerous times from what the owner said was "smacks on her head with a two-by-four for being bad." I didn't need another Belgian, but I dug deep in my pockets, borrowed and scraped, and came up with the money to buy her. I rationalized that maybe, eventually, after bringing her back to health, I could use her as a brood mare. Under all the mud and dirt, I saw some promising conformation.

Christie's history couldn't have been more different than Dixie's. Christie came from a loving home, had the best of care and much preferred being with people than with other horses. She was my first draft horse and she came to the farm a year or so before Dixie. I knew she was special and I knew she would help me safely learn all the ins and outs of owning and driving a draft horse. She never disappointed me.

Dixie, although lacking Christie's people skills and trust, turned into an excellent, caring mother and gave me nice, strong colts each year that she was bred. During a routine visit, I asked our veterinarian to look at Dixie. Something just didn't look right. She was eating, drinking and taking care of Pinkie, the colt she had a month earlier, but she just looked what horsepeople describe as "off."

After taking her temperature we found she was running a fever. Perhaps she had some kind of uterine infection from the birth, although she had no outward signs of illness. We did some uterine cultures and the veterinarian told me to give her some medication to get her temperature down.

But a few hours later, Dixie started getting sicker. Although her temperature was down, she wouldn't eat, she seemed uncomfortable and she wasn't passing stool. She was obviously more distressed and starting to show signs of colic. I put in another call to our veterinarian but our usual doctor, whom I knew and trusted, was not on call. A new, young associate with little equine experience arrived in her place. I wasn't in a position to wait, and figured that she was better than no veterinarian at all.

Several times throughout the evening, the veterinarian returned to administer pain medication, but Dixie's pain increased. She became more and more uncomfortable and finally was unable to nurse Pinkie. Pinkie was confused and hungry, and he didn't understand why his mother, usually so attentive, wasn't paying attention to him. On the veterinarian's final visit of the evening, she gave me a syringe full of pain medication and instructions to administer the shot in three hours. She explained that it was a safe dose of a long acting drug that would make Dixie more comfortable.

I slept in the paddock that night with Dixie, watching her, walking her, trying to help her with Pinkie and hoping to see some improvement. At the appointed hour, I gave her the last shot. Within a few minutes, she seemed more at ease, even making her way over to the fence line that adjoined the paddocks where the other horses were lined up and watching her quietly, as if standing vigil, their hay in untouched piles.

Dixie wasn't a social horse. I seldom saw her show interest in the other horses. She never had anything to do with Christie. Typically, if one of the herd came near her fence she would charge and pin her ears, strongly telling the intruder to stay away.

That night, everything changed.

Astonished, I watched Dixie touch noses with all the horses in line. Next, she stood across the fence from Christie. I thought this was strange, but she seemed so calm now. I began to get hopeful even as Pinkie seemed more confused and upset.

Dixie and Christie continued their silent conversation for several more moments until Dixie turned, looked at the others again, walked to the center of the paddock and lay down.

I kept my distance. I didn't want to disturb her when she needed to rest, so I sat down at the edge of the paddock and just watched her.

I watched as Pinkie, now quiet and subdued, slowly made his way over and stood beside his mother. With a gentleness that belied his anxiety and hunger, Pinkie smelled Dixie's hooves, her legs and her tail, and ever so lovingly nuzzled her mane and pressed his nose to hers. With a final sniff, he turned and walked to the fence line joining the other horses. I knew then that Dixie was gone.

I slowly walked to the center of the paddock and wished my Dixie farewell. Eventually, I glanced over to see Christie still standing in the spot where she and Dixie shared their last moment. To this day, I swear Christie had tears running down her face.

I was numb and in shock. Dixie was gone. I had a month-old colt who needed to eat and no way to feed him. I sought advice from others who had raised orphan foals.

Pinkie would have nothing to do with a bottle. He rejected it, and I worked all day trying to get fluids into him. He had been creep-feeding since birth, eating small amounts of supplemental food, but wouldn't take anything by mouth. He turned up his nose at his favorite grain. He wanted his mother.

As I was working with Pinkie, I noticed how agitated Christie was, running the fence line, calling out. It was a behavior totally out of the norm for her. She had weaned her own colt six weeks before. She hadn't much liked being a mother and wanted nothing to do with him after three months. She had been a good mother but when the time came to wean him, she gladly booted him out of her paddock without a second glance, and her milk supply had dried up in a few days.

Feeling exasperated, I walked outside to try one last time with the bottle. As I passed Christie's paddock I stopped to see if I could figure out why she seemed so agitated. I stood there, not believing what I saw. Her udder, which had been empty and had returned to normal size, was full! I expressed some fluid into my hand—it was milk! She paced the fence line almost frantic, calling to Pinkie and not taking her eyes off him.

Now, I understood the significance of what had happened at the fence line before Dixie died.

I decided to take a chance. I put Pinkie in Christie's paddock. He was exhausted, hungry and depressed. I stood close by in case Christie rejected him. Instead she trotted up to Pinkie, nuzzled him and pushed him around until he was close to her udder. He started to nurse. He drank his fill then quickly lay down and slept with Christie standing vigil over him until he woke up and ate again.

Christie adopted Pinkie as her own. He started creep-feeding again the next day, and with the help of Christie's milk grew into a strong, vigorous colt. A much better mother to Pinkie than she had been to her own colt Pete, Christie continued to produce an abundance of milk for another three months and watched over her adopted son until he went to his new home.

I know I was sent to bring Dixie home and give her a few happy years. I still get tears in my eyes when I remember her at the fence line that night, calmly and quietly touching the noses of the horses she'd previously wanted nothing to do with.

On that sad night I saw a miracle. On that sad night I found hope. On that sad night I witnessed the power of love.

Thank you, Dixie.

Chris Russell-Grabb

A Leap of Faith

Everything depends upon myself and my horse.

Mamie Francis

Babe leaped out at me from a newspaper story about the National Cowgirl Museum and Hall of Fame.

She merited mention as the mount of Mamie Francis, a famous equestrienne of nearly a century ago. The story explained why the museum was moved from the Texas Panhandle town of Hereford to Fort Worth and why an elite coterie of cowgirls, women writers and artists, and leaders are revered and remembered for their contributions to the Western way of life.

Mamie (billed as "Miss Mamie," born as Elba Mae Ghent) and Babe (a white Arabian mare whose real name was Lurlene) made their living diving from a fifty-foot tower into an impossibly shallow, ten-foot-deep tank of water. They performed their high-diving act 628 times from 1908 to 1914, for the amusement of audiences and a paycheck.

The New York American (July 12, 1908) called Mamie's act "the most dangerous of all the circus thrillers." *The Gazette Times* (Pittsburgh, July 25, 1909) gushed: "Her self-poise is the best indication of nerves of steel."

A photo published in Philadelphia's *The Daily Evening Telegraph* (July 8, 1909) proves the peril. Babe and Mamie have just made their leap. Babe's ears are forward and alert, her tail flies perpendicular to the ground. Mamie's long, dark hair streams straight back—testimony to their breakneck speed—as she sits balanced and confident on Babe's back. It was unlikely work for Mamie, a small-town Wisconsin girl who couldn't swim.

Danger was their daily fare. The daredevil girl, always dressed all in white, and her white diving mare stunned the thousands who watched their act. They headlined in Cincinnati, Pittsburgh, Philadelphia, and in the most-celebrated playground of all—New York's Coney Island.

While their leaps provided royal entertainment for revel-ers, it was dangerous business for Babe and Mamie. Each leap, always a leap of faith, made them money and fame, and ready candidates for the obituary page.

Horses are grounded creatures, born to crop grass at ground level, and to run and roam together in social groups . . . herds . . . for companionship and protection. There's safety in numbers, with lots of eyes on look-out for preda-tors lurking behind a bush or in the trees. Bad things come from above and being away from the herd.

But here Babe was, poised on the precipice of a tower, against instincts developed by her forebears from surviving millions of years in the wild. She waited until all was still and quiet, for just the right moment, when she felt as one with Mamie. Then she leaped. Mamie never forced her.

Faith in each other kept them climbing the ramp . . . and jumping. On one dive, the tank collapsed when they hit the water, and they were buried under mud, dirt, canvas and water. Mamie's chest caved in and she was in danger of drowning. Luckily, a Good Samaritan was watching from the wings. He jumped in and pulled Mamie out from under Babe and the debris, and out of the tank. Babe managed to scramble out on her own. As more help arrived, her res-cuer—a man with athletic, quick reactions and a good heart—disappeared into the din and clatter of the carnival. Mamie didn't know him and never got to thank him.

On July 11, 1908, in full view of a happy Coney Island crowd of 30,000, Babe inched to the tower's edge, her skin quivering with anticipation. The moment to leap was upon them. Suddenly, the whistles of a steam calliope pierced the quiet and shattered Babe's concentration. She lost her balance and teetered, and before Mamie could steady her, they tumbled into the water below. The crowd feared the worst. Could they have survived? Attendants pulled Mamie from the tank. But no Babe. She was thrashing about, drowning on the bottom of the tank. Precious seconds passed as workers rushed to get a rope around her. Two minutes passed as Babe kicked and struggled, making rescue impossible. Five minutes passed. Finally a lone diver, a hero among horses, dived into the tank. He swam down to Babe, who was probably unconscious by now, and passed the rope under her body. The men wrenched Babe out as death knocked on her door.

Two hours later, Babe walked out of Coney Island's Dreamland under her own horsepower. Horses remind us, in their simple ways and simple faiths, that there is hope in life. And as long as there is life, there is hope.

Mamie was a sprite of a girl, and on horseback as in life, she was tough as West Texas boot leather. Her grandson Tom Shelton says, "She was afraid of no one and of nothing."

She respected the dangers of the high dive, but embraced the excitement: "Oh, the glory of it all. I just close my eyes, take a deep breath, and await the splash."

Mamie's boss, C.F. "California Frank" Hafley, appreciated her talents and liked her so much he married her in 1909. Mamie is so beloved among cowgirls that she was posthumously inducted into the National Cowgirl Hall of Fame in 1981.

She told *The Gazette Times* (Pittsburgh, June 26, 1910) that she dived for money:

"After a while, I will be able to retire and live on my ranch without bothering over money matters. Until then, I must take the chance of accident involved in the high dive on horseback. But . . . I have minimized the chance . . . not by any trickery or chicanery, but by skill. Everything depends upon myself and my horse."

Mamie might have leaped for money. But Babe leaped for Miss Mamie.

Gayle Stewart

READER/CUSTOMER CARE SURVEY

We care about your opinions! Please take a moment to fill out our online Reader Survey at **http://survey.hcibooks.com.**

As a **"THANK YOU"** you will receive a **VALUABLE INSTANT COUPON** towards future book purchases as well as a **SPECIAL GIFT** available only online! Or, you may mail this card back to us and we will send you a copy of our exciting catalog with your valuable coupon inside.

(PLEASE PRINT IN ALL CAPS)

First Name _____ MI. _____ Last Name _____

Address _____ Email _____ City _____

State _____ Zip _____

1. Gender
- ☐ Female ☐ Male

2. Age
- ☐ 8 or younger
- ☐ 9-12 ☐ 13-16
- ☐ 17-20 ☐ 21-30
- ☐ 31+

3. Did you receive this book as a gift?
- ☐ Yes ☐ No

4. Annual Household Income
- ☐ under $25,000
- ☐ $25,000 - $34,999
- ☐ $35,000 - $49,999
- ☐ $50,000 - $74,999
- ☐ over $75,000

5. What are the ages of the children living in your house?
- ☐ 0 - 14 ☐ 15+

6. Marital Status
- ☐ Single
- ☐ Married
- ☐ Divorced
- ☐ Widowed

7. How did you find out about the book?
(please choose one)
- ☐ Recommendation
- ☐ Store Display
- ☐ Online
- ☐ Catalog/Mailing
- ☐ Interview/Review

8. Where do you usually buy books?
(please choose one)
- ☐ Bookstore
- ☐ Online
- ☐ Book Club/Mail Order
- ☐ Price Club (Sam's Club, Costco's, etc.)
- ☐ Retail Store (Target, Wal-Mart, etc.)

9. What subject do you enjoy reading about the most?
(please choose one)
- ☐ Parenting/Family
- ☐ Relationships
- ☐ Recovery/Addictions
- ☐ Health/Nutrition
- ☐ Christianity
- ☐ Spirituality/Inspiration
- ☐ Business Self-help
- ☐ Women's Issues
- ☐ Sports

10. What attracts you most to a book?
(please choose one)
- ☐ Title
- ☐ Cover Design
- ☐ Author
- ☐ Content

FOLD HERE

Do you have your own Chicken Soup story
that you would like to send us?
Please submit at: **www.chickensoup.com**

Comments

Riding in the Alaskan Bush

Living in Alaska, we often encountered wildlife, especially moose. In the winter, when the snow was deep in the mountains, they would come down into the valley and be thick through the trees. I have awakened and opened the drapes of my room downstairs to be face-to-face with a moose eating grass outside my window. I have waited at the bus stop countless times with a moose contentedly eating a tree a short distance from me. It became second nature to sing or talk for the entire quarter of a mile walk to the bus stop in the dark so that they knew that I was a person.

During cross-country ski trips, we encountered dozens of them. They bedded down on our property with their calves and, on a few unlucky occasions, ate our bushes down to the nub despite our repeated attempts to scare them away by banging pots and pans from the safety of our second-story deck.

Dustee, my lovable horse, was known to be frightened of moose when they would venture too near and he would snort and run at dangerous speeds through his pasture. When I walked out to the balcony and called his name, he would rush over to the fence as close as he could get and fix his eyes upon me. He would stand frozen, not looking away, as if it would all be okay as long as I was there. I would stay out there with him until the moose had gone.

Despite acknowledging their well-deserved reputation, we didn't consider the moose a danger. In all the years, no one in our family was ever hurt or threatened by them. That changed one day as I was returning from a trail ride, traveling down a power line toward home. I always carried a folding hoof pick in my pocket in case the occasional stone or other debris become lodged in Dustee's foot. As we were riding along, I realized that something was bothering him and I stopped to check it out. I stepped off and went to his left foreleg, kneeling down and placing his leg on my knee so I could pry the stone loose.

Suddenly, I froze, the hair on my neck stood on end and I had the distinct feeling of being watched. Instinct told me I was in imminent danger. I remained there, kneeling down and completely unable to move. I have never been one to freeze in dangerous situations. As a matter of fact, I am usually the first to act and address critical issues in emergency situations. But not this time. I was only able to turn my head, and there, over my left shoulder, was one of the most dangerous creatures known to man: an angry moose.

The sight of a moose about to attack is difficult to describe. She stood only about fifteen feet away, teeth bared, ears flat back on her head. Standing six feet tall at the shoulder, she towered over me as I kneeled there, the hair on her back standing up. I had no time to react before she charged. I watched her come, unable to look away from the awesome sight. Then I felt my horse's leg rise off of my knee and out of my hand, and the next moment his front legs landed squarely in front of me. I was directly underneath his belly, looking out between his outstretched legs, watching as his neck stretched down and his head snaked down low toward the ground.

He assumed the posture of the angry moose, but stood stock-still. His teeth were bared and his ears were flat back as he crouched over me, staring at the moose. I only vaguely realized in that split second what was happening. The moose had stopped, ears flat and teeth still bared, her nose only a few feet from my horse's, her angry eyes locked on his. There was utter silence, as only there can be in the wilderness. No wind, no leaves rustling. It seemed that we all were holding our breath.

Then, from over my right shoulder I heard a rustling. It was the pitter-patter of little feet, small hooves moving in the woods. I watched from the corner of my eye as a very young, very cute calf moose walked nonchalantly out of the woods, passed by us and calmly walked by the angry moose that still threatened like a terrible thunder cloud. The calf disappeared into the brush. Agonizing seconds passed as I waited there under my determined protector until the cow moose relaxed her posture and turned to disappear quietly into the woods.

My sweet horse turned his head, looked at me with his beautiful eye and nuzzled me gently as if to say, "It's all right now. You can come out." Words can't express the kindness that glowed in those dark chocolate eyes and the love that was shown.

He stood, quietly waiting, as I crawled out from beneath his belly. He placed his legs back where they belonged, I mounted and away we went toward home. After what we had been through together, our peaceful departure was a relief and a letdown at the same time. For bravery above and beyond the call of duty, Dustee deserved a medal at the very least. But the best I could do, and I think he understands, is award him the trophy of my heart. He never will be forgotten.

Laurie Wright

Instincts of a War Mare

I was born loving horses. As my mother tells it, my first three words were "da-da," "ma-ma" and "horsey." I come from many generations of city folks, my great-grandfather being the only one to have owned a riding horse. So, it's my conviction that God gave me this passion for horses. And it's Marguerite Henry (author of *King of the Wind*) and Walter Farley (author of *The Black Stallion*) who focused that passion onto Arabian horses.

I was blessed with understanding parents, who saw to it that I began riding lessons at the age of six and who bought me a horse seven years later. Because we lived in a neighborhood with less than an acre of wooded land and no barn, the mare lived in the backyard with the screened porch as her stall. She joined in with the family each evening, watching television through the glass doors that separated the den from the porch.

Two years later, we moved out into the country to a small seven-acre farm that had fenced pastures and a three-stall barn. Right next door was this beautiful, green-eyed albino stallion who was owned by an equally beautiful brown-haired, blue-eyed boy. Ah, love was in the air. The stallion was gelded, but the boy and I were married five years later.

Seven years after that, we had our own farm and

eventually, we began boarding horses to help offset the cost of our collection of Arabians. We now have a small herd of straight Egyptian brood mares and a very talented young show horse, Raasuwl SCA. My husband Donald and I do all the work on the farm, which means many long, but rewarding, hours each day.

One cold, windy evening last February, I was finishing up the chores at the barn. Don had already gone to the house to bring in the dogs and cats for the night, and I just had to shift the mares from their pasture to the paddock by the barn. The mares know the routine: I open the gate and they charge through and gallop to the paddock where their buckets of sweet feed are waiting.

They always run through in the same order: first, Hazara, the undisputed alpha mare; then Mataalah, Inaaya, Yum-Yum and, always last, Khatira Moniet. Katie, as we call her, is the lowest-ranking mare within the herd. She is just as pretty as she can be, the image of her great-grandmother the famous Egyptian mare Moniet El Nefous, but this doesn't carry a bit of importance with the other mares. Katie is always made to be last: last through the gate, last to get to her bucket, last to get to choose a flake of hay, last to get to drink from the water tubs and last to get her belly scratched when Don and I are out visiting with the mares.

And if once in a while she dashes ahead and gets somewhere first, she is reprimanded with snapping teeth and flying heels. We like to give her some extra attention when we can, particularly extra scratching and extra carrots, while we make the other mares stay back.

So, on this evening as I went to swing the gate open, the mares were bunched up, waiting for their run to the barn. All except for Katie, that is. She was standing back about fifty feet out of harm's way. As I gave the gate a push, a gust of wind caught it and pushed it right back at me. Hazara had already started her charge and as she dodged to avoid the gate, her shoulder rammed into my chest and sent me flying ten feet through the air. I landed on my back and my head slammed against the frozen ground, knocking me out cold. The first thing I was aware of as I began to come to was the sound of hooves all around me and the pressure of what I thought was a fence post against my side. As my vision cleared I looked up and there was Katie standing above me.

The other mares were milling all around me, but Katie was standing very calmly over me, protecting me. What I thought was a fence post against my side was actually her front leg. It took me about ten minutes to even try to get to my feet, and she stood guard over me the entire time, keeping the other mares away. As I tried to stand, she lowered her head and let me grab her mane and pull myself up. When she was satisfied that I was safely on my feet, she touched her nose to my face and then calmly walked away through the other mares and once again took her place about fifty feet away.

Since childhood, I have read the stories about the loyal Arabian war mares who would stand guard over their riders who had fallen during battle, risking their own safety for that of their masters. I had wanted those stories to be true, but I always wondered if they weren't just exaggerated, romantic tales. Now I know that they are true. I have my own "war mare" who certainly risked her safety to come to my aid. I have loved Katie since we bought her ten years ago, but because of what transpired on that wintry day, she now holds a very special place in my heart. And there is always that one extra carrot in my pocket that is just for her.

Christina Donahue

The Man Whisperer

For three generations, Sandy MacPherson's family had owned a farm in the county of Angus in northeast Scotland. Mainly, the farm had been prosperous, raising black Aberdeen Angus cattle for beef, some sheep and raspberries. Sandy's wife Jean ran a riding school and the horses were her "family."

Unfortunately, as the changing times made farming harder, the MacPherson's farm struggled to survive. Sandy was old-fashioned. He believed that running the farm was "a man's job" and that his wife and children could not really understand the position in which they found themselves.

Sandy found great consolation in spending time with the horses, particularly with a horse named Wallace that Sandy had delivered himself many years before. Standing in the stable in the early evening, Sandy would stroke Wallace, get a whinny in response, and then the man would explain all his worries to the horse. Sandy could unload on the silent but responsive Wallace all the worries he could not bear to share with his family.

Unfortunately, Sandy's other solace was vodka. When he went to visit Wallace and drink from a vodka bottle hidden in the hay, he would explain it as "going to tidy up in the stable and settle everyone down for the night."

Sandy's wife Jean was one of those quiet women, who said

little but saw and anticipated everything. Her cousin was the local lawyer, her nephew was the local accountant, and she probably knew more of their precarious financial position than her husband.

Jean knew that when Sandy went off to the stable heavy with the burden of farm worries, and came back an hour or so later with his burden considerably eased, he had been at his secret vodka bottle. She would ignore the odd slurred word that Sandy never even knew he let fall. She would give him coffee to get rid of the smell that Sandy fully believed vodka never left on his breath.

Standing one day looking into the warm and wise eyes of Wallace, Jean asked him, "What are we going to do about Sandy, Wallace?" As she stroked the horse and he butted her with his head in response, she suddenly began to form an idea.

The clever Jean slipped into the stables every evening while Sandy was out on the farm and took out his secret vodka bottle. She would pour the vodka into a jug, fill the vodka bottle with water and then brush the neck with the real vodka. This way, when Sandy opened the bottle, it still smelled of vodka.

For more than two months, this process went on, and each evening, Sandy would return, his burden duly lightened by his vodka. When one day his accountant finally told him that the farm was no longer making enough money to survive, he stroked Wallace with tears on his cheeks and asked, "What am I to do. How can I tell them?" Wallace moved his head against the troubled man's face almost as if he were wiping the tears away, and Sandy hugged him.

Jean took Wallace out for a ride the next morning, looking over the land they all loved so much. She was about to turn and head for home when, to her surprise, Wallace resisted and went a few steps to his right. Jean frowned, but said, "What is it Wallace. Where do you want to go?"

He trotted in the direction of the old raspberry fields. Once, they had been very lucrative with a profitable raspberry crop. Over the years, the local canneries that had bought the fruit had closed down, and now they were empty. Wallace trotted on, down toward two old farm cottages. In the heyday of the farming life in Angus, they had been homes for some of the farm workers, but now they were in ruins.

Jean dismounted from Wallace and studied where he had brought her. Suddenly she cried out, "Wallace, you're a genius," and she threw her arms around him and hugged him. Like all geniuses, Wallace accepted the praise that was his due and nodded his head a little in acknowledgment.

Jean had a word with her cousin, and two days later he asked Sandy to stop by. "There may be a way to raise quite a bit of capital. Sell the old raspberry fields for a housing development," he said. "You could have quite a few houses there. The demand for country homes in the county of Angus is at a peak. You could make a fortune!"

Sandy took a little convincing, but over the months, he began to see that this was, indeed, going to bring in a lot of money.

Finally, he stood one night in the stable telling Wallace, "Things are great boy. It's like a miracle, as if God knew how worried I was and just solved all of my problems."

The next morning, Jean found the vodka bottle was untouched and it continued that way. When there was some thunder, Sandy heard one or two of the horses crying a little, and he put on his jacket. "I'll just go and see that they are okay. Wallace, in particular, doesn't like thunder."

Sandy came back just as soon as the storm passed over. "He is fine now. I really seem to have a way with horses, particularly Wallace. I calmed him right down. I think my always talking to him has been good for him. Maybe there is a bit of the horse whisperer in me."

Jean smiled and the next morning went to the stable. As she stood there stroking Wallace, he turned his head to look at her and she smiled. "I know, you clever boy. You have helped him and all of us enormously, but particularly Sandy. I think there is more than a bit of a 'man whisperer' in you, hmmm?" Wallace nodded his head and lowered it for his rewarding hug.

Joyce Stark

The Pilon

*Far back, far back in our dark soul the horse
prances. . . . The horse, the horse! The symbol of
surging potency and power of movement, of
action in man!*

Apocalypse

In the Tex-Mex slang of south Texas, the word *pilon* (pronounced peh-lone) means "a little something extra." But because Spanish is a musical language that wraps a rainbow of emotions around a single word, it also has a much broader meaning. A *pilon* is an unexpected gift and an unanticipated blessing, although it probably won't be recognized as such when it is received because a *pilon* will usually come disguised as a problem, a trouble, an annoyance, an inconvenience. Yet, true to the magical nature of a *pilon*, it will turn out to be the silver lining in the dark cloud.

My *pilon* came to me when we decided to buy a mule. We had recently moved to the country and had bought our son a gelding. Because my husband and I had been raised as country folks, we knew it was only a matter of time before we would be faced with the problem of finding a companion for the gelding. Many horses are not happy living alone. We didn't want to invest in another horse right away, so we decided to get a mule, which could do double duty as both a companion for the gelding and as a guard animal for the sheep. After much searching, we finally found what the advertisement said was an "excellent pack animal." As we hooked up the trailer and loaded the family in the truck, my husband and I decided that, unless the mule had only three legs, he was coming home with us, regardless.

We arrived with checkbook in hand and were shown a short, gray animal with long, floppy ears and a black stripe running down the middle of his back

Quickly deciding that this was the mule for us, we turned to the seller to finalize the agreement. As we said, "We'll take the mule," the seller, misreading our eagerness for gullibility, added this stipulation to the sale: "I'll sell you the mule if you take the little horse, too."

What little horse? I wondered as I looked around the pen. All I could see was the mule, but the man was walking toward another pen before I could even voice my question. We followed, full of curiosity at this unexpected snag.

As we rounded the barn, we saw the little horse. It was a foal, about four or five months old, although it was hard to tell. At the sound of human voices, the foal had begun racing around the pen at breakneck speed, trying to escape. She was in pitiful condition. Her belly was swollen with worms, her mane and tail were matted and tangled, she was covered with mud, and I could see several large gashes on her legs, where she had tangled with some wire. Her coat was dull and lifeless. She raced around the pen, nostrils flaring, with a wild look in her eye. My husband had already begun to back up, telling the man, "No, we're not in the market for a horse." My eyes, however, were drawn to that poor foal. She was scared to death, but something, perhaps it was in her gaze or in the arch of her neck, told me that in spite of her pitiful condition, she had pride.

I interrupted my husband and drew him off to the side. "There's something about this foal," I whispered.

"She's a mess," he replied. "The vet bills alone are going to be more than she's worth."

Using my best female logic, I answered, "Well, we need a mule, so let's go ahead and take the package deal." I guess I had that look in my eye, because my husband just sighed and turned around to write the man the check.

It took us four hours to catch the foal. We chased her around the pen, tried to box her in and watched dumbfounded as she sailed over the fence. We clambered over the fence after her. Just as we were about to give up, miraculously, we caught her. We loaded her into the trailer, jamming her up against the mule and tying her securely so she wouldn't try to jump through the roof. I prayed all the way home. When we pulled into the ranch, the gelding had smelled the new arrivals and was trumpeting his welcome. As we turned them all in together, I thought I caught a look of gratitude in the foal's eyes.

The veterinarian was not very optimistic when he saw the foal the next day. He checked her, dewormed her and immunized her, but left the ranch saying that he couldn't guarantee that she wouldn't have a lot of future problems. I named her Senisa, which is the name of a plant that grows all over south Texas. For most of the year, it is a gray-leaved mousy little bush, but when it rains, it suddenly bursts into beautiful purple blooms. I was hoping that with some love and attention, the foal would be like that tough little desert bush.

Senisa exceeded everyone's expectations. Within two months, she had a beautiful, glossy black coat that was as soft as a kid glove. Her wounds had healed and she was healthy. As she grew older, she became very territorial about "her" ranch. She ruled the roost in the barn, with the gelding and the mule content to bask in her glow.

One day, Senisa repaid my rescue of her by rescuing me. I had heard some barking down by the barn and had raced out of the house to see what was going on. Some stray dogs had gotten into the area and were snarling and growling at two lambs in a small pen. Without thinking, I ran into the pen to protect the lambs. As I held the lambs and turned to face the dogs, I realized that I hadn't brought the gun with me and grew scared as I watched the dogs tear at the fence. They were operating as a hunting pack and I knew that if they got into the pen, they would attack me to get at the lambs. I was desperate and alone and wondering what in the world I could do, when I caught a black flash out of the corner of my eye.

I turned my head to see Senisa racing across the pen and charging directly at the dogs! Her hooves were flying and her head was down and weaving as if she wanted to slash and bite them. The dogs didn't realize Senisa was charging them until she was almost upon them. They turned away from the fence with a yelp and ran out of the pen, down the hill and through the pasture, with Senisa chasing them all the way. They slithered out of a hole under the fence and were gone, never to return.

That day, I truly understood what they mean in Tex-Mex when they comfort someone going through difficult circumstances by saying, *"Es un pilon."* Bad times are only "a little something extra" in your life. Persevere and work through the trouble because tucked into every bad circumstance is a *pilon,* a magical pocket of beauty or love that is waiting for you, if only you have the eyes to see it.

Nancy Minor

Shawnee

Shawnee was a high-stepping, head-up, tail-arched three-year-old the first time we saw her. She pranced down the street in the Fourth of July parade, her owner and his small granddaughter on her back. A glowing sorrel with large white splotches here and there, Shawnee had a big white blaze down her face. Her eyes were large, liquid and intelligent; her body tall and beautiful. My eyes followed her and her riders down the street. We were looking for a younger horse because our Strawberry was getting old, and my husband Jim had told me about Shawnee. "She's half Quarter Horse and half Arab," he said. "Hank told me he just broke her to ride this year, but she's coming right along on the cow bit. He wants a lot for her, but I'm thinking hard about it."

I shifted our six-month-old son Dan from one hip to the other and stepped forward to see Shawnee better. "Okay," I told Jim. "But I want to ride her before you buy her." I wasn't much of a horseperson, preferring my own two feet to those of a horse even when it came to chasing cows. "Yeah," Jim replied. "I told Hank we'd meet him at the Blue after the parade and take a good look at the horse." The Blue was where Jim's brother-in-law worked and there was a nice big parking lot behind it.

Jim got on Shawnee and rode her around for about a half

hour. When he returned, he told me, "I'll hold Dan, you go ahead and give her a try." I did, thinking it was a good thing I'd worn clean jeans to the parade that day instead of a skirt and blouse. Shawnee was huge, but I managed to get into the saddle without help, and she started walking along the alley. I turned her into the next street, away from Main and all the cars and people. Shawnee seemed calm, neither shying away from people crossing the street in front of us nor swerving when cars came up behind her and passed slowly. People were accustomed to horseback riders in our small town, especially during the Fourth of July festivities, with the big parade and rodeo going on.

I neck-reined Shawnee down yet another street and headed back in the general direction of the Blue. Suddenly, a young boy ran into the street and tossed a lighted firecracker right under Shawnee! I touched her flanks with my heels and she leaped instantly into a run. The firecracker went off with a terrific bang behind us, but Shawnee slowed to a walk when I pulled on the reins. She never let on she even heard the firecracker. I knew right then and there that we had a new horse.

Hank took our check that day, but said it would be the next day before he could bring her out to the ranch. "Okay with us," Jim told him. "We'll be there."

The next day, Hank came riding in on Shawnee, followed by his wife in their pickup. "I decided just to ride her out," he said with a grin. "She's a real good horse, and it'll be a while before I get another one like her." We had to laugh, knowing Hank said that about every single horse he raised, broke and then sold. I well knew what would come next, so I went inside to start the coffee perking, leaving our son playing in the yard.

"Well, get down and come on in for some coffee," Jim told him. "The wife just baked some cookies a bit ago, and I think they're still warm." They tied Shawnee to the gatepost and trooped inside.

"Where's Dan?" I asked. "Oh, he's playing with that Tonka

truck in the side yard," Jim told me. Dan loved that big old Tonka truck, and because he couldn't do much more than crab-crawl, we didn't worry too much about it. I served the coffee and set out a plate of cookies to go with it, then walked to the door, intending to go out to get Dan. I stopped short, with one hand on the door, and let out a faint scream.

"What's wrong?" Jim came swiftly to the door. I pointed, wordlessly, out the door. Hank and his wife hurried to the kitchen window. Shawnee was standing, front feet spread out, her head down, looking between her legs. And there, standing underneath her belly, hanging on tight to a front leg with one hand, reaching up trying to scratch her tummy, was our six-month-old son!

I couldn't have said a word had I tried. Jim however, was a typical ranchman. He was always calm, cool and collected. And he acted! He went out the door, easy as you please, talking all the time in that slow, gentle manner he used with animals and children. "Easy does it, old girl. Don't you move now. You just stand real still until I can grab that boy under you. Easy now, girl." Jim moved forward, still talking soothingly to Shawnee, until he could reach down and lift our son out from under her. Shawnee had raised her head and given him one rather exasperated look, before lowering her head to that small mite of humanity still trying his cooing best to pet her stomach.

After he had Dan safely in his arms, Jim slumped a little—the only sign he ever showed that he had been worried and afraid. Then he held Dan so he could touch Shawnee's nose. Shawnee reached out and velvety horse nose met tiny boy hand. It was an instantaneous mutual admiration society. The mutual love and respect didn't end until we buried our beloved Shawnee nineteen long years later.

Jan Roat

The Wedding

I have run a small carriage business for about eleven years. We offer a horse-drawn carriage for romantic rides, weddings, engagement proposals—those occasions when something unique makes the moment even more memorable.

Dealing with brides-to-be can be great fun or absolutely awful. I've had some meet me on their wedding day in tears. Others have been just as calm as could be. I've had some say to please take them for a ride somewhere—anywhere— because they weren't up to getting married.

One spring day, I got a call from yet another bride-to-be. She was thrilled that she had found someone who offered a carriage for weddings. This young woman knew exactly what she wanted us to do at her wedding. We were to pick her and her dad up at her house, drive them to the church and then drop them off. That seemed simple enough, I thought. Before accepting the job, I drove to her house to see what was involved.

I always do this because I've gotten into some tight situations by not checking before saying I'd do the affair. I don't want anything happening to the people riding in my carriage or to my horses. It looked like an easy drive along a quiet country road to the desired church and I agreed to do the job. The bride was very pleased and paid for the whole thing on the spot.

On the day of the wedding, we arrived, clean horse, sparkling carriage, in our tuxedos, all set to have a good time. The bride's father came out, looking glum. He told us that something terrible had happened the night before and suggested that we see it before we drove into something that we might not be able to handle. We had no idea what he meant, but my partner took off in a car with the bride's father to take a look. They returned.

"Eh, no big deal," I was told. "There was a little house fire close to the street we would be driving on. Don't worry about it."

Off we went at a crisp walk. My mare Lynn was enjoying herself as usual. She always liked to take drives in new places. Round the hill, all the way to the bottom and out of the woods to the little town we drove. The town was one street in width, with cars parked on both sides, leaving us little room to navigate. I had figured we'd be okay when I first looked at the route, but today there had been a house fire.

The house was right next to the street, not five feet away from where we would pass. It was totally gutted, with timbers still smoldering, some still burning a little. There were fire trucks in the street with engines running, lights on and buckets reaching across the burned cars to spray water on the small fires.

Television newspeople were clustered around their vans carrying cameras. Microphones and cords ran everywhere. It seemed as if every town resident was milling around, watching. Above, TV news helicopters were flying low, people hanging off the sides with cameras. Police were trying to direct traffic through this little street without mishap, and the street now looked to be only six feet wide: just big enough for a Percheron horse pulling a wedding carriage.

Our destination was the church across the street, about fifteen feet beyond the burned house. The whole area was a solid chain of vehicles with no where to drop off a bride-to-be. *Would Lynn ever make it through this chaos?* Talk about sensory overload for a horse! I began to have doubts about proceeding, not wanting to ask my horse to deal with it all. A "little house fire . . . no big deal," my foot.

Lynn got much taller than her actual 17.2 hands when she saw what was in front of her. I imagine her eyes must have been wide open, taking everything in. I could hear what she was thinking loud and clear:

"WHAT in the world is all THIS? Smells funny. Big trucks! Who is that odd looking man in the street and why is he flapping carrot colored things? I don't think I want to be here anymore!"

Lynn hesitated, but kept walking forward, snorting the odd smells, seemingly fascinated by the man waving that orange flag for traffic control. I asked her to walk on and walk on she did, right past the noisy fire trucks, right past the newspeople, over the cords, looking with amazement at the burned house and up at the firemen in those buckets high in the air. She went forward all the while.

When she got to the traffic controller, she stopped. He stopped flapping his flag, thinking she might be scared. *Scared?* After having run the gauntlet of these terrifying sights and smells? Naaah, she just wanted to see if his flag tasted good. When he realized what she wanted, he laughed out loud and let her sniff his orange flag. Obviously, Lynn didn't think too much of it and proceeded down that crowded street to the church.

Throughout the journey, the bride and her father were totally quiet. We arrived on time, stopped in the middle of the street and the bride's dad helped her down from the carriage.

I expected her to rush up the steps to the church. Instead, she walked around to the front of my carriage to see Lynn.

Face-to-face, they stood. The bride told Lynn what a brave horse she was and thanked her for getting her to the most important affair of her life without a problem. Then she reached her arms around Lynn's big gray face and gave her a kiss on her forehead. Lynn lowered her head for this, knowing somehow it was a good thing to do.

We unhitched in the street a little further away from the

hubbub, cooled Lynn off and left, grateful that nothing else bad happened.

Later that month, I got a notice from the post office of a package delivery. The mailman couldn't fit it into the mailbox at the farm. When I picked up the package, it was addressed to Lynn at the farm's address, and sure enough, it was big.

Inside the box was five pounds of fresh carrots and a note. The kind young woman who got married that day a month before hadn't forgotten Lynn's bravery. She had set up deliveries of fresh carrots to the farm every month for a year, a box each month for every minute that Lynn had carried her through that scary town.

I'm proud to say that Lynn shares her treats with the rest of the horses, but I'm prouder still of Lynn's bravery that day. She dug deep and did things most horses would have panicked over and refused. Not that mare. She came through with flying colors and delivered in style, creating special memories for a beautiful bride on her wedding day.

Kris DeMond

Andy's Wish

The first time I saw him was through a small window in a horse trailer. I saw only his eye, but it looked right through me and pierced my soul. Andy, a Thoroughbred stallion, either was going to find a home with me or be ground up into a small can of dog food.

After a four-hour drive in silence, we were home and I had no idea what to do with Andy. I didn't know what to expect. I only hoped that I could handle what was to come. I opened the rusty trailer door and could see long legs encrusted in manure. He was covered by a horse blanket that at one time must have been green, but now it was heavily soiled with urine stains and tied together with hay-baling twine.

This stallion was as proud as any I had ever seen and he had a severe hatred for man. His piercing eyes glared, he was prepared at any moment for the fight of his life. I noticed the blanket was deeply embedded into his skin. I had no idea how long he had been jailed in its clutches. I was able to walk him carefully to a stall while he reared to his staggering height and shouted that he had arrived, never acknowledging my existence.

After the shock of seeing such a poorly managed animal, I was at my wits end with what I should do first, knowing that this stallion needed more than my experience justified. I placed him in a comfortable stall with an attached paddock. Although the stall I made for him was bedded deeply in pine shavings for comfort, Andy had the idea that being able to see the outdoors was his greatest comfort. He stood for hours in the corner of his paddock riveted by the sight of the green mountains that surrounded him. He gulped gallons of fresh air, enjoying a silent thrill that he wasn't willing to share. I knew that the breeding ranch he had come from had kept him in a small, enclosed stall, he was knee-deep in his own manure and he had only a small window at the very top of his stall for fresh air. He was beaten daily with a two-by-four and made to withstand the torture of a chain against his gums. He left his jailed existence only if the ranch manager needed his sperm. Other than that, his life didn't matter. He existed solely for himself.

I had to tranquilize Andy to remove his blanket of torture. The knotted ties had to be cut apart and the embedded fabric slowly peeled from his hide. The wounds were horrendous and I contemplated how I would be able to care for them, considering his obvious hatred for people. But the wounds appeared to be the least of my worries. This poor stallion was so undernourished that I could see every bone in his body, and his coat was in shambles, puckered by sores and lacking any glow. He was green and crusted with old feces. I had to cut off the majority of Andy's tail because it was so tangled. Because of this, he couldn't even perform the simple maneuver of swatting a pesky fly. The simplicity of a horse's life had been taken from him, and it was up to me to see that he found it again.

In the weeks that followed, I spent hours in Andy's stall, talking softly to him, groveling for his attention. At first, he ignored every attempt I made. Then slowly, his ears began to perk up at the sound of my voice. I managed to doctor his wounds by enticing him near the paddock fence with grain. Then I would reach inside the fence line and swipe salve into the open sores. I was able to hose off his coat, and he began to take on the shine of a copper penny with each layer of crust that was removed. His eyes changed their focus and his beautiful sculptured head inspired me as he looked toward the hills each evening at sunset.

After a few months, Andy began to fill out and I could see the elegant form he must have had as a young colt. He was a sight to behold even during this metamorphosis. He began to allow me to brush him and his eyes began to soften more with each passing day. I smiled when I saw him swat at a fly and it brought tears to my eyes to see him roll in the splendor of his clean pine shavings. Regardless of what he had been through, he was now home.

To my amazement, my $1 rescue horse turned out to be a true bargain. I discovered that Andy was an ex-racehorse who had won several stakes races. His sire was a full brother to the great Northern Dancer and his dam a granddaughter of the famous Man o' War. Andy was bred and trained at the Florida farm that had produced Affirmed. His future as a money-earning racehorse was right on track until he suffered a broken knee joint and was put out to stud.

How he ended up in my hands was a pure miracle. I had always imagined owning a racehorse from the time I was a child reading *The Black Stallion*, riding horses in my dreams. It seemed that fate had brought us together in some twisted irony of survival.

As I worked with Andy, it became apparent that he held as much admiration for me as I held for him. He began to nicker when I walked down the barn aisle and he would stand in his paddock to watch me walk away when the day was over. He began a habit of biting the fence when I came near so that he could contain his excitement while I scratched his head and stroked his delicate ears. He didn't know how to handle affection and it was very possible that he had never experienced it before. I was happy to give him what he deserved.

Today, Andy is the ripe old age of twenty-five and he is still full of life. We have come a long way. His eyes now focus on me with sweetness each and every day. His nickers are now soft neighs and his affection for me rivals mine for him. He doesn't hold any grudges. Through me, he has forgiven his abusers. He sired a few colts that look just like him. Andy allows me to heal his wounds, trim his feet and scratch his ears without question. His remarkable spirit shines through and I am able to imagine just how extraordinary he must have been in his younger days of glory. Through him I hear the sound of the trumpets announcing a race, I hear the blast that opens the gate and I feel his powerful strides reaching for every wire. When I close my eyes, he allows me to dream, and when he closes his, I allow him absolute reassurance.

Vikki Marshall

Great Finesse

It was only my second day on the job at a Woodford County horse farm, when my boss stopped by the barn to see how I was doing. "When you finish here," he requested as he peered through the open door of the stall I was bedding, "just pop down to the second paddock on the right and bring in Great Finesse. She is blind, so be careful with her. She doesn't need much to eat, she doesn't move around enough to keep the weight off. Just give her a handful of feed to make her feel like she is getting something. Give her a good old brushing and pick her feet. Then you can put her back out. She needs something to look forward to each day."

When I finished bedding the stall, I did as he'd asked. I had seen blind horses on other people's farms, but I had never cared for one myself. Most of the blind horses I had seen were jumpy and erratic, a bit frightening to get close to. Great Finesse was quite large, and the thought of bringing her through the tight confines of the gate and the barn doorways was a bit daunting. I walked out to where she was standing in the center of the field. As I approached, I noticed that she had a peculiar way of cocking her head sideways, almost as though she were trying to determine my location by tilting her head so that the sounds of my feet in the grass and my voice reached her ears at different times. The expression on her face was a bit curious, but trusting.

I clipped a shank onto her halter and said hello. Then I turned and walked toward the gate. Great Finesse showed no hesitation at following me. In fact, she stepped up beside me and placed her head along my shoulder and arm. I quickly realized that she was using me for a guide, following subtle cues through my arm and shoulder the way a blind person might follow subtle cues through the harness of a guide dog. Not only that, but if I touched her, she stopped. If I pushed against her, she moved away. Most horses push against you if you push, and pull away if you pull. Great Finesse had learned to trust her handlers enough to follow cues even from a stranger.

Suddenly, the gate didn't seem so daunting. I placed her safely along the fence, away from the gate, while I unhooked the chain and flung the gate open. I used my body to hold it open and used my hands to guide her safely through. She didn't even touch the gate, let alone bang her hips. All the way to the barn, Great Finesse rested her head against my arm, walking in exactly the same position as a blind person following a sighted guide. At the barn, I gave her that handful of feed as a reward. Then I groomed her from head to toe, picked her feet and painted them with hoof dressing, and turned her back out.

The next day, when I brought her in for the same routine, I quickly realized that she jumped every time I did something in a different order from what I had done the day before. She seemed to have memorized the way I did things so that my movements wouldn't startle her. As long as I worked the same way I had the day before, she was quiet. When I changed my routine, she was startled. From that day on, I always did things in exactly the same way with this remarkable mare.

When I mentioned her behavior to my boss, he smiled and replied, "We worked very hard to get her that way."

"How did you train her?" I queried.

"Well, we knew it was coming, you see, so we had a bit of time to prepare."

"She wasn't always blind?"

"No, she had a progressive eye disease. She lost the sight in one eye and most of the sight in the other. Because she could see only shadows, she became quite nervous and upset. She was too valuable a mare to lose. She is quite well bred and has produced several stakes winners. Her limited vision caused her enough distress that our veterinarian finally decided it would be kinder to surgically blind her so she wouldn't see ghosts and monsters in the shadows.

"Because I had a bit of time to prepare before the surgery," my boss continued, "I spent a great deal of time figuring out how to make the transition easier for her. She is on a late foaling schedule. She doesn't usually foal until late April, so I began by choosing a paddock that is situated between the foaling barn and the brood mare barn, where we put the late foals. The paddock I chose for her has access to both barns with gates at the nearest point, so she doesn't have to be moved. She stays there year-round. She has good shade for summer and a windbreak for winter.

"I wanted to make sure she wouldn't hit the fences or the waterer," my boss explained. "So I had the maintenance crew lay tanbark six feet wide around every obstacle. Then I began training the mare by walking her around the field, letting her feel the tanbark under her feet and then letting her touch the fence. Soon she knew to stop when her feet hit tanbark."

"That was pretty smart," I said, genuinely impressed. "I have seen some blind horses who would barely shuffle or who would move only in tight circles in the middle of the field. She seems pretty confident out there."

"That was the idea. I didn't want her to be frightened. The last thing we worked out was companionship. The rest of the mares travel around the farm through the year as their needs change. They foal up in the foaling unit, which is rather like a maternity ward. We even have our own neonatal unit next to the office. Once they have foaled, they come to the brood-mare barns. We fill up Broodmare One, up on the hill first. When it is full, the rest come down here. When we wean, the babies stay here in familiar surroundings and the mares go to a big field across the road, where they are too far away to hear the babies fuss. The babies stay here until the yearlings leave for the track, then they go to the yearling barns. Once the babies are gone, the mares come back here until it is time to go to the foaling barn again."

"So I guess you couldn't give her a mare for a companion because they need to be able to travel," I surmised.

"That, and we were afraid a sighted mare might hurt her."

"So what did you do?" I asked.

"We got her a llama."

"Oh yeah, I saw him up in the far corner of the field. A big brown critter! He always looks scared."

"That's Tipper. He is Great Finesse's companion. They don't hang out together much, but at least she isn't alone."

"What do you do when she foals?"

"The first year we put a bell on the foal. She did great. The mare was an even better mother than before she lost her sight. This year, the plan is to use a nurse mare for the baby to give Great Finesse a break. It is a bit harder for her because she can't see."

"You all really did a good job with her. She is very calm and trusting and confident."

"Well, we tried, you know, but what you are describing, she learned herself."

Just then, I heard galloping hoofbeats. I looked up just in time to see Great Finesse galloping across her field! She moved with all the grace of a sighted horse in her familiar territory. When her feet hit the tanbark, she changed course as effortlessly as any horse. *How aptly named she was,* I thought. Through the efforts of her caretakers and her own great finesse she had learned to cope with the obstacles of her condition and to function happily in her sightless world.

Thirza Peevey

A Job for Missy

You never know how a horse will pull until you hook him to a heavy load.

Paul "Bear" Bryant

God, find that little horse a home. All she needs is a job, I prayed, blinking back tears. I watched Missy leave the auction ring on her way to the killer pens. I hefted my saddle onto my shoulder and followed her out.

Missy was deep shiny black with a tiny white spot on her right rear heel. Her big head and light haunches spoke of her mustang ancestry almost as clearly as the Bureau of Land Management (BLM) brand under her mane. I had known her almost a year and she had won my heart with her incredible work ethic and endurance. Originally, her owners had brought her to me desperate to fix her bad habits.

She liked to bite and she was vicious with her heels. She was very hard to catch even in a pen. Sometimes she bucked and only a very severe bit kept her from running away. But, according to her owners, she hadn't always been like that. When they had tried her out, Missy was easy to handle and seemed to enjoy being groomed and ridden.

I called the BLM's Wild Horse Adoption Program and

found out the rest of the horse's history. She had been adopted as a three-year-old by a family that didn't know much about horses. She was too much for them to handle and they sold her to a horse trader who sent her to a feedlot to be trained to work cows. She excelled there under expert handling and hard work, and the trader thought she would make a good pleasure-riding horse.

So what had happened to this mare? Even poor handling as a youngster shouldn't have caused such terrible habits to resurface years later.

I worked at a livestock auction where horses were used to move the cows from sellers' pens to sale ring and then to the buyers' pens. It's a good place to find out what a horse is made of. There are loudspeakers, people running, cows bumping and banging, tight quarters and other horses, and they all teach a young horse a lot in a hurry. I took her to work and rode her. Her earlier training came back in a rush. She was quick to stop a cow from turning back and willingly plowed through the yearlings packed in the alley. Within minutes she remembered the cues to sidepass so I could open gates with ease from her back. I was impressed. Most horses find sale-barn work daunting.

I called the owner with a glowing report.

"Ride her a little longer. She gets bad if you ride her very long," the owner said.

The next sale, I rode her for eleven hours with only a few minutes to drink and one thirty-minute break to eat. Missy never slowed. She loved chasing cows. Finally, ashamed of myself for riding her so hard when she obviously wasn't going to cause problems, I switched horses. For the rest of the auction, Missy tried to chase cows from across the fence, ignoring her feed and water.

Early the next morning when I started catching horses to return to the auction, Missy hurried to the gate.

"You worked hard enough yesterday, you don't need to go today."

Missy whinnied, pawing at the gate. When I walked by

with two other horses, Missy charged down the fence line, screaming her displeasure. Afraid she was going to hurt herself, I grabbed a halter. Ordinarily, it took mental games and time to catch Missy, but this morning, she stood at the gate and shoved her nose in the halter. She danced expectantly at the trailer and leapt in as soon as the door swung wide enough.

Surprised, I shut the door and headed for town. The horse could stand tied at the auction and rest.

Missy refused to stand quietly tied to the post. She bit at the cows through the fence and paced the length of her tether until she wore a hole around the post. She chewed her lead rope. When she started kicking at the other horses, I gave in. Missy stood very still while I saddled and bridled her, but she almost trod on my heels as I lead her into the alley.

Long hours pulled the fat off the mare and built muscle in her haunches. The work also wore her feet down. Missy stood quietly as her shoes were nailed on. She never even offered to kick.

As long as Missy was working, she was happy. If she had a week off, her attitude took a sharp turn for the worse. Her mustang ancestry gave her incredible stamina, but her own spirit drove her to perform. If I was riding Missy, I needed only two horses when everybody else needed three or four. Her work ethic earned her admirers among the cowboys at the auction.

Six months later, I sent her home. She immediately reverted to her old tricks. She hated occasional short pleasure rides. Her owners couldn't catch her. She began kicking again. She bucked. She ran away. She was worse than ever.

They sent her back. She met me at the gate and stuck her nose in the halter, ready to go to work. I tried using her for day work on ranches, thinking maybe it was open space that was causing her problems. Missy worked day after day without argument. I found other people to ride her at the auction, thinking maybe she had bonded with me. Missy didn't care who was riding as long as she was working. I called the owners and explained that Missy needed a job where she could work hard every day. She would never be a pleasure horse. The owners weren't interested in competitive trail riding or endurance races.

"Sell her," they said.

I couldn't afford another horse, and mustangs rarely sell well, especially in ranch country. Sick at heart, I rode her through the auction ring. She gave a flawless performance, but only the killer buyer bid. The gavel fell at $350. Just because she wasn't a registered horse, my hardworking little partner was going for dog food. Almost physically ill, I stripped off the tack and watched her leave the ring.

I tried to forget Missy, but every time I battled some chicken-hearted, lazy blue-blooded colt, I remembered her.

Almost a year later, I was gathering cattle on a big rough-country ranch when another cowboy began talking about a neighbor kid and his horse.

"You never saw such a horse," the cowboy said. "Toughest thing on four feet. Chris may be only eleven, but he is hell on horses. I didn't think they'd ever find something tough enough for Chris, but they picked this mustang out of the killer pen for almost nothing. That kid must ride ten hours a day. If he ain't in school, he's riding. Why, the other day, I saw him fifteen miles from home, halfway to town. He said he was headed into town to spend the night with a friend. That little black mare was loping along, ears forward, happy as she could be, not blowing a bit." The cowboy shook his head in admiration.

My heart jumped painfully. "Any white on her?" I asked.

"She's got a spot on her off hind foot. Other than that, she's glossy black. What a horse!"

Lynn Allen

$\overline{\underline{4}}$

HORSES AS HEALERS

Horses change lives. They give our young people confidence and self-esteem. They provide peace and tranquility to troubled souls, they give us hope!

Toni Robinson

I Got It, Dad!

There are only two kinds of people in the world: horse lovers and the other kind.

I was the horse lover in my family. My sister was a dancer, my mom liked to bowl and my dad liked to golf. My son, Caton Ryder (Caton after the wise man Cato, and Ryder meaning horseman) is a horse lover, too.

Caton was born in Clements, California, in 1983. Shortly after his birth, something didn't seem quite right. Concerned, we took Caton to the pediatrician, who said, "Oh yeah, that's just strabismus," meaning his eyes are crossed a little bit. "His head has extreme molding," the doctor continued, "which happens sometimes when the baby comes through the birth canal."

Still concerned, Caton's mother and I continued taking our son to various doctors. Finally, it was the eye doctor who said, "This is not an eye problem. There is definitely something more serious going on here."

We immediately took three-month-old Caton to Oakland Children's Hospital. By the time we got there, Caton had slipped into a coma. It turns out that he had a condition called hydrocephalus—excessive fluid in the cranium. The duct that normally goes into the circulatory system is closed off, so the fluid enters the brain cavity and has no way to be released. The typical consequence is wasting of the brain and loss of mental powers. The solution for this problem, we were told, was to immediately implant a shunt that goes from the cranium down into the peritoneum in the abdominal area.

After a hurried series of tests and scans, the doctors told us that if Caton lived through the night, he would probably never walk or talk and he would certainly be greatly challenged.

Caton lived through that night and as he grew up he had a number of surgeries, including the shunt surgery and an operation to help his eyes. Life became more precious every day, and things were going pretty well.

Caton's always been a big boy, today, at twenty years old, he's six feet, four inches tall and he weighs about 230 pounds. I think the combination of being big and having certain physical and mental challenges has presented an interesting situation in his development. It seemed to me that rather than crawling then walking, and doing things in a certain order that seemed more normal, Caton tended to get good at fine-motor details before he managed gross-motor skills. He became more dexterous than mobile.

When Caton began walking, he would fall a lot and it would take him a long time to get anywhere. At times, he would start heading north and wind up going west. But even when Caton was very young, I'd snuggle him in front of my saddle and off we'd ride. Riding gave him a sense of rhythm and motion, and by being "tall in the saddle," he could focus on something in the distance. Eventually, Caton became fairly confident, and it was time for him to ride by himself.

At the time, I had a great horse named Sparky. He and I had scored well in reining cow horse classes and the Snaffle Bit Futurity. I used a lot of voice commands in those days to teach horses to walk, trot, canter, stop, back up and turn, so I knew Sparky would focus on me, even with Caton on board.

I remember the first time I put Caton on Sparky. I strapped my son into the saddle with a seat belt arrangement and led the two into the round corral. I couldn't believe how balanced Caton was. It was as though his sense of pride and accomplishment simply overwhelmed any physical difficulties. His balance was extraordinary, as it is today.

I managed to walk more than a few miles as I led the two of them around for weeks. Then I saddled up and rode next to them in the round corral, doing figure eights, turns and stops. After riding alongside for months, I finally sent Caton and Sparky (who pretty much kept one ear on me and my voice) around the corral on their own.

Caton could steer the horse pretty well, but he couldn't get Sparky to go forward without my help. Then, one day Caton had an epiphany. Talk about being a proud daddy! I remember the moment well.

Caton came up with the idea that if he could get his thoughts from his head through his body, down his legs and to his feet, the horse could feel it and would actually move. Caton started putting together thoughts that caused action. Watching this process was amazing. The horse would pick up a foot and put it down and the two of them would gain some yardage. Caton and Sparky now could actually propel themselves across the round corral without Dad's assistance.

Pretty quickly you could predict the process: Caton would smile, think, send his thoughts down to his feet, and Sparky would lope off across the arena, stop at the fence and turn around. A connection between human and horse had reached an understanding, a relationship.

This is when Caton really started to "wake up." It used to take him ten minutes to get across the arena on foot, and now he could do it in one minute because he had a partner named Sparky. Something special had happened, and I knew the horse was responsible.

We rode together more and more, Caton still sporting his seat belt for security. He wanted to accomplish other things with horses, and as fate would have it, the phone rang one day. We were invited to the French Ranch in Salinas, managed by our friends Hira and Corinne Reed. It was time to gather the cows and calves for branding, and the Reeds needed a few extra hands.

Caton, now six, couldn't wait to go. He was so excited about his first real roundup! So we loaded the horses and down the highway we went, two cowboys and their trusty steeds.

We stayed in the bunkhouse that night, just like all self-respecting cowboys did in the movies. We got up at o'dark early (about 4 A.M.), when the sky was still pitch black, of course, and the smell of coffee was drifting in the air. Caton quickly put on his clothes, including his chaps and cowboy hat. That buckaroo was ready to ride. We wandered over to the house and chowed down on a cowboy breakfast (the stick-to-your-ribs kind) of beans, bacon and eggs, and the best biscuits and freshly churned butter any ranchhand ever tasted.

Our two horses came up to the corral gate, ready to start the day. I saddled Sparky, secured Caton in the saddle and ponied them up the draw between two rolling hills. Within an hour it was getting light, and Caton declared, "I got it, Dad." I turned them loose, after saying a quick prayer. We could now see the cows and calves, the cows bellowing at the calves to join up as we started gathering the lot. Pretty quickly, the herd was headed in the right direction, and we started driving them the four-mile journey. "Caton and I and a few other cowboys had a good bunch in front of us, maybe 300 to 400 cows and their 300 to 400 calves.

Caton was riding over here and then over there, helping where he could. It was a beautiful spring morning in the California hills, and I was sure a proud dad that day, watching Caton ride. There was a little group of calves, about thirty of them up on a knoll, bawling for their moms. I said, "Caton, go up there and get those calves." He did a perfect job. Instead of going straight toward them, he went up and around on the hill so he didn't spook the calves.

Caton rode up on this group of calves, slapped his leg a couple of times and shouted, "Heeeyaaa! Get along little doggies, it's your misfortune and none of my own. . . ." A finer, more appropriate cowboy tune there wasn't, and how he remembered the lyrics was beyond me! That brief moment is etched in my memory as though it happened ten minutes ago.

That seemed to be the beginning of the beginning.

Since then, Caton has become a good rider and he's often in the limelight during my demonstrations. He's learned how to swim, ride a bicycle, snow ski, dribble a basketball—lots of things. He drives everything on the ranch—including his father—crazy and he is even learning how to drive a vehicle.

I've carried this story in my heart for twenty years. Horses are the partners who opened the door for my son, transforming him, offering him opportunities. For that I am grateful.

May the horse be with you!

Pat Parelli

Chrysalis

A horse is the projection of people's dreams about themselves; strong, powerful, beautiful and it has the capability of giving us escape from our mundane existence.

Pam Brown

Ellen was a fat girl.

She didn't start out that way. But by the time she was halfway through elementary school, her lack of coordination and competitive spirit had made her the laughingstock of her more athletic peers.

No matter the game, Ellen was always chosen last. Chosen last in kickball, because she couldn't catch or run. Chosen last in badminton, because she had never once managed to hit the birdie over the net. Chosen last in red rover, a game even a klutz ought to be able to play.

Junior high was worse.

There was a real physical education class instead of mere playground games, and every day Ellen suffered the indignities of not being able to shoot a basketball through a hoop or skip rope without tripping or even perform a respectable side-straddle hop.

And so she turned to food for comfort.

By the time she started high school at age fourteen, five-foot-five Ellen was tipping the scales at almost 200 pounds.

Her family's efforts to help her lose weight did no good.

She turned up her nose at the special salads her mother fixed for her. She refused her father's invitations to take brisk walks with him. She ignored her sister's warning that a girl her size would never have a boyfriend.

Ellen would toss her head and roll her eyes at her family. Then she'd grab a bag of potato chips or a box of cookies and flounce on the recliner in the den, where she'd spend hours lost in the pages of a book.

More than anything, she loved to read about horses. And that's what finally gave Ellen's father a brilliant idea.

"There's a woman at work who's looking for a stable-hand," he told Ellen one evening. "Somebody to feed her horses and clean the stalls and things like that. I told her you might be interested in the job."

"She wouldn't want me," Ellen replied.

"Why not?"

"Because I've never been near a horse."

"I told her that. But I also told her you've been reading about them all your life. She's willing to teach you every-thing from the ground up. And she's also offered to pay minimum wage and to let you ride whenever you want."

Ride? Ellen's heart beat faster. Somebody was actually offering to let her ride a real horse?

Don't be silly, the voice inside her whispered. *Had Dad not told this woman that his daughter was a clumsy tub of lard who could barely keep her balance on a bicycle?*

No way would she be strong or coordinated enough to ride a horse. And pity the poor animal that had to carry her weight on his back.

"I told her we'd drop by her place Saturday morning to see about it," her father said.

So that was that.

Pat Cunningham lived on a small farm not far from town.

Dressed in jeans and cowboy boots, she was waiting for Ellen and her father as they pulled into the gravel driveway.

"So you're the girl who loves horses," she said to Ellen, smiling and holding out her hand. "C'mon, let me show you around."

She led Ellen to the barn and gestured toward a wheelbarrow and manure fork. "Every day, these stalls have to be mucked out and then spread with fresh sawdust. The water and feed buckets get scrubbed and filled, the tack room swept and tidied, the gates and fences checked. Think you're up to it?"

"Um . . . I guess so," Ellen stammered.

"Good," Pat replied. "The school bus comes right by here every afternoon. When you're done with the chores, I'll run you home in my truck."

"Where are the horses?" Ellen asked shyly.

"Oh, yes, the horses," Pat said. She gave a long, low whistle and within seconds, two beautiful horses trotted up to the barnyard gate.

Pat pointed to the bay gelding. "That's Thunder. Don't let the name scare you. He's as gentle as a lamb. And the sweet mare beside him is Buttermilk. Which one do you want to ride first?"

Before Ellen could protest, Pat had the horses hitched to fence posts.

She showed Ellen how to lift their feet and use a hoof pick to dislodge sticks and rocks from around their shoes.

She showed her how to use the currycomb and finishing brush and how to remove cockleburs from their manes.

Finally, she showed her how to put on blanket and saddle, bridle and bit.

"I'd like you to ride at least one of them every day you're here," Pat said. "Both, if you have time. They really need the exercise."

Ellen felt tears welling up in her eyes. How could she tell this kind woman that she was nothing but a fat girl who had no earthly idea how to ride a horse?

"But, I've never . . . never actually been on a horse. All I've ever done is read about them."

"Then it's high time you learned," Pat said. "Stand there beside Buttermilk and put your left foot in the stirrup. Then bounce a couple of times on your right foot and spring into the saddle."

But try as she might, Ellen couldn't stretch her leg high enough to get her foot anywhere near the stirrup.

"Hold on a second," Pat told her. "Let's try the milk crate." She fetched it from the barn and helped Ellen climb onto Buttermilk's broad back.

"There are a couple of things to remember. Heels down. Hands on the reins like so. Relax. This is supposed to be fun! Now follow me."

Pat swung into Thunder's saddle and headed toward the pasture. Buttermilk followed, with Ellen gripping the reins so tightly that her knuckles turned white.

But it didn't take long before she began to relax. Pat was right. This was fun. In fact, Ellen couldn't remember when she'd ever had such a good time.

Pat showed her how to go from a walk to a trot, and promised that she'd be cantering in just a short time. "You're a natural," she told Ellen. "I'm sure lucky to have run across you."

So Ellen became a stablehand. Every day after school, she cleaned stalls and scrubbed buckets and swept the floor of the tack room.

After that, she rode. Some days she rode Thunder. Other days she rode Buttermilk. On good days, she rode them both.

And as the days turned to weeks and the weeks to months, Ellen the fat girl slowly evolved into Ellen the equestrian. Her flab became muscle and her clumsiness, grace. She glowed with a self-confidence that was obvious to everyone around her.

It was near the end of the school year when a heavyset girl sat down beside Ellen on the bus one afternoon.

"My name's Stacy. I hear you work with horses," the girl said hesitantly. "Do you need an assistant? I've never ridden before, but I read about horses all the time."

"Why don't you get off here with me and we'll go talk to my boss," Ellen said, smiling to herself. She was pretty sure she could guess what Pat's answer would be.

"We're lucky to have run across you, Stacy. Who do you want to ride first—Thunder or Buttermilk?"

Jennie Ivey

That Kid Is on Zoloft

We've heard the familiar saying that "the best thing for the inside of a man is the outside of a horse." Well, it is true that horses have an uncanny ability to unlock something deep within the recesses of the human mind.

It was spring on the Cocolalla Creek Ranch, nestled in the mountains of northern Idaho, and the warming sun was pushing up a carpet of lush, green grass in the meadows. When my husband Tom and I checked on the horses that morning, we found that one was injured after having gotten into a squabble with another horse the night before.

The injured horse was a Norwegian Fjord named Olaf, a small, stocky draft horse that looks like a fawn-colored teddy bear with a personality to match. No wonder he lost the fight.

Dawna, our barn manager, brought him into the barn, cross-tied him in the alleyway and started to treat his wounds. Although the wounds were not serious, Olaf was bleeding and trembling from the pain. At this time, the North Idaho Children's Mental Health Psychological Therapy Group was also using the indoor arena on the ranch. The group brings in children who have been abused and helps them overcome their fears and problems by working with horses. This hippotherapy program is called the

Healing Partners Equestrian Therapy Program.

A twelve-year-old boy was part of that program. Fair-headed and freckled, with a slight build, Shane had just been released from the hospital and was very fragile, having had a cast removed from his arm the very day of his visit to the ranch. Shane watched for some time from a distance, then hesitantly walked up to Dawna and asked what she was doing. Dawna told him about the horse fight and showed him Olaf's wounds. Shane winced at the sight of the gaping wounds and asked if Olaf was in pain. Dawna replied tenderly, "Yes, it hurts, and he is in pain, but look how trusting he is to let me help him and how strong Olaf is not to cry out or run away."

Reaching up and stroking Olaf's muzzle, the boy whispered to the trembling horse, "I did the same thing, too, when I was hurt."

Dawna then asked if Shane would like to help groom Olaf. Eagerly, he took the brush that was in her hand and allowed her to guide the first few strokes to make sure it wasn't too hard or too soft, but just right. She noticed his knees and hands were shaking.

"What's wrong, honey?" Dawna asked.

"I'm scared all the time because my stepfather used to hurt me," replied Shane in a whisper. "He beat me up just like that bigger horse did Olaf."

At that point, Olaf dropped his big shaggy head and the boy and horse snuggled into a single, quiet mass. Tears gushed like a mountain spring and Shane told Dawna of the pain he had suffered and the wounds inflicted upon him.

Dawna told Shane that whenever he felt scared, shaky, sad or alone, all he had to do was brush Olaf or think of Olaf when he wasn't around. Shane agreed and proudly pronounced to Dawna, "I take a drug called Zoloft that helps calm me down and not be so afraid. From now on, I think Olaf should be called Zoloft because that's what he does for me."

Indeed, this shaggy, four-legged Zoloft became the miracle drug that broke through the darkness that surrounded this withdrawn child and let him come back into the light.

About this time, I walked into the barn and went up to the group to see what was going on and to say hello. I got down on a knee and talked eye-to-eye for a little while with Shane. When I turned to leave, Teresa, a therapist with the group, came up to me and quietly told me about Shane and how his stepfather had sexually abused and badly beaten him. She said that for more than nine months Shane, had not spoken a word about what had happened to him to anyone outside of her and his immediate family.

"With Olaf, I mean Zoloft, it was perhaps the first time Shane realized that others suffer as well," explained Teresa with thankfulness in her eyes. Shane went on to take a short ride on Zoloft that day and every other day he came to the ranch. Although every ride was another step toward recovery, Teresa summed up Shane's magical first ride on Zoloft by saying, "That was the first time in ten months that I saw Shane calm. That horse opened the door to saving this child."

As a postscript to this story, Teresa reports that Shane got tremendous therapeutic value from standing tall in court and telling the truth in front of the perpetrator, his stepfather. The prosecutor said that Shane's incredibly powerful testimony in court made it possible for his stepfather to be charged with two extra counts. He was taken directly to jail. If recommendations are taken and predictions come true, this evil man will be convicted and sentenced to twenty-five years in prison for his crimes. A heavy sentence would truly be icing on the cake for Shane.

Teresa went on to say, "From my experience as Shane's counselor, I know that Zoloft (that is, the four-legged one) helped this injured young man to feel a sense of power, control, calmness and confidence that he did not have before."

Now when you see Shane proudly riding around the arena, you can really say, "That boy is on Zoloft and it's really helping him!"

Marguerite Suttmeier

Hey, Lady!

"Hey, lady, can I walk Tostada?" came the small voice from somewhere in the dark behind me.

I jumped six inches and rapped my knuckles on the gate I was opening.

Spinning around, I searched the blackness. A short, hunched form was barely visible in the reflected light from the distant street lamp.

"Little John," I said. "What are you doing out this late? Won't your mom be worried?"

The small boy, who lived in the housing project about a half mile from the boarding stable I managed, looked up at me and said, "Nah, she's in jail. Can I walk Tostada?"

I had seen Little John hanging around the stable on the weekends. He was a round little boy, who walked with his shoulders slumped and his head hanging down. He always looked at the ground and wouldn't look you in the face when you spoke to him. He never replied to any questions.

However, he did talk to the show horses in their stalls. They seemed to enjoy the little person and would put their heads over the stall doors to snuffle him on the neck. He mostly just stood there and let the horses nuzzle him. Rarely, he would reach out and tentatively touch their soft noses.

Little John's speech was slow when he would stay to talk.

Most of the time he would scurry away when people approached him. Fetal alcohol syndrome was the term I heard from the professionals who boarded horses at the barn.

"Lady," said the insistent boy, his voice breaking, "can I walk Tostada?"

"Sure, Little John," I replied, and I turned back to the gate to halter my gray Anglo-Arabian mare Misata.

Little John had come by to visit her a few times while I was at the barn and had once gathered the courage to ask her name. He couldn't pronounce Misata, but in an attempt to get her name, he hit upon a word he knew. To Little John, she was Tostada.

That night, my normally energetic, spooky horse walked with her head down next to the small person who had his hands wrapped tight around the lead rope. I held the other end, tensely hoping Misata would behave.

Finely tuned and in show shape, Misata was a handful for experienced riders. Her favorite class was the Arabian costume class, where she would race wildly around the arena, bells and tassels streaming out behind her, trying to outrun every other horse in the class.

That night, she stepped calmly thought the gate. I handed the middle of the lead rope to the boy.

Walking with his head down, in his normal fashion, Little John could not see where he was going in the dark. He stumbled. Misata, who usually had to be jerked to a halt, stopped and stood still.

"Look up, Little John," I said softly as I breathed relief that Misata hadn't spooked at the sudden movement.

Little John helped me finish my chores, and then I took him down to the local police station, where a young officer gently talked to the young boy and set him up with a place to stay.

The next Saturday, as I was mucking stalls, a small voice whispered, "Hey, lady, can I help?" Little John stood in the doorway, looking at the ground.

"Tell you what," I said. "You scrub up all those water buckets and I'll let you sit on Tostada." For the first time, Little John looked me in the eye, "Really?"

He diligently set to work with the scrub brush. About halfway through the sloppy job, one of the buckets splashed up water into the boy's face. Words erupted from the small person that scalded my ears.

"Little John, we do not talk that way in my barn."

"Teacher lets me," he said without looking at me.

"In my barn, you do not talk that way, ever," I said. "If you want to talk like that, you need to leave." Through tumbles and falls and bumps and bruises, Little John never let fly a foul word again.

When he finished the water buckets, I took Misata out of her stall. She walked out instead of bolting through the door and stood calmly as Little John ran a brush over her down-stretched neck and front legs.

The mare, who never stood for me to mount, was still as I tried to boost the round, rolled up little boy onto her back. He was like a deadweight.

"Little John," I asked, "do you want to ride?"

He nodded, still looking down.

"You can't stay on a horse unless you look up and ride straight," I told him. "If you look at the ground, you will end up on the ground."

The boy stared up at the normally fidgety horse who was standing calmly just for him, and then he looked up at me. "Okay," he said.

I boosted him onto Misata's back. He instinctively curled into a fetal position and started to slide off her side. The mare shifted her weight to stay under the boy.

"Sit up," I reminded him.

He looked up, wrapped his hands in the mare's thick gray mane and smiled the first smile that I had ever seen on his eight-year-old face.

That was our first ride of many that summer. Little John rolled over Misata's shoulder more than once as he learned the importance of sitting up straight. The mare stopped each time, waiting for her young charge to climb back to his feet and then back on her back, where she seemed certain that he belonged.

"Stay, Tostada," he would croon, as he pulled her next to a fence so he could climb up and on. For him, she did.

He worked his way up from scrubbing buckets to picking stalls. He was determined to earn his way and be responsible for every minute he spent with his Tostada.

He worked in the barn and rode almost every day. He began to walk straight and look people in the eye.

And finally, that August, Little John's Tostada carried a proud young boy in the town's parade. The tall white mare walking carefully through the balloons and bands was not Misata, my fiery show horse, but the calm steady support of a young man who had little else in the world.

Jeanette Larson

Thursdays Are Special

*Horses and children, I often think, have a lot of
the good sense there is in the world.*

Josephine Demott Robinson

Sometimes he would come on Thursday and not even be
able to get out of the car because of the seizures. Still he
came, week after week.

His caretakers said he knew when it was Thursday, even
though he knew little else and could not communicate how
he knew. He could see, but not speak, could not even sit up
unassisted. Yet, he knew when it was his day to go ride. He
was only ten, and he didn't live to his teens.

Nevertheless, his story, which includes horses and
horsepeople who made him smile and gave him something
to look forward to one day a week, must be told.

Many years have passed and many children have bene-
fited from various therapeutic riding programs. But none
touched me as much as this one boy. He required a steady
horse, one with patience with his rider's inability to balance
and an understanding of the boy's need to occasionally lay
his face on the mane and just breathe in horse smells. We had
several wonderful horses that filled the bill.

One volunteer would walk beside this youngster on the right and help hold him in the saddle, one would control the horse and another would walk on his left to steady him and be his instructor for the day. Any breakthroughs, no matter how small, were recognized and rewarded. A smile, an attempt to move a hand or leg in the right direction, even attention focused on the instructor or the horse were considered achievements.

One week, he was in very good spirits. This followed several weeks when he was either too ill to come or he had suffered seizures in the car and was forced to miss his lesson with the horses. But that day, he smiled. He seemed alert and willing.

We were stopped and waiting for another rider to be helped when my young student reached out and touched my hair. My hand was on his leg, so I knew he was steady, even though my eyes weren't on him. I looked around and knew he was trying to tell me something. The horse stood motionless, as if he knew his movement could distract or confuse his rider.

"What?" I asked. It was unusual for him to reach out and touch, to even control his hands enough to do so. He reached out again and stroked my hair, as he sometimes did to the horse's mane on good days.

I realized that my waist-length hair was back in a pony-tail, and that he wanted it to hang down. Perhaps he wanted to see it, like the horse's tail in front of us, free and swinging. Or perhaps I had worn it down in other classes with him and it wasn't the same today. For whatever reason, I knew he wanted me to free that ponytail, so I did. He looked at me, managed to touch his hands together a couple of times in what he used as clapping, and he smiled at me.

Approval.

Our lesson continued and he seemed to have a better time that day than I could remember him having in any other class. He reached toward me and I put my head so he could touch my hair several times while we were walking along.

I didn't know as his attendant carried him back to the car that it would be the last time I saw him. He missed several weeks, then I went back to college. I found out months later that he died not too long after that.

But instead of mourning, I thought of him in heaven, running out to his favorite horse, not having to wait until Thursday or for his attendants to help him. He and his horse would gallop across clouds, with him laughing and the horse's tail streaming freely behind as the wind sang through their hair.

There is a heaven for horses and for little boys who know what day they ride, even when they don't know much else. I'm grateful for having seen that desire, and for understanding that God gave us horses and little boys and that they all aren't the same, nor should they be.

Kimberly Graetz Herbert

A Beach Day

And God took a handful of southerly wind,
blew his breath over it and created the horse.

Bedouin Legend

"We need to go to the beach." Martha was right. We needed it more than anything right now. We were three friends. Three middle-aged friends. In the suburbs. With horses. We'd been riding together for years and didn't ever intend to stop.

Martha was the most accomplished rider. She was tall, lean and supple. Her face was tanned and her eyes sparked with excitement. She had the resources to buy the best horses and the athleticism and drive to excel at dressage. Her horse was Mars, a licorice-black Friesian with a long forelock that draped his face and graceful feathery hair on his fetlocks. With Martha astride, his muscled body glistened and bunched under her command.

Kerry was fearless, opinionated and had a will of iron. Compact and strong, she could lift fifty-pound feed bags onto her shoulder with a smile. Her whole life had been steeped in horses and she had a solution to any horse-related problem that arose. She rode Shasta, a big dappled

Hanoverian mare with an attitude to match Kerry's. Shasta was smart, too smart in my opinion, and had a good sense of what she could get away with.

I was the busy one, working too hard, raising two kids and getting involved in a multitude of community activities. I had spent my adult life trying to squeeze riding into spare moments. I didn't own a horse, but was always negotiating and conniving to get a ride. I was not the best rider of the group, but the most relaxed. Once I found the time to get on a horse, I was totally in the moment and felt Zen-like in my peace. I had been riding Cort, a hardworking bay who pretended, not too convincingly, to hate all humans. He was a sucker for a good neck scratching and gingersnaps. Like me, he also was middle-aged, but sometimes suffered under the delusion that he was a hot-blooded yearling and acted that way.

In this early spring season, life had just thrown all three of us some pretty serious curve balls. Martha's situation was the saddest. Her husband had just passed away from cancer, and she was now facing the reality of a life alone. Kerry, who never feared any horse, had recently hopped on a neighbor's pony in an ice-slicked paddock. The pony reared, twirled and lost his footing, and Kerry was thrown onto her back. Two broken vertebrae and two millimeters from paralysis, she was told never to ride again. She didn't listen. I had just been laid off from a twelve-year office job due to a faltering economy, and couldn't sleep at night, worrying about money and even more, the loss of my professional identity.

A beach day was prescribed. We lived thirty minutes from the ocean, where there was a wide beach with an inviting stretch of sandbars at low tide. So, on that chilly March morning, we loaded the three horses into a spacious trailer and headed out. In the parking lot at the beach, the sand drifted across the asphalt and the salty smell of the ocean made the horses' nostrils flare. They were excited, shifting their weight and stamping their feet while we tacked up. Their mood was infectious and we found ourselves as eager as the horses.

We started out trotting three abreast across the sand as if we were the Three Musketeers, black, gray and bay in beautiful alignment. The gulls screeched over our heads and dogs let off their leashes bayed and loped behind us. We laughed aloud in pleasure and imagined us as a scene in a perfect movie where nothing ever goes wrong.

But it wasn't to be a movie-perfect day. Kerry moved Shasta into the shallow water to avoid a rocky patch and the big mare decided the water was just too cold and veered back out. A war of wills ensued. Martha and I watched in amusement as horse and rider set a zigzag path: in the water, out of the water, in the water, out. Forced once more into the water, Shasta was fed up. She glanced back at Kerry and slowly collapsed onto her side in peaceful, nonviolent protest. Kerry leaped off at the last moment and stood there, drenched to the thighs in the frigid water, holding the reins of a supremely stubborn horse. Shasta had made her point and soon stood up, shook and cheerfully nuzzled Kerry for a treat.

Happy that no one was hurt, we set out again, this time walking straight out into the bay on a narrow spit of rocky sand that was littered with broken shells and terminated almost at the horizon in an abandoned lighthouse. We walked and talked almost to the end, then turned and headed back toward the beach. Now it was Cort, my aged mount, who decided he was once again a yearling and it was time to run. His head lowered and oblivious to the snaffle bit that I was futilely pulling on, he took off at a full gallop. He could not be stopped. I flew past the other two and caught a glimpse of their laughing faces. My Zen-like peace was left a quarter-mile back and I clung to his back in total panic. Back on the main beach, Cort slowed on his own and waited calmly for the others to catch up. I could swear I saw that horse wink at the other two.

It was almost time to go home. Pools of water barely two inches deep were forming all over the sandbars. Martha rode Mars into one large puddle, then stopped. As Kerry and I watched, Martha straightened her back and moved the reins slightly in her hands. Mars tightened his muscles and started a piaffe, perhaps the most beautiful dressage movement, where the horse trots in place almost in slow motion, his feet rising and falling in the same spot. Mars was awesome. He was a black shadow on the sand, moving in a dream-like sequence. And because of where Martha had placed him, with every step, a sheet of fine water sprayed upward from his hooves. I looked at Martha's face and her eyes were gazing far away and I could see that her soul was flying free.

The air had changed from chilly to cold. The sun was low and the dogs and their owners had all gone home. We quickly and quietly loaded the horses and eased our tired legs into the truck. Not much was said, but we knew our problems had been forgotten, for a day at least. Tomorrow we would have to deal with loneliness, health and money. But not today.

"Hey, Kerry?" It was Martha.

"Yeah?"

"What do people without horses do?"

Tracy Van Buskirk

Damsel in Distressed Work Boots

God forbid I should go to any heaven where there are no horses.

R.B. Cunningham Graham

In my mid-forties, I left a safe, perfectly paved, colorless highway and made a hairpin turn that sent me reeling down a rutted route of self-discovery. My rest stop, my refueling place, was a five-acre ranch on a quiet country road. It became my new home. It offered serenity, healing and the company of nature.

The house came together quickly. I unpacked boxes with a sense of permanence. Everything claimed a place of belonging. I worked hard all day and started sleeping deeply at night. The day my son declared that our new house felt like home, I breathed a sigh of relief. It was the first sign that we were going to be okay. The nesting came naturally, and once the house felt safe and secure, I focused on the rest of the property. It was time to bring my horses home.

The day the hay was delivered, my horses moved in. I climbed the stack of alfalfa to knock off the top bales, and looked down a sheer fourteen-foot wall. I realized I was stuck. I called out for my eleven-year-old son, and he braced the ladder as I fearfully eased down. We didn't have wire cutters, so I popped open the bale by twisting a broom handle until the wire weakened. Without feeders or water troughs, I had to toss the hay on the ground and fill large plastic buckets with water. The next morning, as the sun came up, I fed my horses for the first time.

I picked up the manure fork and wrapped my manicured hands around the cool steel handle. My movements were awkward. Time and again, the fork tines stabbed the ground and the flying manure missed the large mouth of the trash can. My arms ached and I had angry red blisters on my hands. I paused to straighten my back and catch my breath. My horses were eating their breakfast contentedly, and I listened to their slow methodical chewing and the soft rumble of their noses as they blew out bits of alfalfa. The manure, some still steaming, simply smelled healthy. My poor horses were corralled in single-rail fencing with wire curling up the rotted posts. They looked as though they'd moved to the wrong side of the tracks. Where was their silver spoonful of white fencing and pasture grass?

In my previous life of Riley, we had a lovely gentleman's ranch with plenty of hired help. I was indoctrinated by the mantra of my marital years: If you had horses, you had help. One of our longtime employees was supposed to move with us. But I couldn't replace his salary, so I was on my own. Kitchen utensils, needlepoint scissors and light bulbs fit my hand perfectly. Tools, shovels and wheelbarrows did not. I felt physically defeated by the sheer work of taking care of my horses. Trembling with dismay at the injustice, I expected to be rescued. Where's Waldo, my knight in shining work boots, when it's time to feed? Blanket the horses? Pick up manure? And what about the disrepair? Who was going to fix everything? More importantly, how was I going to pay for it?

My seven-year-old trail horse, sweet reliable Buddy, became the financial sacrificial lamb. I was consoled when he went to a loving home. I knew he would be well cared for and, in turn, Buddy became the benefactor of safe new fencing, shelters from the sun and pelting rain, and spacious sand pens with permanent feeders and automatic waterers.

My biological clock adjusted to livestock hours. My designer jeans were replaced with Wranglers and work boots. Our dogs, wiggling their morning greeting, led the way to the hay barn. The wheelbarrow became my most cherished tool. I used it to schlep hay, transport manure, off-load supplements and cart tools and trash and firewood. That scratched blue bathtub body, supported in a steel frame with sturdy fat wheels, became my constant companion. I needed it more than the luxury car in my garage. It was as necessary to my job as a wrench is to a mechanic, medicine to a doctor or a case library to an attorney. I couldn't work without it.

An "Aha!" moment came as I was heaving manure cans into the dumpster. I didn't hurt anymore. I was efficient in my chores. I could throw manure as an intact pile or one nugget at a time across a twelve-foot stall. I could toss hay without getting it in my hair and bra. I could feed and clean in less than an hour, brushing off my hands with accomplishment. I paused and realized that if I was willing to do this kind of work, it must be in alignment with my soul. I reflected on my previous life, a socialite with a full calendar, and discovered that nowhere in society were my needs better met than in the company of my horses. Because of them, I'd learned how to work and I was proud of it.

The first winter, I struggled with the weather. It brought drenching rain, sticky clay soil that made me six inches taller with each trip to the barn, and a dumpster overflowing with manure. Twice daily, I bundled up and begrudgingly left the warm house to take care of my horses.

With the next winter approaching, and my memory of the grueling one past, I dreaded the thought of inclement weather. But I treated it like childbirth and I was better prepared the second time around. I had fresh hay stacked to the rafters—it was tiered and I owned hay hooks for moving it around. I had fleece shirts, down vests and heavy hooded raincoats, rubber boots, warm gloves and earmuffs, too. My body was strong and my hands were capable. More importantly, I had come to love the daily contact with my horses. I loved the gentle whinny of their greeting and their soft blinking eyes as they watched me round the corner with my trusty wheelbarrow. I tried to explain it to my mom, "When my horses are blanketed and eating their dinner in clean bedded stalls, when the sounds are contented and the light soft, it reminds me of nursing mothers comforting their hungry babies. It's nurturing and, for me, it offers a deep sense of communion with mothers everywhere."

One early evening, as I stomped the sand off my boots on my way back to the house, my life suddenly felt familiar. It felt good and honest and real. I shrugged out of my coat and boots and paused in our warm kitchen in my stocking feet. My son was quietly concentrating on his homework, our roasting dinner promised comfort and I was overcome with contentment. I felt that I understood Kahlil Gibran's description of comfort, "That stealthy thing that enters the house as a guest, and then becomes a host, and then a master." I knew for sure that I was home.

Paula Hunsicker

Riding the Road to Recovery

As Jane entered her forty-ninth year, her life could not have been more perfect. She had a career in the air force, achieving the rank of senior master sergeant, and she was happily married to a great guy. She was an accomplished musician and equestrian, valued by friends for her warmth, generosity and humor, and admired by peers for her discipline, determination and focus.

Just three years earlier, Jane had won the coveted spot of lead violinist for the U.S. Air Force Strolling Strings. She was the first woman to hold this distinguished position in the group's nearly fifty-year history. As part of this talented ensemble, she performed at the White House and at diplomatic functions throughout the United States and around the world.

In her free time, Jane could be at the barn with her beloved fifteen-year-old horse Clear Screen, also known as Leroy. An elegant pair, this 17.2-hand, dark bay Thoroughbred and his five-foot, nine-inch rider built a successful show record in both the ladies sidesaddle and hunter divisions. Everything was going smoothly until April 2000, when fate had another plan for this beautiful, determined woman. Suddenly, a favorite pastime became the catalyst for dealing with a life-threatening illness.

There was a family history of breast cancer and Jane knew she was considered high risk. She followed the recommended prevention and early-detection plan that included regular breast examinations and mammograms. Until the day she discovered the lump, her exam results always were negative.

A battery of tests led to referrals to several specialists. The agonizing process of identifying the lump and undergoing the appropriate treatment began. Just as in riding, determination and patience paid off. Days waiting for test results seemed like an eternity. The bad news, "You have cancer," was followed by the good news, "Thankfully, you caught it early."

Despite the fact that Jane's breast cancer was diagnosed as Stage I, she opted for a very aggressive treatment plan of surgery, radiation and chemotherapy. With her family history, she didn't want to take any chances.

In early May, she underwent a lumpectomy and lymph-node biopsy. Her first question to the doctor after the procedure was, "Will I be able to compete in a horse show in eighteen days?" Four days after the operation, Jane was riding again, but her ordeal was far from over. Additional testing revealed that the bad cells were a little more widespread than initially thought. As a result, her diagnosis was changed to Stage II breast cancer.

In addition to being an accomplished rider, Jane was an avid runner in top physical condition, but there was no way she could have prepared for the emotional blow. In one of the few times she expressed her doubts, she told me, "The reclassification of my illness from Stage I to Stage II was my darkest moment. I felt totally defeated, like this was the end of the world. How could my body have betrayed me? If my tumor was small and discovered early, how could the cancer have spread so quickly?"

The end of May marked the start of the chemotherapy phase: eight treatments, three weeks apart, concluding with six weeks of radiation, five days a week. All this time, Jane was calculating the show schedule because during the previous year she and Leroy had competed and won ribbons at prestigious horse shows including the Pennsylvania National, the Washington D.C. International and the National at Madison Square Garden in New York City.

By the second treatment, Jane's hair had fallen out. This didn't bother her as much as expected, and wearing a wig offered some unexpected advantages. A lifelong brunette, Jane quipped, "I've always wanted to be a blonde!"

Her winning attitude rarely faltered, and where riding had always been her temporary escape from the pressures of everyday life, it now served the added purpose of enabling Jane to keep control over at least part of her normal routine.

With her doctor's approval, she continued to ride as much as possible. Knowing that Leroy was at the barn waiting kept Jane up and moving. Ever since she had purchased Leroy as a four-year-old, a strong bond had existed between the two. I remember her telling me, "I felt that Leroy rallied to be the strong one. Instead of me taking care of him, the roles reversed, and now he was taking care of me. On days I was sick, depressed or wobbly, he was extra careful."

The road to recovery for Jane was taken one day at a time. Riding and competing with Leroy continued to be the focal point and primary goal. Jane set her sights on returning to the show ring just four and a half months after her breast cancer was diagnosed.

When the big day came, Jane transported Leroy to the Middleburg Classic Horse Show in The Plains, Virginia. The moment she had so eagerly awaited turned out to be uncomfortably long, dusty and hot. Although she was not awarded the blue ribbon that day, Jane was clearly the winner to her friends and fellow competitors present to cheer her on.

Jane's struggle with cancer continued and she faced many obstacles. "When you have cancer, your biggest fear is that the disease changes everything and your world spins out of control. Riding is the best therapy because it puts life into perspective. I know I am still me," she confided.

Two years after she felt that lump, Jane returned to the Middleburg Classic. Her health now restored, she felt strong enough to compete in all three classes of the side-saddle division.

The victory was especially sweet when the tricolor reserve champion ribbon was awarded to Jane and her part-ner through it all—her horse Leroy.

Lisa B. Friel

The President's Escort

The one thing I do not want to be called is "First Lady." It sounds like a saddle horse.

Jacqueline Kennedy Onassis

The four-beat cadence of the riderless horse echoed the beat of a country's broken heart.

On those two November days, Black Jack carried in his empty saddle the grief of a nation. He was vigorous and brilliant, strong, proud and stepping off in his own direction, not unlike the young, fallen American president he was there to honor.

Black Jack was on duty as the riderless horse in the full honor funeral of President John F. Kennedy in Washington, D.C., on November 24 and 25, 1963. The day of the assassination, Friday, November 22, had dawned bright and warm in Dallas, Texas, but a day full of promise suddenly turned dark.

Now President Kennedy was gone and the country was in mourning. The funereal pomp and ceremony befitting a president was playing out, with Washington as stage and the world as audience. Black Jack's role was center stage.

He paraded in a place of privilege in the cortege, only a few feet behind the 1918 artillery caisson that bore the

President's coffin draped in an American flag, and in front of the procession of international dignitaries and family, and the president's widow Jacqueline.

Mrs. Kennedy understood history was at hand. At her request, the funeral reprised many of the rites of President Abraham Lincoln, America's first assassinated president, who died April 15, 1865. Presidents Kennedy and Lincoln both lay in state in the black-shrouded East Room of the White House and in the Great Rotunda of the U.S. Capitol. Church bells rang and a procession trailed through the streets of Washington. Riderless horses—Black Jack for President Kennedy, Old Bob for President Lincoln—provided proper escort.

Black Jack escorted the president's coffin to the Capitol, the White House, St. Matthew's Cathedral, and finally across Memorial Bridge to Arlington National Cemetery.

His empty saddle symbolized an ancient military tradition of mourning the leader who will ride no more. In the saddle's stirrups was a pair of spit-shined black boots, reversed and facing backward, allowing the leader to look over his troops one last time. A silver saber hung on Black Jack's right side. These were trappings of a military officer.

As president, Kennedy was commander-in-chief. Black Jack was military, a soldier on a mission from the Caisson Platoon. The Caisson Platoon is part of the U.S. Army's Third U.S. Infantry, known as The Old Guard, based at Fort Myer, Virginia. The Old Guard is the army's official ceremonial unit and escort to the president. The unit also escorts fallen soldiers and American heroes to their final resting places. The lion's share of its duty is in Arlington National Cemetery, adjacent to Fort Myer.

Black Jack's handler during the Kennedy services was nineteen-year-old Pfc. Arthur Carlson, a six-foot, two-inch tall army soldier from Alabama, who did his best to handle his handful of horse.

"He was spooked," Carlson said more than thirty-five years later.

Black Jack skittered at forty-five-degree angles, and jigged and pranced down Constitution Avenue, Pennsylvania Avenue, Connecticut Avenue, all along the route. At the White House, where they waited for the coffin to be placed on the caisson, he kept circling Carlson. He was impatient with the skirl of the Black Watch bagpipes and the relentless, muffled drumrolls. This was duty different from his typical, quiet missions in Arlington. Thousands of people crowded curbsides to watch. It was all new and noisy. And historical. A loose horse would have sullied perhaps the twentieth century's most solemn ceremony.

Black Jack's anxiety level rose just as the services got underway. Early on Sunday, November 24, the platoon contingent gathered in the courtyard of the Treasury Department building for the first procession, to move the president's body from the White House to the Capitol. A chance encounter with a steel grate frayed the gelding's nerves.

"When we went to leave that courtyard, we were to pass through a street-level tunnel that penetrated the building. There was a grate—a large steel grate that had been left propped up against the wall—and I was following the caisson leading Black Jack," Carlson remembers. "A wheel on the caisson, snagged on that grate and the caisson started dragging it on the stones and making an awful noise, which was magnified being in that tunnel.

"And it just scared that silly horse out of his wits. He decided to stay scared for two days. He danced for two days. He danced and tossed his head."

Carlson said he was hardest to control "when I was supposed to be standing still, like outside the White House, outside the Capitol and outside the cathedral, where he stomped my foot."

Somehow, Carlson hung on to Black Jack and maintained the dignity required of the occasion, a feat he credits in no small measure to the determination inherent in his Swedish ancestry. "Much determination. Not good for much else, but my God, we're determined," he said.

"At the time, I was in full military mode, that is, completely focused on the mission. That was it. I didn't allow anything else in. I was just trying to do my small part the best I could."

Carlson's and Black Jack's "small part" remains an enduring image of the Kennedy funeral.

Black Jack was handsome, not a big horse at 15 hands and not a purebred of any breed. He was a Morgan–Quarter Horse crossbred gelding, who kept his date with destiny when he was transferred from the Fort Reno, Oklahoma, Remount Station to Fort Myer on November 22, 1952, eleven years to the day prior to the assassination.

His tiny feet—"He could have stood on a biscuit," Carlson says—precluded his being ridden or used to pull the heavy caissons. His good looks qualified him for duty as the caparisoned or decorated horse in military funerals. As is required for all GIs, Black Jack was assigned a serial number, his was 2V56, which was branded on the left side of his neck. He was the last horse the army branded with "US," which marked his left shoulder.

Why was Carlson, a private with no previous horse experience, conscripted into the prestigious service as "cap walker?" Easy.

"I was tall, slim and had good posture. Still do."

Black Jack's military resume also featured a shared January 19 birthday with Confederate General Robert E. Lee (Lee was born in 1807, Black Jack in 1947) and a name honoring General of the Armies John J. "Black Jack" Pershing, the American military commander in World War I. Coincidentally, the nickname of Mrs. Kennedy's father Jack Bouvier also was Black Jack.

He served with The Old Guard for twenty-four years and paraded in thousands of funerals for the famous and the not-so-famous rank and file, including Presidents Herbert Hoover and Lyndon B. Johnson, and General of the Army Douglas MacArthur.

The horse from Oklahoma lived a long and full life as the

platoon's patriarch and most famous resident. On birthdays, he enjoyed media coverage and butter-pecan cakes baked by a colonel's wife, who was a devoted fan. He received hundreds of letters and birthday cards, including one hand-drawn birthday card in 1975 from a little girl in West Virginia named Mary Lou Retton, who made her own history in 1984 when she won an Olympic gold medal in gymnastics.

Black Jack died at an elderly twenty-nine in 1976, the year of America's bicentennial. He is buried near the flagpole on Fort Myer's Summerall Field parade grounds. A bronze plaque marks his grave, and the Black Jack Museum in the Caisson Platoon stable honors his memory.

The memories of that November, though it was so long ago, remain seared in America's soul. The red, white and blue of the American flag, whipping in the wind at half-staff. Six matched gray horses pulling the high-wheeled caisson and coffin. A black-veiled widow lighting an eternal flame at the grave. And the proud spirit of a riderless horse. They provided the theater, a place for the country to cry.

Gayle Stewart

Fly, Misty, Fly!

Why am I so dumb, Misty?

It was a sparkling cold winter's day when I came out to ride. In the high mountains of southern Idaho, riding is usually a summer pastime. Winter riding took a certain amount of nerve and preparation, and at the time, I had neither. I just had to get out: out of my house, out of my life for a while. So, I came out to the farm where I boarded Misty, my old Morgan mare. I was halfway through my junior year in high school and it wasn't going well, not well at all.

"I can't see why it makes a word wrong if you spell it a little differently. Why can't they see what I meant, not how I spelled it? F-r-i-e-n-d or f-r-e-i-n-d? They look like the same word to me, so it doesn't matter how many times they grade me wrong. I can't tell which is right. I'm so stupid."

I caught Misty with a halter, brushed her thick winter coat and warmed the bit between my hands so that the cold metal didn't "bite" her tongue. No matter how upset I might be with my life, none of the lessons I had learned about how to care for horses ever left me. They'd been taught to me by Mr. Codding, who owned the farm where I boarded Misty. Mr. Codding would board horses for kids who lived in town, but we never forgot that he had the last word on how they were to be treated.

But it does matter if I confuse greater than or less than, or if I put the decimal point at 00.1 or 0.01. If I say it out loud, I can hear the difference, but they look the same. I understand the math, but I can't write down what I understand. And every time my math teacher makes me take a turn at the board to solve problems, everyone can see how dumb I am. If I have to go up to that board again to work out a problem, I think I will die. Mom'll just kill me if I flunk a math class. Well, no, she won't kill me. She'll just be so disappointed. Why can't I be smart like she is?

Mr. Codding had shown me how to warm a bit before asking a horse to take it in his or her mouth. You took off your gloves and warmed it with your own hands. Better your hands got a bit cold than a cold bit hurt your horse's tender mouth.

I'm not sure he would have approved of my taking Misty out on that cold winter day. Even without wearing slippery shoes, a horse could lose his footing on a snowy road. But I had to get out, get away—far away—from my problems. I hadn't told anyone where I was going. I needed some healing and fortunately, had the presence of mind to seek out a horse.

Of course, Dad says that the only reason to send me to college would be to get my "M.R.S." degree. I wish he hadn't made all those people at his dinner party laugh at me when I said that that wasn't it, that I wanted to go to college to learn. Maybe he's right. I'm too dumb to go to college. I can't even spell, for crying out loud, and I'm flunking math. It's a good thing I didn't tell him I want to go to college to be a scientist. He'd think that was a real hoot.

I leaned against Misty's muscular neck, buried my face in her mane and inhaled her sweet horse scent. Together we stood and breathed. Her strength and calm presence steadied me.

I decided to ride around the section. A section is one square mile, which is how our county roads were laid out. Where I grew up riding, we kids mostly rode in the fields or in the barrow pit next to the roads. (No one knows why those in southern Idaho call the ditch next to the road the barrow pit, but that is the term everyone used.) The barrow pit is not the best place to ride because it can have trash in it, but it was all we had. A dirt road was the best thing, of course. And that is why I headed around the section. The back mile, the one that ran parallel to the Codding's farm, was all dirt for its entire one-mile distance. And there were only two farms on it. So there was a lot of space for us to stretch out and run or enjoy all the kinds of horseplay that teenaged girls could think of. That made it a favorite place to ride.

Only today, I didn't have any girl friends with me and I wasn't in the mood for play.

If I can't do math, I can't be a scientist. That's what Mom says. She says that a scientist needs to be able to measure and test things.

I climbed up the fence and got on Misty's bare back. It's nicer to ride a horse bareback in the winter because your legs are right next to the animal's warm body. My body moved automatically in rhythm with Misty's. My hands connected with her mouth and we were one. All my life, I had been a complete klutz. I couldn't catch a baseball to save my life or kick the big rubber balls we used to play kickball. I couldn't walk on the top of fences the way that my friends did. I was always the last to get picked for any team and my physical education class was torture. But the first time I got on a horse, I found some mysterious coordination that had missed me in every other physical endeavor I had ever attempted. On a horse, I was graceful and strong.

Sandy is going to medical school. She gets straight As. John is going into engineering. He breezed through Algebra II as if it was easier than walking. Whenever they talk about the future, I just tell them I plan to be a goat herder. They think it's funny. I've never told a soul what I really want to do. They would laugh and laugh if I did. But I'll tell you,

Misty. I want to be a scientist and watch animals like Jane Goodall and I want to be a veterinarian. Isn't that silly? It is harder to get into vet school than to get into med school and you need good grades. I'll never get good grades. If I flunk algebra, I won't make it to college at all because my grades will be too low, so I've got to drop it before I flunk it. But if I can't do the math, I can't do the chemistry I would need to be a scientist. You see, Misty, there is no hope. This is a stupid dream.

I want this to all go away, Misty. I want wings so that I can fly. Tommy flies all the time, you know. He's doing drugs again. He says it is wonderful to be high. He says I'd feel happy all the time if I got high with him. But if I did, I couldn't come and be with you. Tommy does dumb things all the time when he is high. I couldn't risk doing something dumb and maybe hurting you. That's a risk I won't take.

We had gotten to the back road. It was a mile long with snow packed over the dirt. Almost no one drove on it and no one knew I was there. If I fell off on that cold winter's day, it would be a long time before anyone would think to look for me there. But the thought that I might fall off Misty never crossed my mind. For me, the rest of my life was risky. This was real and necessary.

I dropped the reins and carefully knotted them so that Misty wouldn't trip over them. I wouldn't need them. The road was straight and ran for a mile before it met the north-south road. Misty would tire and slow before we reached it. If I needed to, I could ask her to slow with my voice and I trusted her to listen. In the past, when I had lost my balance and started to fall, she always slowed and moved to stay under me. Misty wouldn't let me fall now. The rest of my life was falling to pieces all around me: my parents' divorce, my school failure, my friends, my beliefs, my broken dreams. But Misty wouldn't let me fall.

I wrapped both hands in her mane. I leaned forward and gently asked her to run. She surged ahead, powerful and strong. My long hair flew back in the wind, like her mane.

The road blurred beneath us. Cold wind blew tears from my eyes onto my icy face. I closed my eyes and felt her powerful muscles surging as she carried me with her. She was blowing now, emitting a rhythmic puffing sound from her nostrils. It sounded like the beating of feathered wings. Faster and faster, farther and farther, Misty was carrying me away from my hopelessness.

Fly, Misty, fly.

I came back from that ride renewed and determined to continue. A year and a half later, I entered college. My parents sold Misty to some family friends who wanted to use her for breeding and for their daughter to ride in 4-H. So Misty had more souls—equine and human—to nurture. My path was rockier. I entered college as a music major, but switched to zoology, only to find that my mother was right and I didn't have the math skills for chemistry. I switched again to psychology, still hoping to study animal behavior. Fortunately, the college dorms were on the same side of campus as the livestock barns, and whenever things got too overwhelming, I would go and watch the horses. The barn guys got used to me as a regular fixture, perched up on the fence watching the horses eat their evening meal. I completed the psychology degree and started another degree, this time in animal sciences. By this time, I had been joined by Larkin, Misty's son. He would take me flying when everything threatened to overwhelm me.

It wasn't until I was in graduate school that my learning disability, called dyslexia, was discovered. The psychologist who tested me, an old professor of mine, was astonished by the results. "How did you do so well in my class with so severe a learning disability?" he asked me.

I rarely had time to ride while I was going to veterinary school. Yes, I finally made it to vet school, although it was a struggle to get in because no one believed that a dyslexic could pass the grueling curriculum. After hours of classes and studying, I would come home and seek out Larkin in the pasture. I would stand by his shoulder, lean against his muscular neck, bury my face in his mane, inhale his sweet horse scent and breathe with him. His powerful essence gave me the strength to go on.

Riding horses is easy. Climbing back in the saddle of life when you repeatedly fall off, now, that is a lot harder. I kept going because of my mother's belief in me and because my love of animals and my desire to learn about them were stronger than my fear of failure—and because I had a horse carrying me.

Janice Willard, DVM, MS

Like Pegasus, Laughter Takes Flight

The first time I ever saw a group of live horses I was ten years old. A dozen horses appeared at one of the busiest intersections in the city where I lived with my mom, grandparents and a variety of aunts, uncles and cousins. I distinctly recall that each horse carried one of "Newark's Finest" fully outfitted in riot gear. The shields, weapons and boots blended with the horses to form menacing images.

Newark, the largest city in the state of New Jersey, was in the middle of civil unrest that summer and riots had erupted throughout the city. The governor had dispatched the National Guard and the mounted police to restore order. As a child, the sights and sounds terrified me and my first impression of horses would forever be tied to riots, violence and looting. It would take more than a decade for that association to change.

Eleven years later, I was a college student majoring in journalism and working part-time for a weekly newspaper. A prominent resident volunteered her time every week "walking horses" for a nonprofit organization. Somewhere, there was a connection to disabled children who were confined to wheelchairs. "Cover the story," I was told. "It should make good copy."

Somehow, I just could not reconcile the two images in my

mind: a group of fragile, disabled children with a herd of wild, thrashing horses. These contradictory images occupied my thoughts as I followed the directions to Crossroads Farms in western New Jersey. As I drove, I couldn't help but admire the breathtaking landscape with its rolling hills, open spaces and white rail fences. It was a far cry from the congestion, traffic and urban chaos with which I had associated horses.

When I arrived at Crossroads Farms for my interview, I noticed a specially equipped school bus, outfitted with a hydraulic wheelchair lift, parked near the entrance. Inside the vehicle were six children, each occupying his or her own motorized wheelchair. As their teachers and caregivers maneuvered the wheelchairs from the bus, it was evident that the children were struggling to contain their enthusiasm. Laughter, shouts of cheer and hand clapping were evident everywhere. Even to the most casual observer, the looks on these children's faces brought to mind Christmas morning, Disneyland and a visit to the Hershey's Chocolate Factory.

Volunteers, including the woman I was featuring in my story, were waiting to escort the children from the wheelchairs onto a special staging area. As the volunteers pushed each wheelchair up a ramp, the children were gently lifted from the confines of their mobile apparatuses. Below the ramp, six horses patiently waited for their precious cargo to be placed on each of their backs.

Taking in the situation, I was completely awed by the scene unfolding before me. One by one, each child was secured in a special saddle. Three volunteers were assigned to each child: one leading the horse, and two flanking the child. The horses seemed to sense the fragility of their cargo and took special care not to jostle or bump the child.

The children, in turn, were ecstatic. Their faces were not big enough to hold their smiles and their bodies were too small to contain their joy. The horses slowly began walking down the rustic paths and the children were absolutely delighted. As they were led away, they bantered back and forth, "I'm flying!" "I love my horse." " I feel like an angel. These horses are like wings."

From my vantage point, it wasn't difficult to understand their frame of reference. While they were atop the horses, they were freed from the metal, the bars and the arms of the wheelchairs that almost perpetually surrounded them. In addition, their perspective astride the horse was a high one. For once, they were at least the same height as the adults who cared for them. No one was looking down at them. For the next thirty minutes, they were as tall as, or taller than, their caregivers, and their laughter was sent heavenward.

I continued to watch them and pondered the comparison to angels' wings. Although these children were still confined to the limitations of a physical existence here on earth, their horses were, indeed, like angels' wings, providing them with the opportunity to experience a freedom they could never have imagined.

As their laughter continued to ring out, I was reminded of the Greek legend of Pegasus, the white winged stallion. The most beautiful creature in the ancient world, this elegant equine was so revered that Zeus, the king of the gods, created a constellation of the winged horse to light the night sky. I am delighted to report that the descendants of Pegasus are alive and well in northwest New Jersey. For as Pegasus transported the thunderbolts of Zeus across the sky, these "winged" horses carry a more precious cargo—the souls of children, who, for a brief moment, can soar through the air as their laughter is released to the heavens.

Barbara A. Davey

At the End of His Rope
. . . a Winner!

When Jerry Long, of Capitan, New Mexico, first meets the at-risk, emotionally and physically challenged children he counsels in the Horses N' Hearts program at Lincoln County Schools, he directs them to convey a positive first impression, no excuses. Excuses just don't belong in Long's world. And he ought to know.

His directives: "No fish handshakes. Firm grips. Stand up straight. Look me in the eye. Smile."

Then he tries, over three or four days, to match names he's previously memorized with the students who line up to make contact with him. They try to confuse him, to elicit incorrect responses from him in a game of wits for all players, made even more challenging because Jerry is blind. He's also diabetic and fifteen years ago he underwent a kidney transplant.

Long's own twelve-year-old American Quarter Horse, Heza Exclusive Man, nicknamed Duke, plays an integral role in the therapy, just as horses play a major role in this human volunteer's motivation. A champion team roper then and now, Long uses Duke as an instrument to teach lessons of coping with life and its challenges, something Long well understands. He wants the youngsters to learn to be responsible for their actions.

A father and grandfather, Long, holds a Master of Education degree. He was a public school teacher, counselor and administrator for thirty years when diabetes took his sight and caused kidney failure, ultimately resulting in his retirement and in his abandonment of riding and roping. Even though battling depression at the time, he found work and inspiration as transition coordinator with the Texas School for the Blind and Visually Impaired in Austin, helping blind students prepare to reenter that sometimes fearful place, the "real world." All the while, he dreamed of returning to his beloved sport of team roping. In that Western discipline, riders pair up to catch a cow by galloping toward it and then tossing ropes around the steer's humanely wrapped horns.

One day, when Long was with a friend who missed a steer at a local roping, he jokingly told his sighted buddy, "I'm an old, fat, bald-headed blind man, but I can do better than that. Quit making excuses. Just tie some bells on him, and I'll do at least that well!"

He hadn't, of course, planned on following through with his pronouncement.

When the two chums got together next, Long's comrade coerced and chided him into getting on a horse and picking up where Long had left off before losing his sight. With "my heart in my throat," Long recalls, he rose to the challenge. He roped seven times and caught two steers. He was, literally, "back in the [roping] saddle again," and it felt just like old times.

Now, he competes and wins against "regular" ropers, his only concession as a blind rider being a set of bells affixed to the cow's horns. Long is so adept, in fact, that he recently played the lead in an educational video about roping. He ran 108 steers and roped 99 percent of them. In roping, a seventy percent average is considered admirable by anyone.

Long, who's an in-demand public speaker, says he tries to inspire people, to motivate them. "We all face different challenges and our character is determined by the way we meet those and contend with them." He's also a Christian who just wants "to treat people the right way."

He doesn't write down his speeches—he couldn't see them, of course—and he endeavors to speak from the heart. His audiences find much value in his messages and they tell him so.

About his sporting successes, he's reflective. "It takes a pretty brave person to team rope with a blind guy," laughs Long. There are many who might say it's Jerry Long who's not short on determination, drive and courage.

For him, there are more kids to help, more adults to inspire and more cattle to rope. Oh, and if he adds another shiny winner's belt buckle to his collection, that would be just fine, too.

Stephanie Stephens

"I'm sorry, sir, but roping horses are a dime a dozen."

Roping. *Reprinted by permission of Steve Sommer and Francis Brummer.* ©2002 *Steve Sommer and Francis Brummer.*

Don't Fence Him In

A good rider on a good horse is as much above himself and others as the world can make him.

Lord Herbert

I'm standing in the entry hall of a 116-year-old Victorian-style home, the wooden floors creaking beneath my shoes. "What time does his bus come?" I ask, shifting my weight to hear the floors again.

"It stops at our door at 8 A.M.," his mother replies.

The eighteen-year-old high school senior staring out the window chimes in. "No, it doesn't. It comes at 7:50." Then I hear the roar of the school bus as it moans up the hill to the Max Meadows, Virginia, home of David Taylor.

I look at my watch. It's 7:50.

David flashes a smile in my direction as he walks off the porch, makes his way across the yard and climbs up the steps of his school bus. "He loves being right," his mother Judy tells me as she waves good-bye.

Doesn't every normal teenager? I think to myself. And perhaps that's the best way to describe David.

I became friends with David in 1998 when he ran over my foot with his wheelchair while we were at the American

Quarter Horse Youth World Championship Show.

He attends a public school, just outside Max Meadows, where he walks to class like the hundreds of other students scurrying about the hall. He plays sports, plays bass drum in the band, swims, skis, rides an American Quarter Horse and goes to dances. Heck, he even dates. If you didn't know any better, you'd swear that David is just another typical high school kid intent on proving that his parents are never right.

But the fact that David is able to do any of this is nothing short of a miracle. David was born two months prematurely in what his mother describes as a backwoods hospital some sixty miles from Roanoke, Virginia. On the way from that facility to a more modern one, David died and was resuscitated five times. Later, Judy was given the grim news about her newborn.

She was told that he would require surgery to implant a shunt into his head to release a dangerous buildup of fluid on his brain known as hydrocephalus. The doctor said that her son also had seizure disorders and would likely have impaired hearing and speech. Later, David was diagnosed with cerebral palsy, which affected his mobility.

"The doctors told me that *if* he lived, he would be a vegetable," Judy explains. "But I would look into his eyes and see this spark. There was just something about him. I thought with any infant who refused to die five times over, I wasn't willing to accept their opinion."

David is the youngest of four children and the only boy. To survive, he would have to be strong, independent and work harder at the everyday tasks that able-bodied people take for granted.

After learning to walk at four, David had hamstring and heel surgery to help his balance and to straighten his legs. Then his doctors recommended horseback riding lessons.

"This was fourteen years ago and horseback riding as therapy was practically nonexistent," Judy explains. "But we found him a Shetland pony and started him riding."

It wasn't long before David outgrew his pony and

ultimately acquired his first American Quarter Horse.

"Then he started walking better," Judy says. "He started talking better. He even started breathing better, which helped so many other things. I am convinced it was that horse and the way he moved that helped him so much."

Today, David has advanced from therapeutic riding to competing in various shows. He competes at local shows and has been to the All American Quarter Horse Congress every year since 1997. He has competed at the American Quarter Horse Youth Association World Championship Show each year since 1998.

"It doesn't bother me being handicapped in an able-bodied world," David says. "But I don't want people to make me a handicapped person in a handicapped world. That's why I want to ride in Quarter Horse shows. I love my Quarter Horse and hope someday that I can show my skills against other people of similar ability."

Every day except Tuesday, David can be found riding English and Western in the field next to his house or in his neighbor's arena. Tuesdays are reserved for water therapy, another activity that has contributed to his independence. His therapist is an affable, gregarious young guy named Jason, whom David affectionately calls Buddha Belly. As they spend an hour in the water stretching, playing catch, walking against a current and wrestling, Jason tells me that he's never seen anyone work harder than Slim Fast, his nickname for David.

The water also helps his balance once he's on horseback. When David rides, he is not strapped on. He uses no special equipment and for the most part, he does everything himself, short of tossing the saddle up and pulling the cinch. And yes, everything includes falling off.

"Oh yeah, he's fallen," Judy admits with a giggle. "Right in front of the judge once." Like any teenager, David rolls his eyes away from his mother.

David's horse is a twenty-year-old sorrel mare named Judy Meyers. He acquired her in 1997 and is quick to point out that she's not named after his mother.

"I love this horse," David says proudly. "She knows me and we're getting better the more we work together. She helps me run barrels and poles, and do reining. We're practicing a lot for trail and learning English [style riding]."

For safety reasons, David can compete only in individual pattern classes.

David's voice shakes as he and Judy work into a trot and they circle my body as if it's a barrel to prove they're getting faster.

"She won't hurt you," he says. "It's just Judy." *No*, I think to myself, *it's not just Judy. This is an amazing horse keenly aware of who's on her back and where each pound of his nearly six-foot-tall body is.*

After David finishes using me for barrel practice, we head inside, where he sets the table, fixes a quick lunch and says grace before we eat.

During the meal, we talk about his future. David, an avid NASCAR fan who collects signed memorabilia from his countless trips to the races, is expected to have a normal life span with continued riding and therapy. He is not mentally handicapped and will graduate with a regular high school diploma. He is planning a move to North Carolina in the hope of getting a job in auto racing. Judy teases and says that as soon as her youngest moves away, she'll begin remodeling the house, starting with his bedroom. "I've waited a long time to do it," she says.

"Yeah, but I get to keep my horse," David pops back. Then he goes silent for a minute. "She gives me the chance to be part of the real world."

Tom Persechino

Regalito

Regalito is a Spanish name that means special little gift, and he was, in more ways than one.

Little girls who love horses dream of riding great white horses with long wavy manes and tails. Although mostly in the middle part of "middle age," I had never lost that little girl's dream. My husband Arthur gave me Regalito for our thirtieth wedding anniversary. That was the first special little gift. Regalito is a Spanish Andalusian stallion. He is beautiful, noble and above all, huggable.

Since the age of four, I have ridden horses. They are the love and passion of my life—after Arthur, of course!

After his five-day journey from California, Regalito arrived at our farm in Louisiana. He immediately made himself at home. How proud and noble he was. But, with great pain and sadness, I knew I would never sit on his back and share in the exultation of his dance; for, indeed, when Regalito moves, it is like a dance.

For five years, I had been unable to ride because I suffer tremendous pain and lack of mobility from a devastating disease called fibromyalgia. This disease robs you of the joy of movement; every step is a painful effort.

Because I could not ride horses, I started painting them in watercolors. All my feelings for these wonderful creatures came out in vivid shades of green and blue, copper and silver, turquoise and gold. Many of the paintings have sold, but one stays with me: the painting of Regalito that I did a year before I even knew of his existence. I think I must have conjured him up. He was, in fact, the magical horse who changed my life.

After Regalito arrived at the farm, I had a new working student come over to ride him. I taught Bobby dressage and in turn he taught Regalito. The days, weeks, months and then a year went by as I watched Bobby ride my beautiful white stallion. Sometimes it felt as if my heart would burst from wanting to ride him so much. I watched day by day thinking, *If only that were me.*

Then one day as I sat in my usual place in the viewing stand by the riding ring teaching Regalito and Bobby, the thought came to me, *Why not me? Why not me?* Regalito is the kindest horse, so gentle and willing. We had built such a bond in the year he had been with us. I knew he would never hurt me. Somehow he knew that I was fragile.

So today is the day, I said to myself. *If I don't ride him today, I will explode with all this emotion!* Aloud, I said to Bobby, "Wait a minute while I go change into my riding pants. I'm getting on Regalito!"

Of course, Bobby's surprise was immense and he said, "Are you sure?"

I replied, "I've never been so sure of anything in my life. The time is now".

I mounted Regalito with stiffness and difficulty; the mounting block made it easier. Bobby held the stallion's head, but it wasn't necessary. Regalito stood as still as a statue. He seemed to be saying, "What's taken you so long?"

I felt completely at home on his back, almost as if I'd slipped a foot into an old shoe. Regalito and I were made for each other. I sat in the saddle and all the pent-up emotion came out. Tears of joy rolled down my cheeks. I had done what I had thought was an impossible task a year ago. I was sitting on the back of my beautiful white stallion.

It took me a few moments to compose myself. Regalito just stood quietly and waited, and then we walked away into a land where horse and human merge. I was weightless on my horse. I felt no pain and for these moments on his back, I was well again.

Regalito gave me back the second special gift, the gift to be myself. With generosity of spirit and great care, he carried me around the riding ring, doing intricate dressage movements with lightness and ease.

Daily I danced with my horse, daily my body moved and daily I became stronger, regaining a lot of my range of motion and certainly regaining the joy and passion of my life.

Thank you, Arthur, for my special little gift. Thank you, Regalito, for living up to your name and giving me the greatest gift of all: a reason to get up in the morning and feel again and again the joy that riding brings to my life and the healing it brings to my body and soul!

The Bond
For Regalito

I looked into his eyes and saw his soul.
He looked into my eyes and saw my soul.
He was my horse and I his person.
We knew each other's thoughts, each other's feelings.
We trusted one another.
We took joy in each other's company.
He was my horse—I his person!
We shared a bond, a bond of love.

Diana Christensen

Touched by an Equine

Emma arrived at the ranch on a typical Saturday morning about two and a half years ago. She was five years old and absolutely beautiful, with blue-green eyes, sun-kissed golden brown hair and a smile that would melt even the coldest of hearts. Emma came to us because she was clinically diagnosed with autism, a complex developmental disability that typically appears during the first three years of life. This precious child behaved like a windup toy.

"Emma, come here." "Get out of the tack room." "No, don't eat the ball." "Emma, sit down." "NO, Emma," her mother's words rang constantly. It would take two people to keep Emma still. On more than one occasion, she got into one of the stalls and tried to eat the horse's rubber mats. Emma, to say the least, was in her own world.

I'll never forget the day, the very moment that she first got on Horse Angel Dottie. When Dottie began to carry her new rider around the ring, the transformation was immediate. Gone was the uncontrollable child. In her place was a beaming, relaxed confident little girl. Wow!

Ever since I've known Emma, she's spoken only gibberish. "Saa Pa awom nes sapa nom," she would say, smiling and laughing to herself. I longed to know what she was trying to say and I could see in her eyes that she wanted me to understand. We communicated on a different level, thanks to Dottie.

Emma's been riding every week since her first visit. She's an excellent equestrian. She loves to ride and has no fear. I take some credit for her riding prowess and courage, but the real honors go to Dottie.

Emma had been riding for about eighteen months when she came for her usual Saturday lesson on an unusually hot, humid and dusty day. Nobody felt like working on this dog-day afternoon, especially yours truly and our Horse Angel Dottie. Nevertheless, as we stepped into the arena, I instructed Emma to give Dottie a little kick and say "walk," just as I had done a thousand times before. I tugged gently on Dottie's lead rope and started to move forward when, all of a sudden, I heard a little voice say "walk." I stopped dead in my tracks. So did Dottie, whose ears were already pricked to the rear. "Emma, oh my God, Emma, you said walk. You said WALK!" I shouted at the top of my lungs. "Your first word, Emma, your first word, and Dottie and I heard it." I don't know who was more touched by that one fantastic word, Dottie, Emma or I. Emma was smiling and clapping her hands. She knew. Tears were streaming down my face. And Dottie, well, she quietly walked on, just as she'd been told. I felt an overwhelming joy and gratitude for that incredible moment and this wonderful Horse Angel. I believe with all my heart that this is the reason Emma is speaking today.

Emma's vocabulary has increased to include the words whoa, yes, no, peanut butter, red, blue, yellow, green, the numbers one through ten, and Dottie's and my personal favorite, "I love you."

Melody Rogers-Kelley

Going Where No Horse
Has Gone Before

The first time I was invited to bring miniature horses to a nursing home, I asked the activities coordinator if she wanted to schedule an alternate date in case bad weather on the appointed day should prevent the residents from coming outside to see the horses.

What a surprise when she said, "Oh, but I thought they could come inside. Can't they?" And so we did.

Once inside, I handed my pooper-scooper dustpan and broom to the nearest staff member and asked her to bring up the rear. She didn't even flinch.

Immediately, staff members and residents who probably never had expected to have the opportunity to see or touch a horse surrounded us. Once you love horses, you always will, but the responses we've had at the nursing homes are as varied and surprising as the people themselves.

During one visit, we brought two of our little horses into a room where people lined the walls in a semicircle of chairs, wheelchairs and hospital beds.

We told them a little bit about each horse, then walked them around the center of the circle. If someone reached out, we brought the horses over to be petted, but we stayed far enough away so that those who didn't want to touch wouldn't have to.

The lady sitting in the first wheelchair looked up at me, and I thought she was going to say something, but she didn't, so I went past her around the circle. When I came back to her, she looked again as if she were going to speak and I paused, but still she said nothing.

Unexpectedly, my mare Taj stepped forward and put her head on the folded hands in the woman's lap. Underneath, I saw one finger move against the soft muzzle resting there. Then I saw tears on the woman's cheeks. I hadn't known that she was paralyzed, unable to speak or to reach out. Taj, however, had sensed her wishes with unfailing accuracy.

The stories the residents tell us of their experiences—their long-past racing-stable days, the ice cuttings at the river before refrigerators were common, the time the barn burned, or the day their old mare ran away with the plow—give us vivid images of their "good old days" that we enjoy as much as they enjoy our horses.

It's easy to get caught up in the wonderful memories of these visits, but to get back to the real world I need only to remember one quiet man last summer.

He was sitting in an armchair in the circle of residents, his chin resting in his hand, calmly watching the flurry of activity while the horses made their last circuit of the room before leaving that day.

As I approached him, I was asking if anyone had any more questions before we left. He looked up at me when I stopped in front of him.

"Why, yes," he said thoughtfully, "Do you know when we eat?"

Apparently, everyone's world doesn't revolve around horses!

Carole Y. Stanforth

Billie Girl

When you are buying a horse, take care not to fall in love with him, for when this passion hath once seized you, you are no longer in a condition to judge his imperfections.

Sleur de Sollesell

One morning during the summer of 1994, I found myself standing inside the barn in front of one of the stalls. We had recently lost our daughter's beloved first pony, Rounder, to colic, and staring at that empty stall made me feel very heavyhearted. How would we ever replace Rounder?

Since moving to our small rural town of Agua Dulce, California, in 1977, my husband Don and I had filled our lives with horses while raising our four children and running our local water-well business. I knew I needed to find another perfect horse for our family. When my girlfriend called and asked me to go with her to look at a horse, I didn't hesitate to say yes and I hooked up my horse trailer. Little did I know that would be the day that Billie Girl would come into our lives.

As we drove into the feed-store parking lot, I was filled with excitement. There were so many horses to look at. My girlfriend was unsuccessful in her search, but I felt very drawn to a sweet-looking Paint mare. I was able to take her home for a couple of days to try her out. Then, I would get back to the horse trader with a decision.

That night, my husband walked into the barn and was surprised to see an occupant in the once-empty stall. He asked what her name was and I told him she didn't come with one. After a little discussion, we decided to name her Billie Girl after our friend Billy who had died just that day from a five-year battle with cancer.

For the next two days, Billie Girl passed every test I put her through with flying colors. All we had left to do was the vet check. When all was said and done, the veterinarian had shocking news for us. Billie Girl had cancer. My family was devastated and yet concerned about the quality of the mare's life in the future. After much thought and prayer, I called the horse trader with my sad news. His first response was uncompassionate as he told me to just bring her back and I could look at any of his other horses. Trying to hide my frustration, I responded, "I don't want to do that. Billie Girl has cancer and is unsellable, so please just give her to me." But his last response chilled me to the bone. "I can get a dollar a pound for her at the auction, so just bring back my horse!"

Late that night, I walked into the barn feeling extremely discouraged. I went into Billie Girl's stall and wrapped my arms around her neck. Pressing my cheek against her warm velvety coat, I could feel my discouragement start to fade and a peaceful, tranquil feeling came over me. As I listened to her munching hay in the quiet of the night, I asked, "Oh, Billie Girl, what do I do?" At that moment, she pulled back and put her muzzle to my face. As I held her head and breathed into her nostrils, she blew four consecutive warm breaths into my face. It was as if she was sending me a message of love and gratefulness. I knew, in that instant, that Billie Girl was here to stay.

The next morning, I excitedly told Don about my experience the night before with Billie Girl. We both knew we needed to arrive at a price the horse trader would accept.

After much emotional discussion, we agreed upon an amount and put it into a sealed envelope.

As I drove to the feed store and walked into the front office, I could see the puzzled look on the horse trader's face. I'm sure he was wondering, *Where's my horse?* I walked up to him and said, "I don't have your horse because she is at home. I really believe you should give her to me, but since that doesn't seem to be an option, what is the lowest amount you will take?" I will never forget how long it seemed to take for him to respond. He sat back in his tilted chair with hands clasped behind his head. After staring a few moments at me, he simply said, "Nine hundred dollars." I handed him that sealed envelope filled with nine $100 bills and quietly asked for a bill of sale. I still get chills today thinking of that amazing moment.

Billie Girl became a favorite of our family. She was a babysitter for all who rode her, including my nonhorseman husband, our nine-year-old year old son Matt and our five-year-old son Aaron. She was such a good babysitter that one month after she became ours, Aaron was galloping her with a group of riders down a sandy beach—one of his favorite memories.

We were blessed with four fun-filled years, a year for each breath she once blew to me the night she became our Billie Girl!

Laurie Henry

Passages of Time

One pretty Saturday morning in midspring, I stood watching in wonderment as Sheba, our old gray mare, cantered in happy circles around our nine-year-old daughter. Helen was standing in the middle of the pasture, halter and lead rope in hand, looking completely exasperated as Sheba ran circles around her. After all, Helen had awakened early this morning in eager anticipation of riding her brand-new horse for the first time.

But not if she couldn't catch her! I watched as Sheba lightly sailed over a low practice jump hurdle set up in the pasture. With head high, ears pricked forward and tail sailing on the wind as Arabians tails are wont to do, this old horse was the picture of beauty and lighthearted gaiety. I glanced across the paddock and saw that my husband, too, had stopped to watch this scene play out. We had just bought Sheba three days earlier and had found her to be gentle and very approachable in the pasture. But now she was happily evading my daughter's attempt to halter her. However, she was not running away to the far corners of the pasture, just circling within a few yards of Helen. Then, as we stood watching, Sheba simply stopped running and walked quietly over to the water tank for a drink.

A few moments later, while Helen was pleasantly grooming

Sheba, I asked my husband what he thought of the incident. "They looked to be 'happy circles' to me," he said. We both had a tingly sense of having received a message from this animal. She seemed to be expressing her gratitude for having been rescued from the crowded horse dealer's corral and coming to live with us. Indeed, before buying her, I had taken the old horse aside and quietly told her that if she would teach my young daughter to ride, she could have a home with us for as long as she lived. Now, Sheba seemed to be answering me with a resounding "yes!" Little did I know then just how much she would do for us.

It is a couple of years later and I am again standing in the same pasture, watching the same horse, the same gentle canter, but this time my handicapped daughter Mary Elizabeth is astride. Grandpa is with me, watching with tears in his eyes. Shaking his head in amazement, he is saying, "I never would have believed it." Helen went on to become quite an accomplished rider, pursuing such diverse equestrian activities as dressage lessons and exercising young Thoroughbreds on the track. But of my three children, it is Mary Elizabeth who loves horses as much as I do.

Although a couple of years older than Helen, she has always been developmentally behind her younger sister. Mary Elizabeth was born prematurely, deaf and with an impaired nervous system. She couldn't crawl or sit like other babies. She learned to walk with the support of a wheeled walker. She graduated to a pair of crutches in kindergarten. By first grade, she could walk unassisted but fell often. Her run looked more like a controlled fall. She found it difficult to stand without constantly moving to maintain her balance and she usually sat down or propped against something for support. In addition, she has severely reduced sensation in her arms and legs, which hampers her fine-motor control. Her deafness adds another handicap in itself.

But Mary Elizabeth loves animals, especially horses. As Helen began to learn how to ride, it soon became apparent that Mary Elizabeth intended to be included in this new activity. I was aware of riding programs for the handicapped and knew that Mary Elizabeth would benefit from riding. However, with her poor balance, I never thought that she would be able to ride without someone walking alongside the horse to steady her in the saddle. She never has been able to ride a bicycle and the two activities seemed similar in my mind.

One surprise followed another and through it all, I have been astonished repeatedly by Sheba's patience and understanding. Without any spoken words, the horse always does exactly what our deaf daughter "tells" her, such as positioning herself perfectly next to strange objects for mounting, or standing still with a slipped saddle hanging from her belly. Time and again, this old mare has demonstrated her intelligence, instead of the more usual and expected equine behaviors, to accommodate Mary Elizabeth.

Grandpa was right to be moved to tears of awe that day as we stood in the pasture witnessing Mary Elizabeth's demonstration of riding bareback at a canter across the field with only a set of reins clipped to the halter—a feat even her teenage brother wouldn't attempt! Over the years, Sheba has very generously shared her capable legs and willing spirit so that our very special daughter can experience an unaccustomed freedom and equality in her otherwise handicapped life.

Mary Gail Cooper

Aul Magic

A horse can lend its rider the speed and strength he or she lacks, but the rider who is wise remembers it is no more than a loan.

Pam Brown

When Betsy removed his halter, our spirited chestnut stallion whinnied loudly, wheeled away and kicked up his heels, racing the wind around the arena as his golden coat gleamed in the sunshine, obviously delighting the kids in the audience. Afterward, however, the proud Arabian stallion stood quietly at the arena fence as the children gathered to pet him.

I had introduced Aul Magic+/ to the audience as The Red Stallion comparing him to Walter Farley's Black Stallion, an equine hero from literature and the movies. He certainly lived up to that introduction at the special presentation at the therapeutic riding school that day. Schools like the one we were visiting provide physical therapy to the disabled, but they also supply emotional therapy through the bond that develops between horses and people.

Magic, too, is exceptionally good at bonding with people of all ages. He thrives on attention and hugs, and we enjoy sharing him with those who otherwise wouldn't get a chance to interact with such an affectionate and responsive horse.

On this particular occasion, as Magic performed, walking without wearing a halter or any other equipment, his trainer Carolyn Resnick invited an autistic boy into the arena to walk with the stallion.

With the characteristic detachment of autism, the boy stared downward, never looking up, as he was guided by his teacher toward the horse. The boy's head remained down and his gaze stayed firmly fixed on the ground as he stood with the stallion in the arena.

When the proper cue was given, the entire group, including the stallion, stepped forward. The boy, head still down, was gently encouraged by his teacher to walk with the others.

After a few steps, again on cue, everyone stopped walking. Magic, too, immediately stopped and stood at Carolyn's side.

When the group walked forward again, Carolyn eased back, giving up her place at Magic's shoulder to the boy. At first, the stallion lagged behind the boy, remaining beside her as he had been taught. With Carolyn's encouragement, however, Magic soon realized that the boy was now leading the parade and the horse began walking beside him.

The group continued walking and stopping, walking and stopping across the arena, with Magic always at the boy's side. During the entire time, the boy's eyes never left the ground, as though he were not even part of this parade, much less its leader. Yet whenever the boy stopped, the stallion stopped and stood beside him. When the boy took a step, Magic stepped forward as well.

When the little group stopped for the last time, the autistic boy finally raised his eyes from the ground. For the first time, he looked up at the beautiful stallion that had been his walking companion. As I watched from outside the arena, there seemed to be a sudden hush of expectation. If there was any noise from the crowd or any other sound I no longer heard it.

In the sunshine, Magic's coat gleamed like golden silk. I watched, fascinated, as the boy reached upward to stroke the stallion's glistening neck. *Perhaps,* I thought, *if even this boy can manage to reach out to another creature, there is hope for the rest of us.*

The remarkable interaction between the boy and the stallion ended as swiftly as it had begun. The boy's arm returned to his side, his eyes resumed their fixed downward stare and he was led shuffling from the arena.

But I will never forget that glorious day when an autistic boy reached out to caress a gentle Arabian stallion. I'll remember, too, the shining tears in the eyes of those who understood the significance of that gesture.

Sharon Byford-Ruth

5

ON COMPANIONSHIP AND COMMITMENT

Is it the smell of their body as I hug their long neck,
or the scent only a horse has that I can't forget?
Is it the depth of their eyes as they contentedly rest?
No, it's just being around them that I like the best.

Teresa Becker

A Horse in the House

It was more than two decades ago, as Easter was approaching, that my family waited for Martha, our cream-colored Quarter Horse brood mare, to have her annual foal. All of us—my husband Arthur, our ten-year-old son Marc and twelve-year-old daughter Karla—considered the birth of a foal a big event on our farm in Mandeville, Louisiana.

That year, Martha was taking her time. She was already three weeks overdue. When my husband had to go away on business, I was left to oversee the birth alone. I spent many nights sleeping in the stable next to Martha's stall, wondering each evening if this was finally going to be the night.

On the night before Easter Sunday, Martha at last went into labor. When I heard her pacing restlessly, I got up from my folding cot and ran to her stall. Fifteen minutes later, she gave birth to a small golden-haired foal. Martha nickered once, licked her newborn foal and lay down to rest.

But ten minutes later, Martha was up and turning around again as though she wanted to give birth a second time. I couldn't believe it. Equine twins are rare, and from what I knew, when a mare carries two foals, she usually aborts them or they are born dead. But sure enough, Martha gave birth to another foal. This one was dark brown with three white socks and a big white mark on its forehead.

Though Martha's foals were small, I was relieved that they were both alive and seemed healthy. It wasn't long before they wobbled to their feet and began pushing each other to get to their mother's milk. After the foals had nursed, I thought my troubles were finally over and I went back to the house for my first good night's sleep in weeks.

The next morning, the children and I let Martha and her foals out to pasture. We named the reddish-gold filly Amber and her darker sister Ebony. It was a delight to watch them trying out their legs and exploring the world.

But it soon became evident that Martha was having a problem accepting Ebony. When Amber ran, Martha cantered protectively after her, but when Ebony tried to follow them, the mare pushed her away. Then, to our horror, she kicked at the foal, striking her baby on the head.

Though Ebony was thrown off balance, she didn't seem harmed or fazed by the blow. In fact, she continued to run after the two other horses. But later that morning, Ebony began to have what appeared to be a seizure. Repeatedly, her legs stiffened, her body arched and she fell to the ground.

Each episode left her more weak and helpless. It was heartbreaking to see her struggle to her feet only to fall down again.

In desperation, I called all over town to find a veterinarian. I knew if Ebony became too weak to nurse, she would die. But it was Easter Sunday and the local veterinarians were either away or busy with other emergency calls. Finally, at 6 P.M. I managed to reach one. When I explained what had happened, he came straight over.

The veterinarian suspected that the kick to Ebony's head had caused a blood clot that was putting pressure on the brain. He thought that this was the reason for her convulsions, and injected her with steroids to help dissolve the clot. For hours, we watched over Ebony in the freezing barn, hoping for some sign of improvement. But Ebony stayed weak and helpless. Finally, it became so cold, I decided there was only one thing to do: bring Ebony into the house.

I padded the floor of my bedroom with pillows and towels and the veterinarian helped me carry the foal inside. He gave me some formula and told me to feed Ebony from a baby bottle. Then, having done all that he could, he left me alone with her.

Ebony had to be fed every twenty minutes. Between feedings, I lay on my bed, trying to get some rest. The situation seemed hopeless and my mind and body were heavy with despair. I was exhausted both physically and emotionally from the effort of trying to keep Ebony alive.

I must have dozed off, because the next thing I knew I was suddenly awakened by a nuzzle and a soft nicker from a wet little nose.

It was Ebony. She had gotten up and come to my bed for her bottle. Though she still was weak, I was overjoyed to see her on her feet again. As I watched her suck greedily at her bottle, my fatigue vanished and I felt a wave of joy. Ebony was going to pull through and live after all!

Three days later, Ebony was running in the fields as strong and as healthy as any other foal. But when we tried to return her to Martha, the mare again kicked her away. It was clear that I now had another child—an equine daughter—to raise.

At that point, Ebony had to be fed every half hour. To make feeding her easier, we kept her in the house, leaving the patio door ajar so she could come and go as she pleased. Whenever she was hungry, she came into the kitchen, nickering for a bottle.

My son Marc became her playmate. Every day after school, he and Ebony ran in the fields together. When Ebony tired of playing, she came inside and lay down on the living-room carpet to nap or watch TV. It seemed completely natural to have this large and rather gawky creature sharing our home with us.

Then, as Ebony grew older and even larger, we began to put her in the barn at bedtime and gradually reduced her bottle feedings. But during the day, she still had the run of the house. Like most toddlers, Ebony was curious and wanted to get into everything. She walked from room to room, looking for things to play with. One day, she found Marc's school report on the kitchen table and promptly chewed it up. The teacher said Marc's excuse, "My horse ate my homework," was a new one for her. Another day, I caught her gleefully pulling tissues from the box on my bedside table. What a mess!

When Ebony was three months old, we decided that it was time to wean her from the bottle and encourage her to become a horse. We took her out to pasture and left her to play with her sister Amber and our other horses. At first, Ebony protested. But she soon adjusted to her new life and happily settled into the herd.

For many years after her stay in our house, I still considered Ebony my daughter, even though she became a fine, healthy horse, well able to take care of herself.

That's why I was pleased to discover that the feeling seemed mutual because if ever I left the door of our house open, guess who walked right in? It startled our guests, but for us, Ebony would always be welcome—our horse in the house.

Diana Christensen

Side by Side

It had been a great day at the barn. Everything was going smoothly, the sun was shining brightly, everything was perfect. Then the telephone rang and I was shaken back to the reality of my job as owner of a horse-rescue operation.

It was almost midnight when my new charges arrived after their nearly twelve-hour journey. I recall walking around the trailer to get a first look at the two aged mares recently confiscated from their home by authorities.

They eyed me cautiously. We opened the trailer and began to unload them, careful to keep them close to one another to help them feel secure in their new surroundings. The fear in their eyes screamed, "How much more can we take? How long will this nightmare go on?"

We slowly led them down the barn aisle, past the curious eyes of their new stablemates, and placed them in a stall together. Rushing to a corner, they stood shaking, their heads buried. Only occasionally did one of the mares, Dee, look around. Rosie, Dee's companion, seemed the most traumatized. She was unwilling to lift her head and her eyes were hollow and distant—a dull blank stare where blazing light should have been. Lethargic, she refused to look at us. Both of the mares ignored offerings of small amounts of water and hay. I settled in and continued to monitor them through the night, but nothing changed.

I knew Dee and Rosie's history and it was a sad one. When the authorities arrived to investigate a complaint about neglected horses, they found no hay, grain or bedding on the property. Dee and Rosie were literally eating the wood off the barn to try to stay alive. These two horses had been kept not only in the same barn, but in the same stall for nearly twenty-eight years. Tomorrow would be the beginning of my real challenge: to introduce these two terror-stricken horses to the life they had been denied.

For the first two weeks, I tried to gain their trust but my slow, deliberate movements stirred only more fear in their hearts, where fire and spirit should have been. Finally, a few mornings later, I entered the barn to find Rosie looking over her stall gate. When she saw me, her whinnies filled the barn. I approached her, talking softly and through tearful eyes, I saw the faintest hint of a spark in her gaze. She and Dee still backed away and refused my touch, but they were interested in their surroundings and showing signs of life.

I hung feed buckets in the stall, placing them so Dee and Rosie could touch one another as they ate, but they refused. They would eat only if allowed to share the same bucket. The same was true with water.

Five weeks passed before I had gained enough of their trust to attempt to take them outside. Holding a lead line in each hand, I had to be sure they could feel one another before they were calm enough to handle. Their eyes once again filled with fear, but they reluctantly followed me from the barn.

I was told that neither had touched grass since the age of six months. When their hooves touched it, they panicked. The whites around their eyes showing, nostrils flaring, they snorted and screamed as each of them tried to raise all four feet simultaneously. I quickly worked to get them back in the barn and into their stall. There, they once again retreated into the corner where they shivered and shook with fear. I had lost everything I had gained, but only for a short time.

A week later, I tried again. Although the experience was still traumatizing, they trusted me enough to walk with me for a short distance. Over the next fifteen minutes, I learned their fear of birds, butterflies, water puddles and vehicles. From that day forward, a daily trek would be part of our routine.

Soon, they trusted me enough that I could open their stall door and they would run from the barn, make two laps around it and then return to their stall together. What a beautiful sight to see them trying to accustom themselves to a new situation in a world that had been so cruel to them.

Two months would pass before I could separate them and give each her own stall. The stalls were side by side with an open grid between them so that they could see and touch each other. I placed their hay bags back to back so it appeared that they were eating together. Each had her own hay, and plenty of it, but still feared that the other would be hungry. Rosie would take a bite of hay and eat it. The next bite would be dropped to the floor, where she would use her nose to push it under the stall wall to Dee. Any hay that fell to the ground was given to Dee.

Four months after the girls (as they had become known to everyone at the farm) had arrived, I decided to try to turn them out in a small paddock. The experience did not go smoothly. They had seen only one other horse in their lives, so when their stablemates began getting close to the fence that bordered the fields, they once again panicked. The girls would race one full lap of the paddock at top speed and then stand shaking at the gate, waiting for me to save them from their newest danger. Each new experience was an insurmountable obstacle to them, but patience and repetition would work every time.

Thirteen months passed and it was time to try them with the other horses; time to see if they could lead a normal life. I turned them out in a small field with five other horses. The first few days, Rosie and Dee stayed together. Eventually, Rosie began to socialize and seemed to love her new life. She would run and kick up her heels and "talk" to anyone who would listen. Dee, on the other hand, was reserved and feared her fieldmates. But as always, Rosie and Dee were together at feeding time and Rosie always made certain that Dee had enough to eat. At the end of the thirteenth month, Dee also began to socialize with the others and to live her life as a normal horse.

The beginning of the fourteenth month would bring new changes for all involved with our horse rescue operation. For three years, we had rented facilities and now we had purchased our own farm. All of our horses, at that time numbering eighteen, loved the new land—seventy acres of rolling hills for running and grazing and enjoying life! Rosie and Dee would thrive on the lush pastures with their nightmare past behind them. Finally, the light returned to Rosie's eyes, and I could sense the fire and spirit in both their hearts.

The world couldn't have been better, at least until the Sunday morning I went to feed and Rosie didn't come to her bucket. This was unusual because she was always the first to her place. I fed the other horses and then set out to look for Rosie. The search was short. Next to the fence, only fifty yards behind our house, lay Rosie. I called to her and she raised her head and nickered. She tried to get to her feet, but failed.

As I approached her, I called her name again, and once again she tried to stand. Again and again she tried, but her efforts were futile. Exhausted, she collapsed. Looking her over, I couldn't find anything wrong or see why she wasn't able to get up, but on closer inspection, I found what appeared to be a bullet hole between her eyes. It had been covered by her forelock.

I phoned the veterinarian and after what seemed like hours, he arrived. A careful examination determined what I feared: Rosie would have to be destroyed. Both the sheriff and the veterinarian confirmed that she had been shot with a high-powered rifle with a scope. A trespasser with a rifle outlawed in our state had once again shattered Dee's world and had stolen away Rosie's newfound life.

A reward was set and the search was now on for the killer of the beautiful white horse who, after surviving decades of abuse and neglect, had just learned to live. The sheriff advised us that Rosie was to be left in the field for at least four days. In the event that the person was found, the bullet might have to be surgically removed from Rosie's brain as evidence so that it could be matched with a specific rifle.

My concern now turned to Dee. For twenty-eight years she had lived side by side with Rosie. How would she survive now? I covered Rosie with a heavy tarp and tied it for her privacy as well as protection. When I returned the next day to feed, Rosie was uncovered and Dee was standing guard over her body. When I put grain in their buckets, Dee would paw Rosie's body and whinny to her. As I led Dee to her feed, she kept calling Rosie to "come to eat." When Dee finished eating, her guard duties continued.

For five days, I would cover Rosie's body only to find her uncovered the next day with Dee by her side. The fifth day we would bury Rosie, but for nearly two weeks after that Dee would continue to guard the place where Rosie had lain and continue to call her for supper each night.

It has been five years since Rosie's death. Her killer was never found, although other horses within a ten-mile radius of our farm also were shot and had to be destroyed. Dee, at the age of thirty-eight, is now arthritic but otherwise in good health. She still lives her life in the rolling pastures of our farm.

Dee's trust in us has continued to grow. She comes to me when I call her and she can be handled as easily as a newborn kitten. The pain of her past seems to have faded away, but I sometimes see that faraway look in her eyes and I wonder what thoughts are passing through her mind. As she stares across the fields, is she searching for Rosie? Does she realize she'll never have far to go to find her? Rosie will always be with her, standing by her side by side.

Sissy Burggraf

My Friend Bob

I was short. He was tall.

I was white. He was black.

My vocabulary was above average for a third-grader. His . . . . Well . . . . I was the only one who understood him when he spoke.

I was a nine-year-old girl. He was a gorgeous six-year-old Tennessee Walking Horse whose registered name was Bob's Merry Legs. He had the most velvety black coat I'd ever seen. His four white stockings and broad white blaze made him look even blacker than he was. He was at least 16 hands tall which meant that he towered over me.

I wanted him as soon as I saw him enter the sale ring. Daddy had brought me to the auction, but I'm sure he had no idea what would happen.

I couldn't take my eyes off the glorious-looking creature. I was quite certain my life would be nothing but pure happiness if I could have him and, by contrast, I was equally certain it would be nothing but misery if I were denied him.

I knew begging and pleading would get me nowhere. In our family, one made a simple request and then waited for the parental decision.

"How will you take care of him?" asked Daddy. Look at him. He's huge. You won't even be able to get on his back.

"They want $125 for him," continued Daddy. "That's a lot of money, but that's not all. We'll need to feed him and pay for visits from the veterinarian every now and then. We're talking about a very expensive situation here."

I looked him square in the face, eyeball-to-eyeball. "I could give you my entire allowance until he's paid off," I said.

Looking back over all those years, I have no idea how Daddy kept a straight face.

"And how much allowance do you get?" he asked.

"A quarter every week." I responded.

"Hmmm," he said, "if my mental arithmetic is correct, you'll need almost fourteen years to pay him off. That's a long time."

I dropped my head and looked down at the dirt. My visions of having the beautiful black horse in the pasture at our small farm were fading quickly. Now, my focus was to keep my bottom lip from quivering.

"Are you sure about this? A horse is a lot of responsibility, you know. It's different from having a dog or a cat."

I shook my head in the affirmative.

"Okay," said Daddy. "Go over to the man in the red plaid shirt, the one leaning against the fence. Ask him if the horse is still for sale for $125 and ask him if he can deliver him to our farm."

A grin split my face so wide I could feel the shape of my cheeks changing. I ran to the man, began talking to him, pointing first at Bob and then at Daddy. He nodded his head "yes" to both of my questions. I started to run back to Daddy, but changed my mind. I knew he'd take care of the business part. What I needed to do was introduce myself to Bob.

The big black horse had been moved to a small corral. I climbed to the top rail of the fence, threw over one leg at a time and perched there.

"Hey, Bob," I said. "You're beautiful. You don't know me yet, but I already love you. We're going to have wonderful times together."

The horse tossed his head before walking to me. He stopped three feet short, then stretched out his neck and flared his nostrils in an attempt to pull my scent into his nose. Slowly, I held out my hand. Bob snuffled across my small palm, his warm breath the most wonderful sensation I'd ever felt. I knew at that moment we'd bonded. Nothing else was needed. Bob settled in at the farm immediately. No fuss. No special fanfare.

My parents set limits on the freedom we could enjoy. The railroad track one mile east and the bridge three-quarters of a mile to the west were the boundaries. There were numerous dirt roads crisscrossing our farm and I could ride anywhere I pleased on those.

Bob learned my schedule. He began prancing and whinnying sometime between 4:05 and 4:15 in the afternoon, but Daddy made him wait until 4:20 before he opened the paddock gate. Bob walked on his own, with no bridle or rider, down the long driveway to the edge of the cattle gap and waited, looking expectantly in the direction he knew the school bus would come. I would find him neighing furiously by the time the bus door opened and I stepped out.

My daddy wouldn't go anywhere without wearing one of those dapper fedora hats, and Bob loved them. He waited for Daddy to walk past him and, quick as lightning, he darted over, snagged the hat with his teeth and snatched if from Daddy's head. The horse seemed to laugh and was extremely pleased with himself, knowing he'd exposed the man's very large bald spot. Fortunately, Daddy learned quickly that chasing Bob down was not the thing to do. It wasn't a fair match and Bob always won. Instead, Daddy would just ignore the situation, and try as hard as he could not to acknowledge the sight of Bob running around with the hat dangling from his big yellow teeth. Eventually, after being ignored, Bob would walk over and drop the hat at Daddy's feet.

Three years after Bob came to live with us, Mama and

Daddy decided that I could ride beyond the railroad tracks and the bridge. That was really great, but there was one major problem: I couldn't convince Bob that we had permission to expand our universe. He absolutely refused to cross the tracks or the bridge. It was frustrating as well as humiliating. Finally, Daddy came and led him across both former boundaries while I sat in the saddle. Somehow, Bob equated that action with receiving the official okay from an authority figure.

I had my first date on Bob, graduated grade school and moved into high school. Unlike some girls, though, I didn't leave behind my passion for horses in general and for Bob in particular.

He was still my very best friend and he still met me each day at the end of the driveway. Very seldomly did we skip a day of riding, but if we did, I sat in the pasture with him. Our conversations were long and slow and deep. There was nothing about me he didn't know, and he kept my secrets ever so well.

I was completing my sophomore term and Bob was sixteen. His coat was still jet black and his step still had all the fire and prance of a much younger horse. I visited him each morning before catching the school bus, but on one particular morning, something was seriously wrong.

He was on the ground in his paddock, drenched in sweat. He'd swing his beautiful head toward his side and try to nip himself, telling me he was experiencing painful stomach cramps. He looked at me. I knew he was asking for help and I also knew he had a serious case of colic.

I ran to the house, slamming the door behind me, snatching the receiver from the wall phone and dialing the veterinarian. Mama came from the kitchen, drying her hands on a dish towel.

"What's wrong?" she asked.

"It's Bob. Colic. I called the vet." I answered, short of breath from the run as well as from fear and from struggling to hold back tears.

Mama walked to me and patted my shoulder. "It'll be okay," she said. "I'll go get Daddy so he can help." She got into her car and drove to the field where he was working on his tractor. They returned together.

"We need to get him up if we can," he said to me. We set off for the paddock at a run. Daddy put a lead rope on Bob's halter. "You coax him," he said. "He'll listen to you."

"Bob," I sobbed. "Please, Bob. Get up. Please. Please. I need you, Bob."

The big horse lumbered to his feet and when he was standing, I gasped. He looked as if he'd lost a hundred pounds overnight. Daddy handed me the lead rope. "Walk him," he said. I could tell from his look and the tone of his voice that he thought the situation was bleak. With tears running down my face, I started walking the black horse.

The veterinarian arrived, jumping quickly from his seat. He grabbed a stainless-steel bucket from the back of his truck and poured in mineral oil until it was half-full.

Then he stuck a pump with a long, clear plastic tube attached to it into the bucket. He walked over to Bob, pinched his nostrils together and began feeding the tube through his nose, down his throat and into his stomach. Then the veterinarian began pumping the oil into the tube, hoping to dislodge the impaction that was the source of Bob's pain and move it out. He pumped and pumped and pumped, but nothing happened. Bob's front legs started buckling at the knees.

"Don't let him go down," the veterinarian yelled. "We don't want him to roll. If he does, he could twist that intestine and then we don't have a prayer."

I held on to my horse, my heart breaking, knowing he was miserable. I knew how he longed to lie down, but I tugged and strained on the lead rope. "Please, Bob," I prayed. "Stand up, Bob." And, for the first time since the ordeal began, I allowed myself to say the word, the awful word. "Please, Bob. Please don't die," I breathed.

"I can't do anything more," the veterinarian said. "Just keep walking him as much as you can."

Both Bob and I were exhausted, but I walked him and stroked his face. Finally, he touched my cheek with his nose. I suppose I knew what would happen. I suppose I wasn't surprised when he yanked the rope from my hand and crumpled to the ground, looking like a million broken pieces of black glass.

He stretched out his neck, and I lay down on the grass next to him. "I love you, Bob. You've been the best friend I could ever have." He knew what I said. He always did.

Daddy worked all day to dig Bob's grave, way back in the middle of a small thicket of trees and vines. He knew a decent burial was all I'd accept for Bob. I missed school for an entire week, crying every day.

All these many years later, my heart still feels the tug of a lead rope whenever I think of Bob.

Daddy is dead and Mama is more than eighty years old.

The farm has long since been sold and rows of houses cover the pastures and fields.

There's a house built over the grave now.

Sometimes, when I'm home visiting Mama, I imagine the people living in that house. They are unaware of the history the earth holds, but I wonder if every so often they hear a whinny and just for a minute see the silliest thing: a big, black horse with a fedora dangling between his teeth, trying to entice someone into a game of tag.

Diane M. Ciarloni

The Magic Carpet Pony

Gypsy gold does not chink and glitter. It gleams in the sun and neighs in the dark.

Gypsy Saying

At nine, I had already shown my determination to ride through several years of being overmounted until, at last, Daddy got serious about finding me a proper pony. He went looking one day with $300 in his pocket, just in case he found the right animal. At one farm, he saw a 13-hand Welsh pony with a a flashy bay coat that shined like a new penny. Daddy just thought, "Wouldn't it be fabulous to own a pony like that?"

After two months of looking, Daddy realized that he couldn't settle for anything less. He paid $800 for Jupiter, an exorbitant sum in those days. But when I found that note in my Christmas stocking—"Dear Robin, I am waiting for you down at the barn. Please come soon. Jupiter"—I'm sure my ecstasy was worth $800.

As Jupiter and I rode out across the fields, it was as if I'd been given a magic carpet. Jupiter took me anywhere I wanted to go, from the winner's circle to the ends of my imagination.

Of course, he did it on his terms. Jupiter was too independent to be anybody's lackey. He dutifully carried me over hill and dale and post and rail, but only after I'd spent an hour trying to catch him. When I fell off on my first fox hunt, Jupiter galloped away, totally unremorseful. "If you're not good enough to stay with me, that's your problem," he seemed to say.

Jupiter wasn't above asserting his independence in the show ring, either. Every so often, he would refuse a fence just to remind me that I rode—and won—at his sufferance. Most of the time, though, he suffered me to win, providing me with a wall full of ribbons and a truckload of silver trays, plates and goblets.

He ran away from me in the pasture, he ran away with me in the hunting field and he lorded over the dogs and the other horses with his well-aimed kicks, so why did we love him so? It was his indomitable spirit. When it came to that go-for-the-gold, never-say-die, thrill-of-a-lifetime effort, the Black Stallion had nothing on Jupiter.

Jupiter had the right stuff and he knew it, too. I rode that little pony over a lot of fences that I'd hesitate to jump with a horse today. Daddy saw him jump out of a paddock over a four-foot fence in the snow one time, then make a circle and jump back in, just for fun. His exuberance was excessive at times, but you had to love him for it.

There was talk of selling Jupiter when I outgrew him. After all, ponies are expensive pets and they live forever. But it never quite happened.

My friendship with Jupiter actually deepened in high school. Some afternoons I took off cross-country on Jupiter and dealt with the disappointments of teenage life. So what if I didn't get chosen to be a cheerleader? So what if the wrong fellow asked me to the dance? I didn't have time to practice being peppy or agonize over adolescent crushes with a barn full of horses to ride.

Soon it was college and marriage and talk of the day when my little girl would have Jupiter to ride. But instead of a daughter, I had a divorce.

Divorce was still somewhat scandalous in those days and I wrestled with guilt and feelings of failure. One afternoon, I tacked up Jupiter for a long ride. He didn't look much like the magic-carpet steed of my childhood, with his shaggy brown winter coat. He was well into middle age and had mellowed a bit, but I thought he could still save the Alamo. Sure enough, the moment I got on him and felt that familiar step, I was flooded with a feeling of security.

As I began making a life of my own, I found that Jupiter was not just a solace in troubled times, but a role model.

Jupiter never asked how high the fences were or whom he had to beat. He just jumped. After he had demolished the competition in his own division, he cheerfully out-jumped horses that stood a foot taller. Once, I even had the nerve to enter him in a barrel race. When we rode into the ring—a chubby-cheeked girl with pigtails on a fat pony wearing an English saddle—the cowhide cowboys snickered. But Jupiter flew around the course, his little legs a blur as he circled the barrels without even slowing down. He won, beating the state champion barrel racer in the process. It was no more than I expected of him, but those cowboys were flabbergasted.

His attitude rubbed off on me and helped me get my first job. There wasn't even an opening at the local magazine when I called for an interview. Looking like an English pony up against Western horses, I went to see the editor. But, Jupiter-like, I knew I could do the job. The self-confidence must have worked, because the editor hired me.

Years later, my second marriage gave me a second chance at a lot of things, among them recreating my happy childhood. In high spirits, I went to reclaim my pony, who had been loaned to a succession of little girls.

When I found him, I was appalled at the toll the years had taken: He was thin, one ear was crumpled over and he had something wrong with one eye. Furthermore, although it was late summer, he had the long coat of the last winter.

I cried all the way home. When I unloaded him, I really

was afraid he'd keel over and die before I could get him into the barn. I began shoving grain at him and called the veterinarian. Two days of grain feeding later, Jupiter had perked up considerably.

After a week, I couldn't stand it any longer. I got on him. He walked around a bit and then we trotted. Then he broke into a little canter and, to my astonishment, tried to run away. Oh, you spunky pony!

My husband quickly became enamored of the pony, and together we nursed and fed and groomed him. For three years, I enjoyed seeing my old pony in the pasture, knowing he was loved and well cared for.

Jupiter was twenty-eight the day he lay down in a quiet corner of the pasture and died.

I spent the day much as anyone making funeral arrangements for a loved one. I called my husband in tears, and he began to look for a backhoe. Daddy called and we cried together. "Remember the time . . . ?" In between calls, I braided a lock of Jupiter's tail to keep.

Daddy came over for the wake and we told Jupiter stories. I kept waiting for the neighbors to come calling with pies and hams.

I got out some old pictures, but the best images were in our minds. Daddy shook his head and laughed occasionally at some memory. And we all got choked up. I'd never seen my daddy cry before. In fact, I wondered a bit at his sentimentality, driving thirty miles on a weeknight just to talk about an old pony.

"I'll always picture him jumping the paddock fence in the snow," Daddy said. "You know, that pony had more heart than any horse I've ever seen. He had to, because he didn't have enough leg to jump half the things I saw him go over."

"Is that why you never sold him?" I asked. Daddy shrugged sheepishly.

I reminded him of his motto about owning horses: "You should never have a horse that isn't for sale."

"Oh, I put a price on Jupiter," he said. "But fortunately, no one took me up on it." That was the first I'd heard of that. "What were you asking for him?" I inquired.

Daddy smiled, his eyes shining again. "I figured one day that watching you and that biggety little pony take on all comers was worth about a million dollars. Maybe nine hundred thousand. I didn't want to be unreasonable."

Robin Traywick Williams

Handled with Care

The name Buttercup evoked visions of a small, butter-yellow flower. The horse with the same name couldn't have been more different.

My daughter Lauren is six years old. Three months premature, she was diagnosed with spastic diplegia, a form of cerebral palsey. Lauren uses a walker for mobility. Her balance is too poor for Lofstrand crutches. Now, though, after a surgery meant to reduce her high muscle tone, Lauren's balance should get better. Horseback riding will be her first true test.

Therapeutic horseback riding is Lauren's release. It gives her something to do on a weekly basis that most children only dream of doing.

Her first horse, Robin, was a rather smallish pony. Brown with white spots, Robin plodded along faithfully week after week. The next year, Lauren rode Jeannie, the one-eyed wonder, gentle and small. She rode Jeannie up until the time of her surgery. For about ten weeks, she did not ride at all, then in the fall, she returned in time for the last lesson before the year-end show.

It was then that Lauren met Buttercup, who is well-groomed, caramel in color and BIG. So much for my image of delicate yellow flowers.

Lauren seemed calm about the whole idea of riding a big horse. I, on the other hand, was busy trying not to have a heart attack.

I have trusted these virtual strangers with the safety of my daughter, but now I questioned putting her on the back of this big horse. My sanity was intact. I was calm, cool and outwardly in control. With that reality check, I decided I had good reason to be worried.

"Where's Jeannie?" I asked, trying to keep the quiver of nervousness out of my voice.

"Jeannie has a sore foot."

Buttercup was led around the ring a couple of times to warm her up in preparation for Lauren's lesson. This gave me a chance to see the horse in action. She appeared calm enough. Her eyes were kind. No doubt about it, Buttercup was beautiful and big.

Lauren was thrilled. Her little body stiffened with excitement as it always does when she is happy about something.

Buttercup was brought around to stand in front of us. I swallowed my reservations and fear and lifted Lauren onto Buttercup's broad back. Marcella, the occupational therapist, rounded up Lauren's side walkers as Buttercup craned her neck as if she was checking out my daughter. With the zeal she normally shows, Lauren snatched up the rainbow reins and placed her hands on the green section. Her side walkers were prepared, arms up, with Lauren's legs pinned beneath their forearms to prevent her from sliding off.

"Have fun," I croaked, heart pounding. As she rode around the ring, Buttercup behaved herself. Lauren looked so tiny on her back. Once, twice they circled. Lauren sat up straight and tall. My heart pumped with every hoof fall, though I knew Lauren's side walkers would prevent her from slipping off. Still, she is my baby. My only child.

At the far end of the ring, they stopped. Usually this meant that Lauren was leaning too far to one side in the saddle. To my eye, she was still sitting straight. I wondered why they stopped and watched as Marcella spoke to Lauren a bit. As they started moving again, to my disbelief, the side-walkers LET GO.

Marcella! You're joking, right? I wanted to shout. Why didn't someone warn me that they were going to do this? Don't they know heart attacks can happen anywhere, to anyone at anytime? Lauren sat straight and tall, as proud as a peacock of her accomplishment and newfound freedom. Buttercup calmly chewed her cud, or whatever horses do, and around the ring they walked, Marcella talking to Lauren the whole time. I smiled to greet Lauren's wide look-at-me-Mom grin. All the while my heart was beating hard, not from fear now, but from excitement and joy and, yes, pride.

When the lesson finally ended and I stood at Lauren's side waiting to catch her as she dismounted, I knew Lauren had made great strides forward that day. The days of side walkers would be over soon. It was a sign of healing. Her surgery had now been proven a success.

Lauren slid off into my arms and begged to pet Buttercup. I reached out as well, rubbing the horse's proud arched neck. I wondered if Buttercup understood the gift she had given my daughter. I owed much to the horse and to those who sponsor her so that she is fed and cared for throughout the winter.

Buttercup bobbed her head and looked back at Lauren and me. Maybe she did understand. Thank you, Buttercup, for carrying my princess gently.

Sandra Moore

To Chutney, with Love

A *light hand is one which never feels the contact of the bit with the bars.*

François Robichon de la Guérinière

There is an ancient proverb that advises us to "hold a true friend with both your hands." Centuries after that line was written, its advice still rings true. In our busy, chaotic world, a trusted friend is like a fine gem. I'm fortunate to have one such gem in my life—a beautiful mare by the name of Chutney.

In the beginning, Chutney and I were clearly a mismatched pair. I was a shy, insecure teenager; she was a fiery, opinionated mare. Diagnosed with scoliosis, I was forced to wear a back brace for three years. It was a clumsy apparatus that caused me to become the laughingstock of my junior high school class. It was not uncommon to hear kids ridiculing me as I walked by. Some would even go so far as to knock on the brace. Needless to say, whatever self-esteem I did have, plummeted as a result.

Riding was meant to be my escape from such problems. I began the sport at age thirteen, a relatively "advanced" starting age. In the beginning, I rode at a small, backyard-type barn and competed in the friendly atmosphere of 4-H sorts of shows. As I advanced, my pony and I moved to a large hunter and equitation barn, where my lack of skills became apparent. I was a low intermediate at best, while the majority of my new stablemates were elegant equitation riders who had been involved in the sport since toddlerhood. Many competed regularly at high-caliber competition, far beyond my abilities.

The granddaughter of a racing legend, Chutney had been purchased as a weanling at the prestigious Keeneland sale and she had been brought along steadily by a professional. A "hot" horse, she was accustomed to a precise, accurate ride that would best showcase her talents and athleticism. She was far too advanced for me at the time. Nonetheless, I fell in love with her on the spot.

She was stunning, a flashy blood bay with the most expressive, feminine face I'd ever seen and powerful yet floaty gaits. She jumped with her knees up to her nose and with a round bascule that threw you right up out of the saddle. I liked the fact that she was a challenge. A true diva, she'd pin her ears at any horse that passed by.

Showing Chutney was a valuable, though sometimes frustrating, learning experience. She wasn't about to put up with novice mistakes. If I asked her for a certain distance to a fence, she took it, right or wrong. Automatic lead changes? Out of the question. If I asked too roughly, she'd hop; if I didn't ask firmly enough, she'd fail to swap behind. This mare was a perfectionist, which was the one trait we shared. Perfectionism aside, we somehow complemented each other. Where I was weak, Chutney was strong; where I was shy, she was bold.

When I rode her the way she demanded to be ridden—relaxed, with a soft leg, hand and seat—she could, and did, win with the best of them. If I made mistakes, however, she'd express her displeasure, which was usually enough to keep us out of the ribbons. Our show results were based upon how I rode on that particular day, so it was not uncommon for us to be champions one weekend and come home empty-handed the next. These were great lessons beyond the show ring. Life, as we all know, is what you make of it. It's also a series of ups and downs.

While I was riding with an extremely difficult trainer who told me that Chutney and I would never be a suitable pair, a well-known professional rider came to visit the barn. When the pro rode Chutney, he agreed that she was a very complicated ride for an amateur. However, as soon as my trainer left the ring, the rider took me aside and whispered, "I really like this horse, you know. These other kids will learn to look pretty. You, however, will learn to ride." With his words of encouragement, I became even more determined to ride this horse well.

Chutney has been with me through all of the milestones in my life—first prom, SATs, college acceptances, first car, and when my first book was accepted for publication. When my father died of a heart attack when I was eighteen years old, I once again found comfort by Chutney's side. And when the pressures of showing became too much, we'd often sneak across the street into an open field, where we galloped to our hearts' content.

We know each other as well as any lifelong friends do. I know that she loves peppermints but won't give sugar cubes a second thought. I know that she'd give anything to stand outside during a rainstorm, and that when she curls her upper lip, it's a sign that she's not feeling well. And she knows that I sometimes take life, especially riding, a bit too seriously. Whenever I'm feeling low or insecure, I bury my face in her wonderful neck and feel as if nothing in the world could ever hurt me.

Even after being my friend and riding partner for fifteen years, my beloved mare continues to teach me. I recently took up dressage after years in hunters and equitation. As we competed in our first Training Level test, I began to put the familiar pressure on myself. I tensed up and Chutney, in typical fashion, reacted to it by throwing out a huge buck right in front of the judge's box. Years ago, I probably would have cried. Now, sitting on the back of my twenty-two-year-old friend, I could only laugh. It was as if Chutney, in all her wisdom, was saying to me, "It's only a show. Lighten up! It's our friendship that matters." Once again, she was right.

Together we have shared victories and disappointments; celebrated love and lamented loss; and have been there for each other through thick and thin. And somewhere along the way, a shy, insecure teenager became a confident writer, and a novice rider became a capable and effective horsewoman. I'd be lying if I didn't credit much of that success to Chutney.

Regardless of whatever success I've had, I sometimes get that familiar twinge of insecurity. On these occasions, I head straight to Chutney's stall and wrap my arms around her neck—and once again, I feel completely safe and secure, for Chutney is the type of friend that's worth holding onto—with both hands.

Kimberly Gatto

New Life for Rosie

"Mommy, Mommy, can we please keep her?" pleaded my daughter Jackie as the beautiful white pony nudged her pockets looking for treats. Rosie was every little girl's dream pony. She had a beautiful face with big, inquisitive brown eyes and long white eyelashes.

"I'm really in a pinch here," said the young owner. "I'm leaving for college in four days and she can't stay here. There's no shelter and no one can drive out here to feed her. I just need to find her a good home. She's a wonderful horse, I promise!"

"But we haven't even ridden her," I argued.

"Just take her home and try her. You won't be sorry."

"Oh, please, Mommy! I love her! I can't believe it, we're both ten years old!"

I sighed. I was outnumbered.

We moved Rosie to an old dairy farm, where the retired farmer rented out pastures to a few horses. We couldn't catch her during her first couple of days in the pasture. She was having fun, galloping past us with her tail flying. In no time, Jackie—and sometimes her younger sister Chelsea—was riding Rosie around the pasture and on the adjacent trails through the falling leaves for endless hours of fun. Jackie and Rosie were quite a pair. They dressed up for a neighborhood holiday parade and we brought our precious little pony a treat of warm mash on Christmas morning.

Finally, the days were getting warmer and longer and Jackie was making plans for summer fun with Rosie. She had become a member of our family and Jackie's dream of having her own pony had finally come true. Rosie seemed happy, too. It had been a wet and warm spring, making the endless acres of new grass especially luscious. When Rosie wasn't off on adventures with Jackie and Chelsea, she was eating. She had a grass belly, but she wasn't the fattest horse in the pasture, so I wasn't especially concerned.

One day I got the call that every horse owner dreads. "You better come have a look at Rosie," said Roy, one of the other horse owners. "She doesn't want to walk, and she leans back when she's standing. She doesn't seem to want to put any weight on her front feet, but I don't see any signs of any injury."

I thanked Ray and rushed out to the farm. After seeing Rosie, I called our veterinarian. He told me to take her out of the pasture and put her into a smaller space until he could get there. When he arrived, it didn't take him long to diagnose her with laminitis, a condition that affects the internal structures of the hoof. Indeed, Rosie's hooves were very hot and she was leaning back in an effort to take as much weight as possible off of her painful front hooves.

"How did this happen?" I asked Dr. Pickering.

"Marla, simply put, the horse overloads on rich food, which can't be digested normally. A fermentation process in the intestines produces a toxin that enters the bloodstream. The entire body is affected, but certain sensitive structures in the hoof are most prone to damage. When it is extensive, the coffin bone within the hoof can lose its attachment to the hoof wall, and that's very serious."

Dr. Pickering hesitated, then continued. "Sometimes, it even causes the hoof to fall off. Hopefully, we caught this case early enough. Be sure to continue her on these medications and keep her on the diet I've outlined. You'll have to keep her in this small paddock for the next few weeks. Call me if there are any changes at all. Keep me posted, Marla."

Rosie did not like being separated from her little herd and she especially didn't enjoy her new diet. She repeatedly tried to tell us it was all a big mistake.

"Gee, Mom," said Jackie, "I wish there was some way to explain to her that this is for her own good."

"I know, it's pretty frustrating, but she's getting so much better, and we can put some special shoes on her and maybe start riding her again if she continues to improve."

During the sixth week, Rosie got her shoes with a special cushioning on the sole. It looked like she'd be good to go for the summer. But unfortunately, that was not the case.

"Look Mom, Rosie's lying down," my youngest daughter Chelsea exclaimed. It was a hot midday in May and it seemed a bit odd that she would be lying flat out in the middle of her paddock. She didn't look up as we approached.

"Something's wrong—dreadfully wrong. I'm calling the vet," I said.

"It's very hot, try putting some wet towels on her until I get there," advised Dr. Pickering.

We were all glad we could do something helpful while we waited. The veterinarian arrived in no time. "She's crashed," he said. "I had hoped this wouldn't happen. It's impossible to predict which direction laminitis will take. This isn't good, Marla. She might survive today, but her feet may never recover. You might have to consider some other options. Even if we pull her through, she may be unable to walk for the rest of her life."

Dr. Pickering worked tirelessly on Rosie throughout the hot afternoon. We kept busy fetching equipment, holding tubes and refreshing the wet towels. Jackie spent most of her time comforting Rosie through her tears. "Please girl, don't give up. You'll be okay, Rosie. I'll take care of you." Once in a while, Rosie would let out a big sigh. We knew she was in a lot of pain.

Hours later, as the sun was getting lower in the sky, Dr.

Pickering said, "We need to move Rosie. Can she stay in that enclosure next to the barn?"

"Sure," I said, "but how are we going to get her in there?"

"We're going to have to help her the best we can," he replied.

We pleaded with her to get up. She didn't want to step on those tender hooves, but the four of us couldn't carry her. As a last resort, Dr. Pickering picked up her leg and started moving her hooves one step at a time. We did our best to lead her and encourage her and discourage her from lying down. Finally, we made it to the stall that would be her home for the next few months.

"Now you'll have to watch her carefully. She'll need a shot twice a day at first along with these other oral medications. Can you give shots?"

No, I thought. "I'll learn," I said.

"There's one other thing," our veterinarian said, out of earshot of my daughters. "There may come a time when it's too much to ask from Rosie. It may be too much suffering with very little chance of recovery. She may get an infection in her feet. Horses aren't meant to lie down this much. They can develop sores."

"How will I know?" I asked.

"Rosie will let you know," he said. "She'll groan from the pain and she won't be able to get up. She'll let you know when she can't take any more."

Armed with Rosie's multiple treatments and medications, I almost felt hopeless as I watched our veterinarian drive away.

"She'll be okay, Mommy. Don't worry," reassured Jackie when she saw my face. "We'll take care of her. I love her, Mommy. Rosie has to get better."

"We'll do whatever we can. I promise. Now let's get home to get some rest. She's resting peacefully now."

Jackie and Chelsea spent that evening decorating get-well posters for Rosie. The next morning we went to see her and

I gave her the daily medications while the girls hung their signs and posters.

"I know she can't read, Mom," said Jackie, "but I want her to know we're thinking about her when we're not here. It'll make her feel better."

For those first couple of weeks, she didn't show much interest in anything, but she didn't seem to be getting any worse. The veterinarian's words echoed in my mind when I asked, "What if she's in too much pain?" He said I would know.

In the evening, like wolves at the door, a pack of coyotes watched us from across the meadow. Would they come close to the barn? Rosie was unable to defend herself in this weakened state. Was she safe?

Each day, as we arrived at the barn, I started making excuses to keep the girls in the car for a few minutes while I checked on Rosie's condition. I wanted to protect them from the worst. Rosie would glance my way from her stall floor, but when she would see my daughter Jackie come around the corner of the barn, she would struggle to her feet and give a soft nicker. The sparkle would return to Rosie's eyes and I knew this little pony had a chance. But that entire summer we had no idea what each morning would bring.

We had to rebandage her feet every few days with layers of pads and multiple layers of wrap. We worked quickly because it was so painful for her to bear the extra weight on the resting foot while we lifted the one being bandaged. We became quite proficient with the routine. We were Rosie's pit crew.

"Jackie, will you please crush Rosie's pills and mix them with molasses for her before we go?" I asked one morning.

"I already gave them to her," said Jackie. "She eats them out of my hand if I feed them to her one at a time."

The pills were enormous and obviously tasted terrible to Rosie. Most horse owners had to find increasingly clever ways to disguise the taste, and here was Rosie eating them whole when they were offered by Jackie. Because they were offered by Jackie. No one, including Dr. Pickering, could believe how much trust this little pony held in my little girl.

It took more than a year, marred by setbacks, but eventually Rosie's entire front hooves regrew. It took a dedicated veterinarian and a talented farrier and a whole lot of love to get Rosie back on her feet again. And it took a little girl who never stopped believing in her and never stopped encouraging her. It took Jackie.

Jackie showed Rosie at 4-H that spring. Eventually, when Chelsea grew to Jackie's size, Rosie carried her, too, on a couple of Pony Club ratings, which included jumping. Now, Rosie works at our horse camps for five weeks during the summer, taking young horse lovers on some of their first equestrian adventures. Her feet still require special shoes and more frequent shoeing and we pay extra attention to her diet.

Both Rosie and Jackie have reached the age of seventeen together. I have no doubt that the reason Rosie is with us today is because of the total love and devotion supplied by a girl named Jackie who simply wouldn't give up on the incredible heart and spirit she knew existed in her little pony. It was a spirit that Jackie could somehow see in Rosie's eyes.

My youngest daughter Chelsea—who is now riding Rosie and is responsible for her care as her older sister Jackie gets ready for college—put it best when she said, "What I learned from this experience is quite simple—that animals know when you love them."

Rosie is alive today because my daughter believed in her and because she believed in my daughter. As any mother, I always want to see things in my daughters that fill me with pride and wonder. I still remember the get-well posters my girls made for Rosie and realize that they had hope when mine was failing. They showed compassion and helped ease Rosie's suffering. And they learned how trust can be a powerful medicine as Rosie's soft lips took the bitter pills from my daughter's hands and ate them.

What my daughters did for Rosie was to give her back her life. What Rosie did for my daughters was teach them powerful lessons of trust and compassion that will shine on everyone around them for the rest of their lives. I never anticipated when I brought this little white pony into our lives what an incredible gift my family was receiving.

Marla Oldenburg with Bill Goss

Lessons from Lou

A single tear rolled down Lou's face as I talked to her about that boy. Maybe I shouldn't have been surprised by her show of emotion, but Lou was my Quarter Horse mare, and that boy was King, her handsome five-week-old colt.

My husband had bought Lou, a retired racehorse, to occupy my time and mind while I waited out medical disability with a minor heart condition. Lou was four and a half months pregnant, and we both felt stymied by inactivity. Still, we needed to take it easy for a while, and although I couldn't ride, I showered her with love.

Lou had an impressive pedigree, and even with a sway-back pulled low by her ever-growing belly, she was regal. I knew her foal would be spectacular.

We drifted through the days, settling into a comfortable routine while my children were in school. I brushed Lou and scratched her growing belly while I talked and sang to her and cooed to her baby. It seemed to soothe Lou when I sang. I rubbed her head, lightly touching my nose to hers and breathing deeply, willing my spirit and soul into her.

A few weeks before Lou's delivery date, I visited with her former owner. He warned that she might be moody and shield her baby from me. I didn't believe him. He knew Lou as a racehorse. I knew her as a cherished friend. Over the next few days, I watched and waited, wanting to be at her side when she gave birth. Our veterinarian, who had been coming monthly, then weekly, now came almost daily.

Lou waited until we were gone one evening to have her baby. When we drove in, the car's headlights caught the blaze on her face. She seemed to be calling to me, "Come see what I did!"

Then I saw him. A tiny light sorrel colt with a star and a strip on his face and four tiny white stockings on his legs. He was lying on the other side of Lou, peeking out from under her belly. It was love at first sight. I felt as if he were my baby. I walked to the gate, just talking to Lou for a few minutes. Then I inched in and over to her side. She watched me, but she didn't make any menacing moves. Still respecting Lou's maternal privileges, I kept my distance from her baby, talking as I would to any newborn. He recognized my voice and fought his way up onto those little wobbly legs, walking around to nuzzle me as Lou watched.

We bonded closely, Lou, King and I. We were three imperfect creatures sharing one perfect love—an innocent, childlike love that was complete and unconditional. As the days wore on, it became obvious that something was wrong. King's umbilical cord wasn't sealing off as it should and he didn't have the energy to nurse. Although he shadowed his mother, every movement took great effort.

I talked with our veterinarian, who was making frequent visits to check on King. He tried to be encouraging, but the truth was, the chances for recovery weren't good. King had navel ill, a serious blood infection that can occur in newborn animals when bacteria enter the body through the umbilical cord. It typically results in rapid debilitation and usually death.

When King was five weeks old, it was obvious his pain was getting worse. His suffering was comparable to that of a person stricken with severe rheumatoid arthritis. Although the veterinarian gave him cortisone injections to lessen the pain, they never helped for long. The kind practitioner offered me time to think, but there really wasn't anything to think about. I shared King's pain and loved him too much to allow him to suffer. I had kept him alive, hoping, but any longer would be cruel.

On a beautiful, sunny spring morning, with the Houston air still crisp and the world full of new beginnings, I decided on an ending.

First, I talked with Lou. We were both mothers, and my heart ached for her suffering. They say nothing hurts as much as losing a child, and I felt we were both losing one. Although I didn't know how much she could comprehend, I knew Lou was distressed. Her anxious glances in King's direction told me she understood too much to ignore.

I walked over to her hay-strewn stall while the veterinarian talked softly to King. Lou's intelligent eyes examined my tear-stained face as I explained that King was very sick and the doctor was going to take good care of him. I told her we would miss him, she and I. Together, we watched the veterinarian administer the injection that would bring King peace.

I rubbed Lou's velvety muzzle, and she softly snorted. Then I saw the tear roll down her face. We put our heads together and stayed that way for a long while.

When King was finally out of pain, his spirit set free, my husband and I took his body to the back of our pasture to his freshly dug grave, which was under a tree showing the new growth of the season. Lou stood beside me, as still as stone. She watched silent and sad as we gently lowered her baby into the ground.

I stood by the small mound, quietly sobbing. Then the ground around me began to shake with the rhythmic pounding of hooves. Lou circled the pasture, beating the turf hard and solid. She threw her head back, whinnying in the air. Wondering whether she had gone mad, my husband questioned what she was doing.

Through streaming tears, I answered. "She's grieving."

However, I wonder if maybe a little sorrel colt, with a star and a strip and four white stockings, his mane blowing in the evening breeze, ran beside his mama. And if, just maybe, Lou felt King's free gentle spirit racing beside her in the wind.

Edwina Lewis

Bit by the Bug Thanks to Finger Paint

It was a mildly toasty fall afternoon when my mom and I pulled up to my little sister's day-care center to pick her up, just as we did every day. The sized-down schoolhouse sat at the front of a huge farm edged with a crisp white fence. As the tires crunched the gravel driveway, I leaned my head against the car window, closed my eyes and invited the warm rays of sun to dance on my face. The next few moments were so predictable that I knew there would be no reason to open my eyes. The car would stop with a little squeak. My sister would skip from the front door of the day-care building to the car, waving some sort of macaroni art-work and humming an annoying cartoon theme that would repeat like a broken record in my head until I went to sleep. The car door would open, allowing the chatter of chirping birds to flood the hushed interior. I'd soon hear a shuffle as my sister scampered up to her seat. The door would slam and we'd drive away, but only after my mom honked the horn.

This day would be different.

"Oh my goodness," I heard my mom whisper. I opened my eyes and followed her gaze to the front door of the day-care building. A little girl in a yellow dress with disheveled blonde hair and streaks of paint blazing across her face like an extremely colorful army commando scampered up to the car holding her teacher's hand. As the pair came closer, I recognized the mess in a dress as my little sister in disguise.

"Mom, come see. It was finger-painting day!" my sister shrieked with excitement.

"You have quite the finger-painting artist here," affirmed her teacher. "The masterpieces are still a little wet, so we're not letting them go home today, but they are on display."

Powerless against the coercive tactics of the finger-painting artiste extraordinaire, my mom parked the car and followed my bouncing sibling into the gallery. Given this opportunity to scan the grounds of the farm as I leaned against the car, I realized what a great exploration site this would be. The thick, gnarled trees were practically calling my name, inviting me to climb up their branches. I figured my mom would be a while, judging by my sister's exuberance, so I ventured out beyond the day care's boundaries.

Fluttering around the farm like a butterfly riding invisible currents of wind, I ended up in front of a solid wooden gate. On the other side, a vast expanse of sweet-smelling grass and dozens of horses invited me closer. Back at home, I would sometimes pet the neighbor's horses when they hung their heads over the fence to peek in on our backyard family picnics and talent shows. That was the extent of my interaction with these hooved beauties.

I stifled my initial impulse to slip under the fence and boldly cavort with these unfamiliar animals. Instead, I carefully climbed up the fence and sat along the top of the gate. Although I tried to move stealthily, the horses noticed my characteristic lack of grace and subtlety. Some of them popped their heads up from grazing and shot suspicious stares my way. They were eager to continue stuffing their already swollen bellies, so I was able to return to my curious observations undisturbed.

It didn't take long for a chestnut mare with a gray streak in her tail to waddle over (she was quite fat) and welcome me. Not sure how to respond to her surprisingly friendly nuzzles, I jumped to my feet in case I had to run. Then I reached over the fence and allowed my fingers to brush her nose. She tickled my hand with her whiskers. A sudden wave of courage swept through me as I pulled myself back up onto the fence. The mare took a few steps forward, guiding my hands to her long, muscular neck. She welcomed my pats and scratches and, pretty soon, we were engaged in a silent conversation.

After a few minutes of chatting with her, my inhibitions disappeared and I began to wonder what it would be like to gently grab my new friend's mane, slip onto her back and cruise around the pasture.

Looking back on this experience, I don't recall one ounce of doubt or hesitancy. I like to think that the bond formed quickly and with it came unfamiliar confidence and new-found ability.

Before I knew it, my actions zoomed past my thoughts and I slid my right leg over the mare's back, gently rustling her dusty, red coat. The added weight didn't phase the mighty steed. She just stood there, waiting for me to do something.

I think I sat there for about two minutes before my mom came storming out of the day-care building, hands flailing the air. With a hushed but firm voice she tried not to startle my mount while emphatically demanding that I get back on the ground. I wanted to do what she asked, but I wasn't sure how to get down. Before I knew it, a man named Jack, who owned the farm, strolled up to the pasture gate, calming my mother along the way.

"Princess will take care of her," he assured us both. "She's been around the block a time or two."

His weathered hands helped me down, and before I could extend my arm to give Princess's neck a grateful pat, my mom had me by the collar.

The moments that followed went just as you'd suspect. Through the well-deserved verbal lashing (which continued through the drive home and into the night), I peeked over my mom's shoulder and saw Princess standing in the place where I'd left her. She didn't even blink at all of the commotion.

As my mom dragged me back to the car, my teary-eyed sister following behind, I wish I could say I carefully listened to every word like a dutiful daughter, but I'd be lying.

On this day, the car door slammed and we drove away without my mom honking the horn. Although she had no idea how the past fifteen minutes eventually would shape our lives (and our pocketbooks), she noticed something different about me as I stared out the window, desperately trying to catch one last glimpse of my new friend. If she would have stopped screaming, I probably could have told her about the bug that bit me.

All horse lovers know the bug. It doesn't buzz or chirp or hop around. It doesn't stare back at you with big bulging eyes. It lands on your heart, does its job and disappears without a trace. You're not left with a painful sting, itch or welt, just an inexplicable passion that shapes your thoughts, your habits and your dreams. The horse bug was now a part of my fabric.

As my sister sobbed in the backseat, I silently thanked her for the finger-painting masterpieces that weren't dry enough to take home that day. And so, the journey began.

Tiernan McKay

His Special Gifts

During the summer of 1998, my eleven-year-old daughter Liz moved up from a pony to her first horse, and she named him Koda. As is the case with many little girls and their first horses, Liz and Koda immediately bonded and became inseparable.

That fall, after a ride with a friend, Liz did not get the gate latched all the way and the following morning she found that Koda had gotten into the grain. He didn't show any signs of developing founder—an internal deformity of the hoof that is the end result of a complex series of events triggered by overeating. But he had eaten a great deal, so we thought it best to call the veterinarian and take him in to be checked over. Koda was sent home with instructions to keep him moving. If he didn't founder by the weekend, he would be all right.

The weekend came and we thought we were home free. Think again. Sunday morning, Koda was stiff and sore and could not get around. He had foundered. The veterinarian was called, and this time we had medicine to administer, and orders to walk him every two hours and give him shots every four hours.

Liz was devastated. Her horse was dangerously ill and it was because of something careless she had done. She slept with Koda while we took turns on the couch, getting up every two hours. When it rained, she walked him inside the barn. She did everything in her little-girl powers to encourage him to eat. But he steadily got worse.

Neither Liz nor this little horse would give up. He responded only to her. Only she could get him to lift his head or stand. He would nicker for her when she was not there. I would look out the window to see him lying in the yard with his head in her lap and her tears falling on his face. I prayed to God to please not separate these two.

After two weeks and no sign of improvement, our veterinarian suggested that we put Koda down. My daughter was hysterical and I asked him if there was anything else we could do. He told us about a Mennonite horseshoer by the name of Mr. Martin, who lived three hours away and who was known to have had some success saving foundered horses.

After talking it over with Liz's grandpa, we called Mr. Martin and described the devotion of this little girl to her horse, and how hard both were trying. We explained that he was our last hope for pulling Koda through. Without hesitating, Mr. Martin simply said, "Bring him down and let me take a look at him."

The next day, my daughter met her hero. When we arrived at Mr. Martin's, Koda wasn't able to stand in the trailer. The kind horseshoer looked Koda over carefully and in words that were music to our ears, said that he thought he could save this horse. He explained to Liz that she had to be willing to work hard because things were going to get worse before they got better. Liz told him that she would do whatever it would take and, given the sacrifices she already had made, I had no doubt that she would.

With Liz's commitment made, Mr. Martin and his sons welded metal plates onto the bottom of the horseshoes. They applied a homemade concoction to Koda's hooves, then packed them with cotton and nailed on the shoes. Koda was hauled to Mr. Martin's every two weeks for his hooves to be trimmed and the procedure to be repeated. This biweekly regimen went on for three months, then it became every four weeks, then every six weeks for an entire year.

Liz followed every instruction that Mr. Martin gave her, and Koda did everything that Liz wanted him to. With time and lots of love, Koda healed completely and you would never know that he had foundered. Mr. Martin now admits that he wasn't sure Koda was going to make it. What he did know without a doubt, was that Koda would give it his best to stay with his girl.

I think God has a special place in his heart for a mother's prayers and little girls and their horses. He's given men like Mr. Martin extraordinary knowledge and empathy to do good work, and he's blessed us with the power of love. Because of his special gifts, Liz and Koda are inseparable to this day.

Debbie Hollandsworth

Horse at Harvard

Legally Blonde's Elle Woods had her Chihuahua called Bruiser. I have a young Hanoverian gelding named Donovan. So when Harvard Law School accepted me into its fall 2002 entering class, I never questioned whether Donovan would go with me.

As a college student at the small-town, agricultural University of California at Davis, I always had a horse with me, always rode every day, always competed during the school year. Except, that is, for my first quarter, which, not coincidentally, was the least-happy term of an otherwise enjoyable undergraduate career. So I was no stranger to juggling competitions with term papers, veterinary emergencies with final exams and training with daily reading. *I had always done this*, I thought, *what could be so different?*

Turns out, a lot of people thought it would be different. When I told friends and acquaintances, even other students I rode with at Davis, that I planned to take my horse with me to law school, their reaction was invariably, "You're crazy!" "It won't last!" "You can't possibly ride every day while in law school, and especially not at Harvard!" The other law students at Harvard, many of them from big cities, were equally disbelieving. "A horse," they would say in surprise, "How cool! Do you have time to see him most weekends?"

"No," I'd say, "I'm at the barn six days a week!" Then I'd try very hard not to leave a trail of mud from my paddock boots in the dorm hallways and I always removed the horsehair from the washing machines after laundering saddle pads and polo wraps.

But as the semester progressed, I began wondering if everyone was right. Life was so busy! The owner of the barn said she was taking bets on when I was going to collapse. Was I really crazy to try to do this? Then I began to realize that it didn't matter. My friends at the law school would get burned out from the daily pressure of endless reading and paper writing. And I would too. I'd despair that there was no way I could ever do all this work and come out alive. Then I'd go to the barn. Donovan would be there, waiting for me with a look that seemed to say, "What took you so long? I've missed you! Do you have any sugar cubes for me?" I'd groom him, and as I curried his shiny black coat, law school would seem farther and farther away. Then I'd lead him to the mounting block and law school would vanish from my thoughts altogether.

For an hour each day, Donovan and I are the only ones in the world. We ride a supple shoulder-in, a floating medium trot, find that perfect distance to a square oxer or hack through the woods. *Promissory estoppel, res ipsa loquitur, in rem jurisdiction*—who's worried about any of that? All I know is that I am calm, focused and at peace. I am whole.

And each day, upon return to my dorm in Cambridge, the work I had left to do always seems far less daunting, much more doable, even more engaging. I come home every day with renewed serenity and zest for my studies that many law students around me sadly never find.

All during that first semester, widely thought to be the most difficult of three years of law school, I continued to see Donovan nearly every day of the week. His training continued to progress. Twice we met our Los Angeles-based trainer six hours away in New Jersey for a weekend of concentrated instruction. I even drove Donovan by myself, twelve hours each way, to Virginia to compete in a year-end championship. And we finished reserve champion, a mere fraction of a percentage away from the champion. Much to everyone's surprise, I did all this while keeping up with my daily reading, finishing all my assignments on time, going to class religiously and giving respectable answers when called on by professors using the dreaded Socratic method.

Now that I'm finished with the first semester, I realize that I didn't make it through my first term at Harvard Law *in spite of* having a horse. I made it through *because of* having a horse. Unlike my peers, I have a daily opportunity to escape the stress of school and city life. I have something that relaxes and rejuvenates me and makes me excited to get out of bed in the morning. For this, I realize I am very fortunate. Thank you, Donovan. Thank you for helping me thrive at Harvard Law School.

Jennifer Chong

Tall in Faith

At four pounds, five ounces, umbilical cord wrapped around her neck and delivered five and a half weeks early, Ashley seemed to have more than three strikes against her. Diagnosed with Turner's syndrome and Ollier's disease at age three, this happy-go-lucky child showed little evidence of having endured the trying time of diagnosis and then daily growth-hormone injections and medication to keep her thyroid under control. Her prognosis was good, and although Turner's syndrome could be cruel, Ashley was spared, with only short stature and thyroid disease.

Life seemed to be relatively normal for Ashley until fifth grade, the age where all youngsters seem to hit a growth spurt. Ashley was left behind. She not only felt small in stature, but with all of the kids teasing her, she began to feel small in worth. Ashley was starting to withdraw. As her mother, I was worried. Would she snap out of this funk or would it follow her forever? I had to find a way for her to find herself and be happy with herself.

We had always had horses. Before Ashley and her younger sister Casey were born, my husband and I raised Quarter Horses. After our divorce, I managed to hang on to four precious equine family members. Even though they were the kindest of animals, they were just too big for the girls. I found a riding instructor and the girls began taking riding lessons. This seemed to be a positive experience for Ashley. It didn't matter to these animals that she was smaller than other children. In fact, the horses kind of liked it that way.

Ashley had discovered her passion, but something was still missing. While around the horses, she was bright and happy, but back at school she would retreat into her quiet little world. Ashley didn't have any friends and her grades were barely passing. Then I had a crazy idea. Maybe a pony of her own would give Ashley that friend she so desperately needed.

The search began. On my income as a single parent with a child with more than her share of medical bills, I knew we could not afford a show-ring hunter pony. So we decided to look for a companion that would be honest and form a bond with this child who so needed a friend. Days turned into weeks, weeks into months and we just couldn't seem to find that one special horse. I prayed every day, "Lord, I know you know best. If you see that it is the best thing for Ashley, please help us find her a pony to love, one who will love her in return. And God, she sure would like a white one if you could arrange it." I figured if I was going to ask, I might as well go all the way.

We had almost given up hope. I was now ready to buy the first gentle pony that came along because Ashley was losing faith. She wasn't even excited anymore. We were scheduled to go see a pony one afternoon after work when a friend of mine peeked into my office to tell me about a pony that a friend of his was selling. This friend, Mrs. Jones, had brood mares coming in for foaling and she didn't have room for the pony anymore. The pony had been a brood mare, but she didn't particularly like having babies, so she would have to go. I called Mrs. Jones that very minute and set up a time to see her that afternoon. Mrs. Jones asked me several questions over the phone, wanting to make sure that the pony and her rider would be a good match. After I told her about Ashley, she said, "Lucy is definitely the one." She also was within our budget. Then I inquired about the pony's coat color holding my breath. Mrs. Jones replied, "She is considered a gray, but she is actually all white." I tried not to get my hopes up too high because I didn't want Ashley to suffer yet another disappointment.

When we arrived at Mrs. Jones' farm that afternoon, there stood Lucy in all her middle-of-March glory. She was overweight and hadn't yet started to shed her long winter coat. She also looked as if she'd played in a mud puddle. Even so, I saw potential in the Welsh pony. My daughter did not.

"Let's just look," I pleaded. "We're already here." Trying to be a sport and humor her mother who was trying so hard, Ashley reluctantly got out of the car.

The experienced horsewoman that she was, Mrs. Jones recognized that Ashley could not see Lucy past the mud. "Why don't you go catch her and groom her then you can saddle her up and try her out," Mrs. Jones said, trying to encourage the less-than-enthusiastic little girl. That was enough to do it. If this horsewoman trusted her to be able to handle this task, Ashley would show her that she could do it.

Lucy was a trouper and on her best behavior. Did this pony know something that we had not yet realized? Ashley rode the pony mare in a small arena, where she proved to be a solid, if uninspiring, mover. Ashley was still not excited. "Why don't you take her home and try her for a week?" Mrs. Jones asked. "I think Ashley will like her after she rides her a few times." We scheduled a time to pick up Lucy the following evening.

The next evening when I came home for work, I asked Ashley if she was excited. "I guess," came the reply. Had Ashley given up? "Ashley, will you please trust me on this? I just have a feeling that our prayers have been answered." Again, Ashley seemed to humor me, but she also appeared unable to find the courage to get her hopes up. You see, Ashley really had been wishing for an expensive little show pony that would win blue ribbons—a horse we just couldn't afford.

We brought Lucy home for the trial period and after

Ashley rode her, hope turned into love. We made the purchase and our journey began. Spring finally arrived and we discovered there really was a white pony under all of that dirt and hair. Lucy was put on a diet to get her womanly figure back and she and Ashley began their partnership.

We took Lucy and Ashley to their first show—a backyard affair that we thought would be a good testing ground for them both. Ashley had been taking lessons for about a year, and we had found out that Lucy, in her prime, had shown on the "A" circuit. Lucy now had become the instructor because Ashley's skills had to be polished to ride such an experienced pony.

I held my breath during the first class. I was hoping that this pony would take care of my precious cargo. I must say, during the lineup when I was finally able to breathe, I was quite floored when they announced the first-place winner. This was Ashley's first first-place ribbon. The look on her face was worth all the fortunes in the world. After congratulations were extended, I excused myself for a few minutes to go around to the back of the trailer and let my tears of joy finally fall. I also whispered a thankful prayer.

Lucy has been in our lives for more than two years now. The bond and love between Lucy and Ashley is incredible. They have won many ribbons together and won the champion title in their division at the 4-H state fair this year. Ashley has found a sport where being tall doesn't matter and it has filtered over to other areas in her life. Her grades have gone up to honor roll. She is the vice president of her 4-H club. She was voted Student Council class president, has made the high school cheerleading squad, and we just found out yesterday that she has been nominated for the homecoming court.

Once upon a time, it was hard to get this child to go to school, and now she is talking about which college she will attend. One thing hasn't changed, though—Lucy is still her best friend.

Mitzi Santana

"I suppose it wouldn't be a bad job if
they didn't run those steel rods through you."

Carousel Horse. *Reprinted by permission of Steve Sommer and Francis Brummer.* ©2002
Steve Sommer and Francis Brummer.

6

AND . . . THEY'RE OFF!

In the darkest days of depression and war,
a horse named Seabiscuit elevated
our country's spirit and embodied
the qualities we cherish in our horses;
heart, drive, loyalty, love and playfulness.

We respectfully dedicate this chapter
to the memory of

SEABISCUIT
May 23, 1934–May 17, 1947

A true champion that still inspires us today.

© CORBIS BETTMANN—SEABISCUIT LEADS WAR ADMIRAL BY TWO LENGTHS

An Unlikely Trio of Hope

Horse sense is the thing a horse has which keeps it from betting on people.

W.C. Fields

"Floss, tell me the Biscuit story again, please," I pleaded. To the day she died, none of her grandchildren called my wispy Irish grandmother "nana" or "grandma." She was Floss, short for Florence, to all of us—same as she was to everyone else.

Floss settled back in her chair and her eyes saw something far beyond our tiny living room in Philadelphia. I sat at her feet, ready to travel back in time with her, to relive the magic of her memories.

In the early 1900s, making a place in a new world meant marriage and a family for every beautiful Irish-Catholic girl. Floss was no exception. As the Great Depression gripped our country, Floss struggled, as many did, with raising a large family. Her struggle bore an atypical twist—her husband had left her for another woman.

In those days, few options existed for an abandoned woman raising six children on her own. Fortunately, some of her neighbors suggested an unusual opportunity and before long Floss became a part-time bookie. Her work put food on the table and kept her brood in good graces with people she knew would protect her and her family.

Every time she shared a story from her past, I felt the bittersweet emotion that filled her soul. I knew the empathy she felt for the underdog, empathy engendered from her own experiences. Empathy acquired from doing what had to be done to get by.

I reached up for her hand and squeezed it as much in anticipation of the good story as to let her know I was there. She smiled, squeezing back, then began.

"Lass, the Biscuit was the ugliest horse you'd ever laid a pair of eyes upon. His first race was down in Florida at Hialeah but he didn't break his maiden for another sixteen starts, and almost fifty before he won a race of any consequence."

"First time I heard the name Seabiscuit, some fool wanted a deuce to win in an allowance race at Rockingham. I could tell this fella didn't have that kind of money to be wagering, but I gladly took the bet, thinking of my vig. As I was paying off the win the next day, I remember thinking to myself, *I want to get a look at this Seabiscuit.*" Her eyes twinkled at the memory.

"'Twasn't a problem getting into the barns and paddocks in those days. When Seabiscuit was on the card, I made the races and started paying attention to the Biscuit and his handlers. Pretty soon, I had lots of company."

"The trainer was a ghost of a man—looked like smoke, like death warmed over. That horse was a handful most of the time, and a lazy son of a gun the rest." Shaking her head softly, Floss gave a short chuckle. "The trainer, Smith, he had a gift. You could see that horse and the ghost talking to each other without words. Like both of them knew they were out of second chances and this was the end of the line."

"They had this handsome jockey, a redhead named Cougar, who used to pick up boxing matches when he couldn't find a mount. He was tough as nails and had desperation in his eyes. I knew that look—saw it a lot in those days."

Floss paused, and I knew without her having to say so that the desperation she had seen in the eyes of many during those days had just as often been in her own. She continued, "Turns out Cougar was an Irish who had ended up in Canada. His real name was Johnny Pollard and I don't know whether I was more taken by the horse or the jockey. Both of them had the mischief in their eyes," she chuckled softly again.

"When Pollard was up, the Biscuit settled. Pollard knew the Biscuit's quirks and let him have his rein. He ran like a duck and liked to mess with the other horses—horses do that you know, play with each other. The Biscuit, he'd lay back and let them come right up, side-to-side, get them feeling like the match was theirs, then he'd look them in the eye and take off like a bullet." Floss laughed out loud at that.

"It was something to see, those three. 'Course most folks just saw Cougar and the Biscuit. Only us that liked the ponies paid any attention to Smith."

"Folks who didn't know anything about horses were betting money on the side they didn't have. Naturally, most of the time I was happy taking book on the Biscuit. That horse was a blessing on four feet. Don't know what we would have done if he hadn't come along. Folks loved betting when they were pulling for the underdog. Being the underdog was something they understood."

I nodded.

"Seabiscuit wasn't a sure thing, ran hot and cold for a long time until he came into his own. I think he got bored and liked to stir up the pot now and then. Then that darn Smith would scratch him from big races when folks had traveled hundreds of miles just to see him run."

"Those three—they were fixed on winning and they paid some high prices for that desire, but lassie, they put on a show. They saved a lot of souls in those years. I know some folks believe those souls were damned from doing the jig with the devil and betting good money they didn't have, but that horse gave people something to look forward to, something they could dream about. Never saw so many people without hope get so excited about a horse."

Floss's eyes cleared and she focused on the sights and sounds outside the little living room in Philly.

"Yeah, I fell in love with that horse. Never been another like him before or since, and you know, girl, I've been watching the ponies all my life."

"I know, Floss," I whispered.

"Not another like him," she said again. "Nary a one kept me dreaming or filled me with hope like that, that's for sure."

Theresa Peluso

[AUTHOR'S NOTE: *In November 1938, 40 million people listened to the radio broadcast of Seabiscuit's victory in a much-anticipated matched race with War Admiral. The Biscuit set a track record at Pimlico for the mile and three-sixteenths, winning by four lengths in just a minute fifty-six. Two years later he captured the elusive win at the Santa Anita Handicap and retired to Charles Howard's Ridgewood Ranch where he passed away peacefully in 1947 at the age of fourteen.*]

Ride the Yule Tide

When your ship comes in, it just might be a horse.

Jan Jasion Cross

It was some kind of cosmic thing that took me there. I certainly did not go for the money or the atmosphere. Pocono Downs in late November was, in fact, quite depressing—the temperatures averaged about twenty-five degrees by post time for the first race each evening. Plus, there was a nice, comfortable job waiting for me in Florida for the winter months. A leading New York trainer had offered me a position as an assistant trainer and exercise girl. It was a job I had prayed for. I finally had fallen on my head enough times to realize that my waning career as a jockey was becoming more dangerous than lucrative.

I would have gone straight to Florida and strolled the sunny blessed beaches for a few weeks while I waited for the New York outfit if I hadn't gotten sidetracked by two of my best friends. Russ and Jackie were a hardworking young couple, and I had won a few races on their cheaper horses at a Philadelphia track. They were heading to Florida, too. But first they were going to ship part of their stable to Pocono

Downs, in Wilkes-Barre, Pennsylvania, to win some races and lose some of their cheap claimers—horses who compete in races in which all entries are up for sale at a specified price. Somehow, they convinced me that I should accompany them. We were staying for only a few weeks, they told me, and we would win lots of races. I packed halfheartedly.

We shipped in one afternoon the week before Thanksgiving. The roads were becoming slick from the falling sleet. Our little caravan slid through the stable gate and down a hill that bottomed out at our assigned barn. My little car had no snow tires. If it had, I probably would have made a quick U-turn and hightailed it south, but there was no way my car was going to make it back up that hill. We unloaded the horses from the van and headed for the little apartment that we would share for three weeks, sipping hot chocolate laced with whiskey and dreaming of the big bets we would cash.

I had made a pact with myself not to ride for any trainer but Russ at Pocono Downs. There was that job waiting for me in Florida and I did not want to risk getting on horses I did not know for trainers I did not know. But pacts are made to be broken.

Stabled next to Russ and Jackie's string at barn "T" was an odd sort of outfit. The Boyd racing stable had traveled to Pocono Downs from a little track out West. A few days after our own arrival, their battered old Ford pickup had chugged in, toting a rusty two-horse trailer. The entire stable consisted of two aged geldings. The two old warhorses received plenty of attention, because the trainer, Sally, was accompanied by her husband, elderly father and young son. The little boy, Scott, was a towheaded, courteous and attentive eleven-year-old. I asked how it was that he got to skip school and live at the racetrack with his folks. Scott told me that just as soon as the family could get some money together, they would be going home for Christmas. Then he would return to school. Home, Scott told me, was in Arkansas.

Sensing that the Boyd stable could not afford an exercise

rider, I volunteered to gallop their two horses for them. Sally readily accepted my offer. One horse, Bart, galloped an easy mile every morning, but the other horse, a black gelding named Coaly, was a wee bit off in the left ankle and usually was ponied alongside Russ's stable pony for his daily exercise.

Within hours of arriving at the track, little Scott asked Russ and Jackie if he could work for them for wages. I am sure that Russ had no clue as to what duties Scott would perform, but he did not hesitate to put the little boy on his payroll. From then on, Scott hustled about the barn all morning, cheerfully holding horses for baths, bedding stalls, raking the shed row and helping me clean tack. Russ paid his little right-hand man his wages daily. Scott would thank him politely and hurry off to join his folks down the shed row. The entire clan would then stroll over to the track kitchen for breakfast. I don't think they ever left the race-track grounds.

Three weeks went by, and my calendar was lined with Xs that ended with the date of my departure for Florida. By December 15, Russ had run and lost the last horse he wanted to part with. He was making shipping arrangements, and I was planning to get my gear out of the jocks' room and settle up with my valet Paul. Our neighbors down the shed row had not yet raced Coaly or Bart.

On December 16, I went to the jocks' room after morning workouts to retrieve my belongings. But when I requested my tack, Paul gave me a look of consternation. "You can't leave," he said. "You have a mount tonight in the ninth race." He pulled a folded list of the day's entries from his back pocket and passed it to me. He was right. I was named on Coal Bay in the ninth. I asked Paul if he had seen the form on Coaly. "Uh-huh. If this horse wins tonight, there are snow-men in hell," he replied. "Gonna take off?"

I nearly let the word "yes" slip through my badly chapped lips when I caught sight of something out of the corner of my eye. It was little Scott. The racetrack cherub had come dashing out of the racing secretary's office with the entries list in his hand. He was jumping up and down like a young antelope as he raced back to the barn area. "No," I said. "I guess I'm riding tonight."

That evening before dinner, I borrowed Russ's *Daily Racing Form* to study Coal Bay's past performances. He had not seen a winner's circle since he was seven, and he would be nine years old in a few weeks. The chart writer had summed up Coaly's last three efforts as "dull," "outdistanced" and "tired early." These performances had been in cheap claiming races. Tonight, Coaly was entered in an allowance race, a higher level of competition.

At 6:30 I went to the jocks' room to await my last ride at Pocono Downs. God, was it cold out! As I donned my riding garb, I thought to myself that riding a 60 to 1 shot on a night of freezing temperatures was not a terrific way to end one's race-riding career. Such was fate. When the call went round the jocks' room for the ninth race weigh-in, my valet informed me that it was ten degrees outside. I put on an extra-heavy turtleneck shirt after weigh-in and stuck my gloves and boots into the sauna for a last minute toasting before venturing out.

In the paddock, my teeth chattered as Sally told me that Coaly was a cold-weather horse. The old gelding did look good. His coat was thick and shiny. His large hazel eyes were bright with anticipation. I glanced over at our competition. One horse stood out: the betting favorite, Fast Exit, had just shipped in from New Jersey, but I knew him well. I had ridden Fast Exit when he won his first race a couple of years before at a Jersey Shore track. With that race, I lost my "bug," the weight allowance given to apprentice riders until they chalk up a certain number of victories, and the trainer I was riding for promptly fired me. Another memorable day in my career. The same trainer still saddled Fast Exit, and I waved stiffly at him as he met my stare. Suddenly, Coaly and I had a mission. We had to beat Fast Exit for old times' sake.

When the gates opened, Coaly shot out like a bolt of black

lightning. We easily took the lead, with Fast Exit alongside. My old Coaly was running like a fine-tuned sports car. In fact, Fast Exit seemed to be having trouble keeping up. I signaled to Coaly, and we easily left the favorite in the dust. From the quarter pole to the wire, we raced along, just Coal Bay and me. At the eighth pole, I started grinning and posing. To the wire we coasted, four lengths ahead of the favorite.

Coaly pulled up kindly and galloped back to the winner's circle like a gentleman. He was my hero, and I patted his glistening neck tenderly as we posed for the picture. Sally, her husband, father and little Scott were surprisingly calm during the brief victory ceremony. "We knew he could do it!" Scott declared. I thanked them all for a most memorable ride.

The next morning, I went to the stables at eight. I was packed and ready to head to Florida. But before I hit the highway, I needed to see my new friends one last time. I headed over to the two stalls where Coal Bay and his stable-mate had been bedded. The stalls were empty. I was quite upset to find the Boyd stable gone without notice. Russ walked down the shed row and stood by my side as I stared misty-eyed at Coal Bay's empty stall. "They were already gone when I got here this morning. They must have loaded up in the middle of the night," he said. "I think something was left for you on their tack-room door."

I walked slowly to the end of the shed and pulled the piece of white construction paper from the door. It was a crayon drawing depicting a huge black horse in a winner's circle; his jockey had been given a large red nose like that of Rudolph the Red-Nosed Reindeer. A family of four was grouped at the horse's head.

I smiled as I read the neatly hand-printed caption at the bottom of the picture: "COAL BAY—WINNER—WE ARE GOING HOME FOR CHRISTMAS," and, in smaller letters, "Thanks, Jan. We love you, [signed] Scott." Only then did I realize why I had come to Pocono Downs.

Jan Jaison Cross

Racehorse Poor

"Why is he eating his mama's manure?" I asked my daddy as we stood looking through the fence at our new weanling. "That means he's a good one," he replied in his all-knowing tone. That's all I needed to hear because my daddy knew everything there was to know about a horse. While we stood in the barn that morning, Daddy wrote the check for what would be our first racehorse. "I'll have a winning racehorse if I have to sell everything we have," I remember him saying. That didn't seem like such a sacrifice in my seven-year-old mind. After all, horses were the only thing that Daddy and I considered sacred.

We sat around the dinner table that evening trying to create a name that would sound good being bellowed from a track announcer. It was a family ritual. With each new horse we purchased, Mama would create a masterpiece for the palate and as we ate, everyone jotted down on bits of paper what the newest little one should be named. Our new weanling's grandfather was Misty Flite, so we tried every combination using Flite and finally came up with something we all agreed would sound exciting as it echoed around the track. And so it was. The little sorrel colt with no particularly outstanding features was named Starflite.

As the brisk spring turned to summer, Starflite grew while

he stood lazing in the warm sun. We moved him to my grandfather's dairy farm, where we had created a makeshift horse facility. Starflite lived next to the Holsteins and shared a fence row with my prized pony Patty. The only growth he seemed to experience that summer was in the region of his head and belly. "He sure isn't much to look at," Daddy would say as he meandered out to get him for another lesson in ground work. It was during those lessons that Daddy was exposed to the restive side of Starflite. Watching from a perch on the fender of our horse trailer, I offered moral support as Daddy cussed and spit and tried in vain to get the youngster to enter the trailer. But nothing moved that horse any closer to getting in. Daddy tried coaxing and then he tried to direct Starflite in with a whip. Exasperated, Daddy finally lost all sense of rational thinking and kicked the horse in his big hind end. As Daddy wailed, my grandfather appeared from nowhere, quickly assessed the situation and immediately fell to the ground rolling in laughter. "It's broken!" Daddy yelled. "Help me get this boot off while I can," he squalled.

Summer faded to fall and all too quickly fall was transformed into a cold Ohio winter. The horses were put up out of the ice and snow in a spacious garage that had been converted into a horse barn. With high-protein grain and all the alfalfa he could eat, our baby was becoming a beautiful young stallion. His ground lessons continued and Daddy's toe mended nicely. Only a slight bend to the left and a black toenail were left as a reminder. When Starflite was moved to a training track, he walked quietly into the trailer like a perfect gentleman.

As the earth started to melt from the long cold winter and teacup-size tulips took their place in my mother's garden, the time had come for the fine young stallion to have a rider on his back. The trainer Daddy hired was a stout older gentleman, "One of the finest horsemen in this county," according to Daddy. Bill really seemed to get inside the mind of a horse. He had some of the finest horses I had ever seen, and we were sure he could "get the run" out of Starflite.

The first task was to get a saddle on the horse's back. And a task this was. "Whoa!" Bill would holler. "Easy, now." Starflite moved in ways I didn't know were possible for a horse. He made an art of dodging the saddle that Bill was trying to toss on his back. Up, back, kick, strike. *Whoa, that hoof was too close to Daddy's head!* I had never seen anything like the circus that I was watching here. The men and the horse were covered in sweat, slobber and even a stray sling of Bill's chewin' tobacco. The battle went on for hours, until finally the great horse gave way. Bill eased the saddle onto Starflite's back, and the horse gave the last snort he had in him. "If he has half that much heart on the track, we've got ourselves a winner," Bill said.

Lessons became much easier for Starflite in the months that followed. Once he was saddled, he was asked to do what he loved best: run. Several mornings a week he was exercised by our new jockey, Jerry. Each time he would come off the track, Jerry would compliment the workout. "*She* did a great job today!" he would shout from Starflite's back as he lazily strode past us. I hated the very sight! I wanted to be a jockey, sitting proudly on Starflite as he burst from the gates. I wanted to feel the wind in my face so fierce that it would bring tears to my eyes. Most of all, I wanted to be on Starflite's back the first time he stepped into the winner's circle. There was one slight problem. I was only nine years old. Daddy allowed me to hand walk our horse after his workouts and remove his protective leg wraps. Then I would feed and water him. I felt important in the grand scheme of things, so I settled for what I could get.

For a young stallion, Starflite was gentle and never gave anyone who was kind to him any trouble. Jerry, in particular, was very fond of him. "She's going to be a great one!" he'd say. And Starflite proved that in his schooling races. Jerry pushed him to be a winner as they prepared for their first real race together. "She's ready," he said one morning as they came in from a fast workout. "Why does Jerry always call him 'she'?" I asked Daddy. "Maybe he calls them all she, like people do when they refer to a boat," was Daddy's answer. I didn't like it, though, and insisted that Daddy talk to Jerry about it. My perpetual complaining finally got to Daddy and he casually asked Jerry one day why he called Starflite "she." "My apologies Slim," he said to Daddy. "You mean to tell me that horse is a stallion? All this time I thought he was a mare because he is so quiet!" "Just thought you should know," Daddy said, even though he didn't care if Jerry called him Mutt as long as Starflite crossed the finish line first.

The big day finally arrived: our first official race for our first real racehorse. My mother was all aflutter, cooking fried chicken right outside his stall on a Coleman stove. Mama always has believed everything should start with a good meal and, wow, can she lay one out! Starflite stood patiently in the crossties as I brushed him. He was so large now that my head came only to the middle of his chest. Although everyone around him was bouncing around, Starflite was the picture of calm and serenity.

As we devoured my mother's feast, Bill prepared my parents for what was to come. "Don't be disappointed if we don't run in the money today," he said. "He's young, this is his first time out and the crowd here today may startle him."

Before long, the call came for the eighth race and the post parade emerged from the tunnel as the bugle began its familiar tune. My heart was beating so fast I could barely breathe. The announcer made his way through the list of names—which included those of the horses as well as their trainers and owners. When he got to "Starflite, owned by, trained by, and ridden by," I decided we had chosen a great name for a racehorse, after all. Once through the field, the horses cantered off toward the gates, every horse that is, but Starflite, who casually walked and then sped up a bit into a Western pleasure-type jog.

He had drawn the Number 3 position, so he and two others entered the gates quietly and waited for the other horses to load. The horse in the Number 9 spot was giving the gate men all kinds of trouble. He reared and kicked, and it took several men to shove him in. "This isn't good," Mama said. "Starflite will get upset. He hasn't seen anything like this." Simultaneously, we looked down the gate to the Number 3 position. We could just see the top of our horse's ears because he had his head so low, and I couldn't believe my eyes. "His legs are crossed Mama!" I yelled.

Starflite was standing quietly and appeared to be thinking, *Calm down so we can get this over with and get back to the barn.* The announcer called, "And they're off!" and the young horses leaped from the gates, trying to find their personal path to victory. Every horse in the race, that is, except Starflite. Apparently, all the commotion had caused him to dose off.

Suddenly, he leaped from the gate with such a stride he was right on the tail of the other horses. What happened in those next eighteen seconds was a blur. The blood was rushing through my head at such a powerful rate I couldn't hear or see what was happening down on the track. Then, as if being awaken from a nightmare, I heard my mother scream, "He won!" I was standing frozen in time, as if all the blood had been drained from my body. I couldn't move.

My mother, on the other hand, was winning her own race. She had taken the stairs out of the grandstand three at a time, knocking over women and small children. When she got to the turnstile, she discovered that it had collected several people exiting the stands, so she jumped it—cleared it just like a fine Thoroughbred. I didn't know Mama had it in her. She was running as if there were the possibility that the winner's circle would disappear if she didn't get there in an instant.

When she finished her endurance course, she was standing alone in the winner's circle. Starflite was still on the backstretch and Daddy was with Bill, standing out on the track waiting for the winner to arrive.

There is no feeling that equals the one that overcomes

you on your way to the winner's circle. It is the culminating moment of years of planning and hardwork that begin with the decision of which mare to breed to what stallion. Through the foal's arrival and his passage from fractious weanling to clumsy yearling, you plan, you dream, you hope. All of the joy and heartache that accompany raising a racehorse can never be expressed in words, but it all comes together in that tiny piece of dirt.

There is nothing like it. Starflite's first win picture—along with all his other win pictures and accomplishments—still hang in our study today. Those mementos are surrounded by similar pictures of his brothers and his offspring. Each has an individual story—some of humor and some of sadness—but none will ever take the place of Starflite. He holds a special place in the heart of everyone he encountered. He possessed a certain kindness with which only a few of God's creatures are blessed. We were "racehorse poor" in Daddy's words, but rich beyond compare with what matters most: love.

Carol Wade Kelly

Happy Horses

Surely, I don't believe superstition brings you good luck! But I'm told it works even if you don't believe in it.

Niels Bohr

I took a friend of mine, George, to the races one sun-splashed Saturday afternoon. Our weekend sojourn to Santa Anita Park was George's first trip to a racetrack. It was also the first time he had ever laid eyes on a Thoroughbred. The day proved to be educational for both of us—teacher and student—as the racehorses once again proved what great equalizers they truly are.

Spending an afternoon at the racetrack is nothing new to me. As editor of a monthly horse-racing magazine, it is among my chief responsibilities to chronicle the races. There are few things I enjoy more in this world than watching Thoroughbreds compete. During a good day at the races, we all try to catch a flash of brilliance here or there, a hint of promise that tomorrow big dreams will come true, that the horses we're watching today will be champions at year's end. "Hope springs eternal," they like to say in this business. It's true.

My passion for Thoroughbreds dates back to childhood. In fact, I can't recall a day I didn't trot off to school without a *Daily Racing Form* in my backpack, tucked in along with all the other semester's required reading. As the years progressed and my knowledge and understanding of the industry expanded, I delved into studying pedigrees and their influence on a Thoroughbred's performance at the racetrack. Today, more than two decades later, and after more than ten years in the business, I am still learning this fascinating game and all of its nuances.

Anytime an opportunity presents itself to introduce someone new to the sport of Thoroughbred racing, I leap at the chance. George, in his seventies, had always admired the majesty of horses, but only from afar, from books and what he'd seen in movies. His hands had never touched the strong neck and thick shoulder of a Thoroughbred. His eyes had never met the eyes of a racehorse or witnessed a furious stretch drive between two rivals, each bent on beating the other. I wanted our afternoon at the races to be something personal for George. I wanted him to make a connection. I wanted him to see how magnificent these racehorses are up close and personal. I wanted him to appreciate the teamwork, the strategy, the preparation and dedication that go into a winning or, for that matter, a losing effort at the races.

As the runners prepared for the second race, a six-furlong turf sprint, I walked with George down to the saddling enclosure for a better vantage point from which to view the jockeys saddling up before heading out onto the track. The horses bounced around there, some of them on their toes, ready to strut their stuff on the track. Trainers offered last-minute instructions to the riders as eager owners and friends gathered around for a listen. Crowds of fans leaned against the white fence framing the saddling ring, hoping to catch a glimpse of something that might possibly point them in the direction of a winner: a thumbs-up from a trainer, an owner's especially large entourage, the look in a horse's eyes, anything at all that may signal that a winning effort is on tap.

I spent much of the time in the walking ring with George sharing the backgrounds of the horses competing in the race, talking about their bloodlines, their siblings, trainers, jockeys, past performances and running styles. I even went so far as to point out what I know about a horse's body language and how various actions translate into terms easily applicable to any athlete readying himself for competition. George absorbed it all like a child at his first baseball game. He was making a connection.

Despite my occasionally lengthy dialog, George had his sights set on a long shot. I alerted him to the host of risks and questions associated with wagering his money on a horse with 20 to 1 odds. My warnings, however, fell on deaf ears. George stood firm. I, on the other hand, backed the classiest runner (at least on paper) in the field. We returned to our table in the clubhouse and continued our discussion of the race as we waited for the runners to make their way to the starting gate.

As the horses began to load, George said that he felt a little nervous. I told him not to worry, six more races remained on the day's program, and he would surely cash a winner before we were through.

I kept close watch of the race's early stages through my binoculars, describing to George that his runner was racing along in midpack. As the field entered the far turn and headed for home, George switched his focus from my race call and fixed his gaze to a nearby television set which offered him a much clearer view of what was transpiring on the track below.

As the runners charged through the stretch, my 2 to 1 favorite slid through an opening on the rail. He appeared full of run and was, without question, on his way to a resounding victory. I was confident that he was the right horse, so confident that I took the liberty of betting a small saver ticket on the favorite for George, just so he'd have a winning ticket to cash first time out when my selection streaked across the finish first.

But before I uttered a word, George's 20 to 1 shot kicked into high gear in the middle of the racetrack. With an apprentice jockey up, the long shot collared us inside the sixteenth pole and posted the upset. George couldn't believe it. I was stunned. With George shaking his head in disbelief at his good fortune, we watched the horse jog back for his winner's circle snapshot. The young jockey's smile was as large as the one on the face beside me. I was smiling too, hoping George had bet a saver ticket on his horse for me.

There is no greater feeling for a new fan at the racetrack than cashing a ticket for the very first time. With George clutching tightly to his winning ticket, I escorted my friend down the stairs to the mutual windows. After some convincing, George parted with the ticket. In exchange, $43.80 came back across the counter. He pocketed the return on his investment and we headed back up to our third-floor table.

As I began poring over the *Form* to study the runners in the next race, I asked George what led him to his winning selection. Without missing a beat, he replied simply, "He looked happy. He just looked happy."

So much for pedigrees, power ratings, past performances, track variants, trainer–jockey combos, post positions and the like. Years of working around horses and the racetrack, and all it took to cash a winning ticket that day were a gut instinct and happy eyes.

We departed the track a couple of hours later. George had given $20 back in losing wagers, but left in the plus column for the day, a victory for sure. As for me, my years of handicapping experience delivered as many winners as George had on the day—one. My winning horse paid $7.20 to win.

As we exited the track, I stopped to purchase the next day's *Form*. George asked why. After a dismal showing at the windows the logic made perfect sense, and I replied, "Looking for happy horses George, looking for happy horses."

As the adage says, "Hope springs eternal."

Michael Compton

Down the Stretch He Comes, Hanging on for Dear Life

*There is something about the outside of a horse
that is good for the inside of a man.*

Sir Winston Churchill

Like many of life's bad decisions, it seemed a good idea at the time.

We have all made them: choices that in retrospect seem, well, kind of crazy. Youth is often involved.

Some might think of people they dated or, worse, married. Every August, when the ponies are running up in Saratoga Springs, I think of a date I once had with a horse with no name.

It was fan appreciation day, an annual event when the New York Racing Association throws open the gates to the historic Saratoga Race Course and welcomes horse-racing fans to an afternoon of food and fun, and maybe a death or two. But I'm getting ahead of myself.

I had been asked, and for some reason had agreed, to be a jockey for a day, joining seven other members of the area press. The media race was to be a highlight of the afternoon. It's clear to me now it was just someone's not-too-subtle revenge on the local newshounds.

When I arrived in the paddock area, eight of the sorriest-looking horses I've ever seen were tied to the whitewashed fence—a reassuring sight to a guy who had ridden but twice.

I remember being instantly drawn to a gray horse with a swayback and hooves too large to lift. She seemed older than the rest, content perhaps just to saunter around the racecourse at her own leisurely pace. My kind of gal.

I never got her name. She only gave me that you-are-such-a-fool stare—the one animals like to share with people on such occasions.

I willingly signed a waiver that said if I were killed, crippled or crushed, it was all my own fault. I couldn't sue for damages. And then I was handed one of those head-hugging helmets favored by jockeys. I put it on, snapping the strap under my chin.

As my friends lined the rail, waving and laughing as friends do when they know someone is about to make a fool of himself, I slowly rode onto the deep dirt of the track, my knees tucked tight to my chin. It's a position I could not get into today. I barely got into it then.

My horse entered the starting gate without protest, unlike some of her feistier competitors who balked and backed away. I sat smug and silent, happy with my choice.

And then, without notice, a bell rang, the gates flew open and my old gray mare suddenly morphed into the racehorse she once had been. I don't know if it was the bell, the gate snapping open or if someone had blown a dart into her rump, but she took off down the track, lickety-split. A bullet.

There wasn't enough time to see my life pass before me, let alone to scream. I clung to her mane, and the farther we flew down the track, the more I could feel my body leaning to the right. One more furlong and I would be hugging her belly. My only consolation was that I would be rounding the first bend by then, riding away from the twenty thousand people who had come to witness this media massacre.

Just about the time I was sure I was going down, the old gray mare pulled up short, veered off to the rail and abruptly came to a halt. She was done. Finished. So was my racing career.

I didn't win that August afternoon twenty years ago, but I had no regrets.

Instead, as my friend Nancy likes to say, I had "a moment." Even better.

Craig Wilson

Track Meet. *Reprinted by permission Steve Sommer and Francis Brummer* ©2002 *Steve Sommer and Francis Brummer.*

Allez Mandarin

My English mother was a wartime bride. My father, an American, worked for Mobil Oil. I lived in several countries until I was four, then we returned to England. On one visit to my grandparents in Kent, when I was nine years old, I first became aware of my uncle Fred, and my passion for horses was born.

My grandfather was a private trainer for a Kent fruit farmer. Uncle John was Granddad's assistant and he kept scrapbooks of his brother's riding career. After lunch I sat with John as he added clippings from Fred's exploits of the previous day into his fourth overstuffed book. I began to thumb through the other books and was in awe that a relative of mine could get so much press and ride so many winners.

On the drive home, I quizzed my mother about her brother's career. Mother told me about going to the movies with my father in Morocco in 1957. To her surprise, The Pathe News showed Fred winning the Grand National on a horse called Sundew. This was the first she had heard of Fred's win. I was in awe that my uncle was on the news in Morocco, and I wondered what it would be like to be a jockey.

Many times as I pedaled down the road to school, I would race people walking on the sidewalk or driving in a car or truck behind me to the nearest landmark. I imagined I was Fred, driving to the finish on one of his great wins. I usually held on to win.

One day, I looked behind me and saw a bus pulling on to the road I was on. I began peddling like mad, imagining I was Fred riding a horse named Mandarin in the French Grand National. I was lost in the moment, hearing the whirring of the chain, the rattle of the fenders, the singing of the tires on the hot road, the pounding of my pulse in my head and my labored breathing. The winning post was still far off. I was beginning to tire. The roar of the bus got louder and louder. The smell of the diesel fumes got stronger. The harder I peddled, the louder the noise got. But I was Fred riding Mandarin, the bus was the French horse Lumino. The heat of the day starting to take its toll, my legs started to shake. I wasn't going to get beaten. I kept peddling, refusing to give in. As I reached the winning post, the bus roared past me. Too tired to peddle any more, I imagined how Fred must have felt after his epic ride aboard Mandarin in 1962.

Uncle John had devoted several pages to Fred and Mandarin. On the first page was a photo of Fred and Mandarin coming off the course at Auteuil. Mandarin had his head down. Fred looked exhausted. "What happened here?" I asked my uncle. "Have a closer look at the picture," John answered.

I noticed Mandarin's bit hanging by his side. "That was Fred and Mandarin in the Grand Steeplechase de Paris," he explained.

"Surely, he couldn't have raced with a broken bit?" Slowly, we began to thumb the next pages of the scrapbook. My uncle John told me the story. "Your uncle Fred and Mandarin had a lot of success before going to France to try to win France's biggest race. They had won the Cheltenham Gold Cup in England and several other top races together.

"The day before the race, Fred came down with a terrible stomach virus. He felt absolutely wretched on his arrival in France the day of the race. He was in no condition to ride in a race, but he wouldn't give in. By the time of the race, Fred was still feeling pretty sick. Once he got on Mandarin, he was grateful to find that his old partner was feeling well. At least one of them was fit to race. Fred was very much aware that the reputation of English racing hinged on their performance.

"Once the race was off, Mandarin settled in among the leaders. At the third jump, disaster struck."

"What happened?" I cried.

"His bit snapped," John continued. "It happened just as they approached the six-foot privet hedge, one of Auteuil's most difficult jumps. Mandarin and Fred landed safely, but what lay ahead was truly daunting: three and a half miles around a twisting, turning track and twenty-four jumps with no way to steer except for Fred using his legs and slapping the reins."

"Didn't Mandarin try to run off or run out? Surely, he could have run out if he wanted to?" I asked.

"No. He was normally a free-running horse, but he never varied his speed. There were four fences before the next bend. Mandarin was always a bold jumper and he jumped these well. One jockey turned his horse into Mandarin. That, along with Fred's strong legs, got Mandarin around the first turn. Mandarin was now settling down into a rhythm. It was as if he was determined to do his best despite the setback.

"The other jockeys weren't helping now, but they didn't hinder Mandarin either," Uncle John continued. The next part of the course had no railing and it split in three different directions. Mandarin was going left when he needed to go right. Fred put all his weight on one side and was just able to get him to keep the correct course.

"Then Mandarin made a jumping mistake, almost falling at the water jump. He pitched Fred up his neck. It actually was a good thing though. It gave them a lead around one of the turns.

"With about a half-mile to go, Mandarin was going well within himself. Fred began to think that he might have a chance to win. Then fate dealt another cruel blow. Mandarin bowed a tendon. Fred felt his mount falter for a few strides and lose about four or five lengths on the leaders. But Mandarin was not about to give up. Fred had no way to stop him.

"Coming to the last fence, Mandarin was in front. Fred, weakened by a stomach virus, and Mandarin, hurt but refusing to give in, were about to win. Then from out of the pack came the French horse Lumino with a strong run. Fred was urging Mandarin on. The broken bit was dangling uselessly by Mandarin's shoulder, his brow band stuck between his ears. Push kick, push kick, Fred encouraged his brave partner on. They had come too far to let Lumino catch them now.

"The closer Lumino got, the louder the crowd got. *'Allez Mandarin. Allez Fred,'* the crowd roared, 'go on Mandarin, go on Fred.'

"Mandarin was going slower and slower. Horse and rider were fatigued beyond the limits of their endurance. Push kick, push kick, the ill Fred reaching down into reserves of strength only a few champions possess; Mandarin doing likewise. Neither horse nor rider was willing to admit defeat. Lumino was catching up with every stride. Fred could now hear the thud of his rival's hooves on the turf, the rhythmic squeaking of the saddles, the heavy breathing of Lumino at his knee, and the pounding of his pulse in his helmet as the winning post inched ever closer. Just past the winning post, Mandarin came to a walk. The old campaigner knew where the winning post was.

"Walking off the track, Fred was exhausted and dejected. Mandarin had his head down. Neither jockey knew who had won. A loud murmur spread among the crowd. Had Mandarin held on? Only the photo finish would tell. The loudspeaker clicked on and the crowd went silent. Then the roar of the crowd told the story: Mandarin and Fred had held on to win."

The final picture in the scrapbook told it all. The jubilant team: Fred, giving weak smile, and Mandarin, picking up his tired head as if to say, "We did it Fred, we did it." My passion for racing was sparked that day by the great feat of Mandarin and my uncle Fred in France. Separately, Mandarin and Fred were champions. Together, they proved to be immortal.

Thomas Peevey

The Fastest Mule in the West

She has thirteen-inch-long ears and a distinctive birth-mark on her rump that inspired her name. Although she measures just 14 hands tall and weighs only 800 pounds, she has carried imposts of 134 pounds and won fifty of fifty-seven races. Her exploits have made her the darling of northern California racing fans and have even earned her space in *The New York Times* and *Sports Illustrated*.

She is a ten-year-old female mule, or mollie, named Black Ruby. Some people have even called her the Secretariat of mule racing. It's a title that emits a chuckle from her proud owners, Mary and Sonny McPherson.

"Black Ruby's won a lot more races than Secretariat ever did," they tell everyone.

Foaled in Utah, Black Ruby is half donkey, half Quarter Horse–Thoroughbred mix. When she was barely three, she fell out of a moving trailer and severely injured her hind legs. Her right hind ankle still bears scars from the ordeal, but it hasn't bothered Ruby one bit. Like the Energizer Bunny, she just keeps on winning and winning and winning.

Although the record books credit her with fifty-seven races, Black Ruby actually has made closer to eighty starts. When she was a young mule burning up the bush tracks in Nevada, she was often called on to race more than once on a given afternoon, but the rules state that only one race a day can be counted. In the unpredictable sport of horse racing, she is considered such a sure thing that most tracks accept only straight win bets on her and some tracks even refuse to take bets on her at all.

For the McPhersons, the Black Ruby saga began in 1996. They live in Healdsburg, in the California wine country, and share a twelve-acre ranch with about twenty racing mules and an occasional Thoroughbred. Twenty-one years ago, Sonny lost the lower part of his right leg when his truck collided with a tree, but that has not stopped him from becoming an activist for the mule-racing movement in northern California.

He and Mary first became aware of Black Ruby's prowess when they sent their best mule, Fancy, to race against her in Winnemucca, Nevada. Fancy was a champion in her own right, but Black Ruby simply smoked her.

"Sonny looked at me and said, 'I want that mule,'" Mary remembers.

They bought that mule and her legend has continued to grow. So did Black Ruby's legion of fans. Blessed with an incredible winning spirit, she is almost impossible to catch once she makes that charge for the wire. This fierce competitiveness has made her a five-time world champion and pushed her earnings to $185,850, a record for a racing mule.

A few years ago, the McPhersons discovered for themselves just how difficult Black Ruby is to catch when she got loose at their ranch and headed for the hills. Sonny jumped on his John Deere tractor and gave chase.

"Every time I'd get close, she'd take off again," he said. "All you could see were her ears. I was afraid she'd hurt herself before I could catch her. She had a race in four days. She won it anyway and set a track record."

Another who knows all about chasing Black Ruby is her archrival Taz. In forty-three races together, the eight-year-old jack has finished second to Ruby approximately thirty times.

He is also the only mule to beat her more than once.

Their rivalry succeeded in making mule racing quite popular during the summer of 2002. Thoroughbred tracks even started clamoring for personal appearances by Black Ruby and Taz. The first to step forward with a proposition for a promotional event was Del Mar Racetrack in north San Diego County, which offered to stage a betless $10,000 winner-take-all matched race between the two mules on September 8, 2002.

For the first time, mule racing left its humble but spirited roots in Nevada and the northern California fairs to enjoy the rarefied atmosphere of Thoroughbred racing. Del Mar has been the scene of quite a few memorable match ups, Seabiscuit's 1938 victory over Ligaroti being the most famous. No one expected how seriously this seaside track would be infected with mule mania. The match took on greater importance when Taz defeated Ruby in a race at Sacramento two weeks prior to September 8. The two mules moved into Del Mar and became instant celebrities. Even the most die-hard Thoroughbred trainers wanted to have pictures taken with them.

Ruby's fans were hungry for revenge, and revenge is what they got. She jumped out of the gate running and never gave Taz a chance to catch her, winning by a comfortable two lengths. Black Ruby and Taz met again six days later for another $10,000 winner-take-all matched race at the Los Angeles County Fair in Pomona. Running without blinkers for the first time and carrying five pounds more than Taz, Black Ruby appeared beaten in the final fifty yards. But her great fighting spirit kicked in at that point and she came back and caught Taz right at the wire to win by a nose.

"Black Ruby knows exactly where the finish line is, and she just refuses to lose," Mary said after that particularly exciting victory. "She always seems to find that extra gear, call it 'mulepower' if you will."

Black Ruby made it three in a row against Taz before she called it quits for the season. And what a finale it was.

Carrying seven to fourteen pounds more than her competitors, including Taz, she won the 440-yard American Mule Racing Association Gold Cup at Fresno in world-record time.

After that race, Black Ruby removed her running shoes and settled down for the winter at Mary and Sonny's ranch. Just as she has done for six previous winters, she bossed the other mules that share the pasture with her and enticed them to join her in games of chase. She was always the one flying in front.

"Even when she's playing, she's competitive and the others just let her have her own way with things," Mary adds. "She has made it a hard-and-fast rule that she eats first at feeding time. She's the queen bee, and she knows it."

Debra Ginsburg

Mules-R-Us

Mules-R-Us. *Reprinted by permission of Boots Reynolds.* ©2003 *Boots Reynolds.*

Da Hoss

The Breeders' Cup was always a legendary event in my mind. Ranking alongside the World Series and the Super Bowl, it truly is the culmination of a racing season, with the greatest champions in the world on hand to challenge one another in a test of speed and stamina over several distances and a variety of surfaces. I remember watching it on television while growing up. As the only horse lover in a family of nine, it wasn't easy gaining access to our only family television set for four straight hours on a Saturday afternoon. When I was successful in this endeavor, however, everyone else refused to join me and I was forced to take up the role of announcer of each race, convinced that everyone wanted to watch it with me, but they were heavily engaged in other duties at the time. Therefore, it was my obligation to verbally broadcast each race as it unfolded to the entire household with great enthusiasm.

I was a racing fanatic. I grew up with The Black Stallion and his unforgettable conquest of Sun Raider and Cyclone. As a boy, I would drag the piano bench into my bedroom, fasten a Western riding saddle to it and envision myself in the greatest races of the day aboard any number of the greatest racehorses of the day.

Now here I was at the Breeders' Cup, not merely in

attendance, but actively engaged in a necessary role along-side all of the Breeders' Cup employees. How I had landed that internship, I still do not know. Nevertheless, I was there. My duties were to attend to the needs of the horse-men, the trainers, the grooms—anyone who had anything to do with the actual horses.

As fortune would have it, my position afforded me the opportunity to gain unprecedented access to the greatest horses of our time. It was 1998 at Churchill Downs, and the likes of Silver Charm, Skip Away and Gentleman had gath-ered in Louisville, Kentucky, to test their mettle on racing's greatest stage.

It just so happened that in a rather quiet barn, one gone fairly unnoticed and fairly undisrupted by the ever-present media, was a horse on the verge of legendary status. I could vividly remember calling a race a few years prior in my living room that featured his name, a name that will go down in my personal racing history because it belonged to one of the greatest milers of all time. It was Da Hoss.

To call him a warrior is an understatement. Plagued by injuries throughout his career, with aching knees and swollen ankles, Da Hoss had charged his way into the history books with a dominating victory in the Breeders' Cup Mile at Woodbine in Canada in the fall of 1996.

But this was 1998, and Da Hoss was getting along in age. At seven or eight years old, he was considered by many to be past his prime. It had been two years since I'd even heard his name, and yet he was here. "What a joke," I heard people say. "This reminds me of Rick's Natural Star," another added, referring to a horse who did not belong and who fared rather poorly in a prior Breeders' Cup, causing quite a ruckus among the media.

I couldn't believe what I was hearing. Da Hoss was a champion—a proven champion—yet it became apparent that his fan club had dwindled significantly since his last championship appearance. And who could blame them? We're talking the Breeders' Cup here—a racing extravaganza that had catapulted the careers of Cigar, Sunday Silence, Ferdinand and more. It was a day that had offered the public some of the most awesome showdowns in racing history. This was the big time. It was for real, and I began to fear for my friend in Barn 39.

But fear or not, I watched each day as Da Hoss made his way to the track. He churned up the turf course like a real competitor. Nothing that I could see would stop me from believing that this would, indeed, become the comeback of the decade. I became so confident that I even began to make my predictions known among the Breeders' Cup crew. "He's back," I touted. "It's Da Hoss in da mile," was my battle cry of the week.

The day we had all been waiting for arrived, sunny, crisp and ripe for the challenges that lay ahead. Churchill Downs was everything I had imagined. The trademark twin spires gleamed and the fans streamed in. This was the day champions would be made. As the races progressed, I worked steadily between the winner's circle and the paddock, assisting in a variety of ways, including having the winner's blanket and flowers on hand after each race. But my thoughts were on Da Hoss. The papers had reported and I had personally witnessed his trainer, Michael Dickinson, walking and studying the turf course for the perfect route Da Hoss's jockey would endeavor to travel. Mr. Dickinson, the "Mad Genius" they called him, had even asked his girl friend to walk the turf course in stiletto heels so that he could measure how hard or soft the going might be.

I don't recall the exact order of the races that day. Things happened so fast and without pause that the only thing clear to me to this day is that the mile race was upon us, and the horses were making their way through the track tunnel, out onto the course. As the horses passed my position I whispered, "One more time, big guy. Just one more time."

The horses loaded into the gate, which was an incredibly intense, beautiful and emotional experience. Then the gate flew open and the athletes emerged, a colorful blur. They were gone and churning around the clubhouse turn before I could even locate Da Hoss's position in the race. I turned to find the television monitors, strained to hear the announcer over the crowd, searched intently for anything to indicate his progress.

Down the backstretch they charged, all well in hand and approaching the halfway point. As they sped into the far turn, they came together, fourteen horses in all, each with superior breeding, superior care and training, and each within range of grasping the greatest prize of all. Not a horse among them was decidedly out of the race at this point. Yet they were so tightly bunched that no clear leader could be determined as they sprinted into the stretch.

I raced to the rail and saw my hero. He was there among them and as I had predicted, he had charged to the front in an awesome display of talent and fury. On he drove. And then he was second. A talented chestnut by the name of Hawksley Hill had taken over and was now in charge of the race. Maybe seventy-five yards remained, and my hero's fate seemed to be decided. But this was no ordinary horse, and this was no ordinary race. Like Ali on the ropes or John Elway backed up on his own three-yard line, Da Hoss rallied. He rallied like a demon.

If you look at the Breeders' Cup's archived pictures today, you will see photographs from the stretch run of this race. You will see two horses leading the field, nearly dead even and only strides from the finish line. One horse on the outside clearly is running his heart out, but the one on the inside is different. The fire of his effort is palpable. With his head and neck stretched to their limits, Da Hoss is visibly gritting his teeth against his competitor on the track as well as against years of toil and punishment. The look of determination in his eyes is unmistakable and inspiring, so much so, that it will make you weep. For courage, for love, for fun . . . it is impossible to imagine just what force made him move on. But he did. He won. He earned his victory by the narrowest of margins, and it took several minutes for the track officials to evaluate the finish before a decision was announced.

Upon hearing the results, I wept. I wept for joy, for the pain my hero must have been feeling, for the winning ticket in my pocket. Then I ran down the paddock tunnel to my friends and embraced the first one I saw. "Da Hoss in da mile!" I screamed. It had truly been something to behold.

My hero doesn't race anymore and as a gelding, he cannot be bred so there is no possibility that he ever will have offspring in racing's limelight. However, he is still around. You can see him for yourself should you ever journey to the Bluegrass State. They've got him on display in the Parade of Breeds at the Kentucky Horse Park. Just down the path is the Hall of Champions. Da Hoss, two-time Breeders' Cup Mile Champion. What a horse.

Ky Mortensen

Girly's Gift

Tom and Bonnie Gerdes were as excited as two kids on Christmas morning. The cinder-block paddock they stood in at Hawthorne Race Course in suburban Chicago didn't reflect their festive mood. It was December 15, 2001, but there was nary a wreath, ribbon or bow anywhere. There weren't even any chestnuts among the seven fillies waiting to be saddled for the sixth race. But there was one, nick-named Girly, who was responsible for the gleam in the Gerdes's eyes. She was the first Thoroughbred born and raised by the couple's modest racing operation.

The bay filly's registered name was White O Morn, coined after John Wayne's cottage in the movie *The Quiet Man*. The two-year-old was preparing for an improbable start in the Illinois Breeders Debutante Stakes.

The race, restricted to fillies conceived or born in Illinois, carried a $91,350 purse, by far the richest race for the Gerdes. Bonnie knew that the contest would be a tough one for her untested filly. But Girly was in great racing condition both physically and mentally. Maybe her effort would be good enough for her to finish among the top five and get a check for her owners. Even a fifth-place finish (which represented three percent of the purse) would be more than enough to recoup the $250 gamble the couple had taken in nominating the filly to the race in July. Because so many things can go wrong with a Thoroughbred, Bonnie considered it a moral victory just to have made it to the race.

The Debutante would be the third start in only twenty days for the daughter of the sire Seattle Morn. White O Morn's first two races came against state-bred maidens (horses who have yet to win their first race) at six furlongs (three-quarters of a mile). In her debut, the bay finished eighth in a ten-horse field at odds of 18 to 1. She won her second race by a half-length at odds of 10 to 1 in a pedestrian time (1:16.43). Today, she would race after only a week's rest and run in her first event of more than a mile. It appeared that the odds might be stacked against her.

The wagerers demonstrated little faith in White O Morn at the betting windows. The odds board listed her as a 30 to 1 shot. The field was topped by several tough-looking competitors. The odds-on favorite, Summer Mis, was a daughter of Preakness Stakes-winning Summer Squall. Earlier in the year, Summer Mis had zipped past Illinois-bred maidens by fourteen lengths at Arlington Park, Chicago's premier racecourse. Another Debutante starter, Penny Pit, entered the race undefeated in two open-company starts.

With many of the competitors coming from high-profile stables, White O Morn's more humble origins also did little to stimulate interest among the betting public. The Gerdes, after all, were relative unknowns in the Illinois racing community. Trainer Mike Mokry had been on and off the backstretch many times during his career. Uriel Lopez was a regular in the Chicago jockey colony, but he struggled for race victories.

But that didn't bother Bonnie and Tom, who began to fall in love with each other and with horse racing in 1980.

Following their marriage in 1982, they claimed a sprinter named UC Awarewolf. He won his first race in their racing colors. They were hooked.

Despite their early success, the couple figured that their lark into racing would be costly. So they entered with a realistic understanding of the risks involved and, with their trademark good humor, they named their racing operation Three Good Legs Stable.

Though races are handicapped on paper, they aren't run that way. The Gerdes felt White O Morn would be competitive despite her odds. As the horses were saddled, Bonnie was gripped by the exciting and nerve-racking emotions that most owners experience. Not once did she think about the farm, where the financial situation was so bad, that she had made the last property-tax payment with a credit-card check. Nor did she think of that day, five years before when she'd nearly lost her life.

It was 1996. The Gerdes owned six horses. Each day after work, Bonnie, a postmaster for the U.S. Postal Service, and Tom, a buyer and seller of warehouse equipment, happily tended to the horses' needs at the public stable where they were boarded.

One night at the stable, Bonnie noticed that UC, now a pleasure horse, was reluctant to put weight on his rear right foot. Lost in her concern, Bonnie broke a cardinal rule. She approached the Thoroughbred from behind without letting him know she was there.

UC Awarewolf startled and kicked with both rear feet. His right rear hoof hit the left side of Bonnie's face. After getting the horse back in his stall and telling someone to call 911, Tom sat with Bonnie. As she struggled for breath, Tom repeatedly cleared blood from her nose. The injuries were quite serious. Bonnie's left eye had been displaced from its socket, and her face swelled to four times its normal size. Before the ambulance left the stable, paramedics shocked Bonnie's heart several times to get it into a regular rhythm.

In a coma, Bonnie was given a fifty-fifty chance of making it through the night. Even if she did, the prognosis was not encouraging. The injuries to her brain could cause altered vision and hearing, and trigger changes in her long-term memory, personality and behavior. The chance of permanent brain damage was likely. For the first three nights, Tom never left Bonnie's side in the hospital.

Bonnie awoke after nine days in what Tom described as a childlike state. She improved dramatically during her three-week hospital stay, which included surgery and two weeks of physical therapy. She then went to a rehabilitation center for ten more days to improve her motor skills.

The results of her recovery were miraculous. She suffered no brain damage. After three plastic surgeries, the only visible reminder of the accident was a small depression beneath her left eye. However, Bonnie would learn to live with the loss of most of the vision in her left eye.

Through it all, the couple never lost their resolve or their love of horses. With Tom's help, Bonnie got back up on a horse only two months after the accident. In 1998, they bought a cow farm outside Chicago and began the long process of converting it into a horse farm. They had realized their long-held dream of living a life with horses. They were off.

Yes, they were off, Bonnie now thought as the fillies broke from the gate for the Debutante. Bonnie had taken great care to position herself in her new lucky spot inside the Hawthorne grandstand. That's where she had stood when White O Morn won her first race.

Summer Mis took the lead with Penny Pit close behind. White O Morn was settled in fourth along the rail, seven lengths back. The field never changed positions through the first half-mile of the 11/16-mile race.

On the final turn, White O Morn began to move, but she was still four lengths behind Summer Mis with only about a quarter of a mile to race. Bonnie was in a tizzy, even more so because her breath against the cold glass in the grandstand had fogged her eyeglasses. She used track announcer Peter Galassi's race call to paint a mental picture.

In the stretch drive, jockey Lopez angled White O Morn to the outside, but Summer Mis still looked strong. The Gerdes and their twenty-five-person entourage were lost in the thrill of the moment. Girly moved into second, but still had to make up two lengths on the leader. Suddenly, Summer Mis began to weaken. Under Lopez's continued urging, White O Morn surged ahead for the victory.

The winner's circle scene was pure joy. Improbable victory is the sweetest of all.

The impact of Girly's achievement caused the gleam in the Gerdes's eyes to glow long after that memorable day. The $54,810 winner's purse solved the couple's money problems at the farm. And there was a little extra financial windfall. The tickets held in most of the party's trembling hands were worth $63.40 for each $2 win ticket.

White O Morn was voted the Illinois two-year-old filly reserve champion of 2001 and brought her owners more recognition with an award from the Illinois Thoroughbred Breeders and Owners Foundation.

Ever since the accident one simple poem has never been far from Bonnie's mind. It reads: "Yesterday is history. Tomorrow is a mystery. Today is a gift. That's why it's called the present." Every day the Gerdes squeeze every drop of living out of their beloved life with their horses. And every day they can't help but think about their icing on the cake: Girly's gift.

Dave Surico

The Destiny of Edgar Brown

A chorus of "Amazing Grace" lifted skyward as the mourners gathered around the grave to pay their last respects.
Edgar had lived a long life, eighty-eight years before the
Lord called him home. Many stories of his life were told in
the days and hours preceding Edgar's funeral in March 2002
and it was impossible to hear a story about him that did not
involve his horses.

Edgar's life, most of which had been spent in the mountains of Montana, revolved around horses. After he and Jo
married, they began raising cattle on the Helena valley's lush
meadow grasses and, with the purchase of Shammy and
Shalali (Sha-lay-lee), Edgar began developing a reputation as
a horseman.

Shammy and Shalali, both American Quarter Horses,
were nearly identical twins. They were big, stout sorrels
with white strips from forehead to nostril. Under Edgar's
tutelage, they developed into confident ranch horses capable of quietly sorting cattle and dragging calves to the
branding fire.

Over the years, Edgar's horse herd grew, as did his reputation as a horseman. His early equine protégés were
mounts for Edgar and Jo's four children, who participated in
youth and amateur rodeo events and qualified for the

National High School Finals Rodeo on horses their dad had bred, raised or trained.

Soon after, Edgar turned his full attention to training horses and moved his family to the old homestead just south of Helena, where he built an indoor training facility and purchased a young stallion that he felt had promise as a sire. Destiny Leo Jag was only a yearling and an injury had rendered him unable to be ridden. However, his pedigree, his temperament and his conformation were exceptional, and Edgar knew this horse would produce champions. Edgar contracted a sign to be painted, and then he hung it beside the highway a short distance from his training facility. The sign read, "Producing horses with a Destiny to show, to run, to win."

And win they did. Edgar's horses had a definite influence on the Quarter Horse industry throughout the western United States. Edgar spent the late 1950s and 1960s training show horses while breeding and raising colts sired by Destiny Leo Jag. On a bet, he once hushed a crowd by entering the showring on a horse wearing no bridle and then, following a flawless reining performance, exited to a thundering ovation!

It was near this time that another sorrel, strip-faced horse entered Edgar's and Jo's lives. They knew this foal was special the moment they laid eyes on her. Destiny Leo Jag and the mare Herfano had produced an exceptional filly. When she was a mere yearling, Edgar hauled this gem they named Destiny Jagetta to numerous Quarter Horse shows, where she was undefeated and occasionally was selected the show's Grand Champion. As Jagetta matured and developed, Edgar added more events to her repertoire: Western pleasure, reining and dally team roping. She excelled in all, rarely placing out of the money.

By now, everyone in Montana's Quarter Horse circles knew of Destiny Jagetta, yet few realized how close she was to becoming a legend. Jagetta had earned enough points in halter and performance classes to meet the criteria established for the American Quarter Horse Association's most coveted prize, Supreme Champion. Yet there was one remaining criterion to fulfill: racing.

Not one to sidestep a challenge, Edgar forged ahead with his prized mare. Her siblings were performing well on the racetrack for some of the northwest's most noted trainers, and Edgar knew Jagetta also was special. Unfortunately, he didn't know beans about training racehorses. As fate would have it, his son-in-law did.

Like the rest of Edgar's and Jo's children, their youngest daughter married a man who shared her interest and devotion to horses. A reputable racehorse trainer in his own right, their son-in-law was certainly capable of training Destiny Jagetta. However, Edgar chose to work with his son-in-law and others, all the while keeping close tabs on his beloved mare and doing the majority of the training himself.

The sun shone brightly on that warm July day when Edgar's and Jo's horse career reached that juncture between showing horses and racing them. Just the day before, Edgar had shown Destiny Jagetta in halter at these very same fairgrounds. She had won yet another Aged-Mare class and was named the show's Grand Champion Mare. Now, in nervous anticipation, the family waited as she paraded to the starting gate for her first race, an old maid of five years among the breed's two-year-old maidens.

In a rush, it was over. The gates had sprung wide, and the horses had hurtled toward the finish line as the crowd roared. Jo was so nervous she couldn't watch, yet when the starting gates flew open and the announcer called, "They're off!" Jo sprang to her feet screaming, "Come on baby! Come on baby!" encouraging her sorrel, strip-faced mare to give her all.

The dust settled and photos were developed, and in an amazing display of versatility, this Grand Champion show mare had won her first race! Destiny Jagetta, Edgar and Jo were on their way to a Supreme Championship, and just as they were well known and respected on the horse-show circuit, Edgar and Jo were on their way to becoming a noteworthy team in horse-racing circles as well.

It took nary a year, but soon only one more AAA rating stood between Jagetta and her Supreme Champion award, so Edgar entered her in a race in Helena.

She didn't win that race, although she certainly tried. She always tried. But this time it didn't matter that she didn't win. Jagetta ran fast enough to earn the speed rating she needed for her second AAA. Edgar and Jo had bred, raised and trained a Supreme Champion!

It was these stories the mourners told: the stories of sorrel strip-faced Quarter Horses that, in turn, told the story of this horseman they had come to honor.

When the priest began the graveside service, the stories ceased and a hush fell over the small cemetery overlooking Edgar's hometown. In grief and sorrow, the mourners prayed, when, in awe and disbelief, someone looked up and saw a figure on the hill just above this little country cemetery. With a polite interruption of the service, the mourners were invited to look toward the skyline, where on the edge of the old homestead in a pasture long-ago ridden by a grand horseman, stood a single sorrel, strip-faced horse watching the proceedings.

The family had chosen to cover the casket at the end of the service, so when the final blessing had been offered, the mourners' voices sang one final verse of "Amazing Grace" as the casket was slowly lowered into the grave. Shovels then appeared from horsemen's pickup trucks as Edgar's family, friends and neighbors joined in to bring closure to a life well-lived. And when shovelful after shovelful of granite had covered the casket, the sorrel horse on the hill quietly turned and disappeared over the horizon.

Jeff C. Nauman

A Tap on the Shoulder

In mid-1992 my uncle went into the hospital for the last time. His health was failing rapidly, and there was little left that medicine could do. JD, as we called him, was my father's older brother, now in his eighties. With still-black hair and a quiet manner, he loved "the horses" and followed the game daily.

When I'd go to visit him in the hospital, we'd just sit and pass the time. JD never talked much to begin with and he was no more talkative now. So any chance I had to create a diversion, I did. One day, I noticed in the next day's entries a horse named Pass the Vazul. Now, that's not a great name for a Thoroughbred, but it was worth a hunch bet for an eighty-five-year-old Italian.

"Hey, JD, I'll bet this one for us."

"Yeah, okay," was his unenthusiastic reply.

I bet $10 and sure enough, this hunch was a good hunch. The horse paid $11.80 to win, and our ticket was worth $59. Although that's not a lot of money, it was worth a story and a good laugh on my next visit.

Now, I didn't get back to the off-track betting shop to cash the ticket. There was no rush to cash the ticket, so it stayed in my wallet. Actually, I forgot about the ticket entirely until a few weeks later when JD passed away. It was only then that I remembered the bet and pulled out the ticket. I decided then that I wasn't ever going to cash it. A few days later it was placed in my favorite uncle's jacket pocket at his wake. It seemed only right that a horseplayer should leave with a winning ticket in his pocket, even if it was worth only $59.

The unreasonable fondness for the ponies that my uncle and I shared was not lost on those who know us. Shortly after the funeral, my aunt approached me and gave me an off-track betting ticket she had found in a drawer at home. JD had made the bet before he went into the hospital for the last time. She asked me to check and see if it was a winner. It read: $6 to Win, Letter B, 4th Race, Belmont, June 28, 1992. I checked it. It was a loser. But I didn't trash the ticket. It was the last bet JD ever made, so I put it in my wallet and forgot about it.

That ticket stayed in my wallet among other scraps of paper until sometime the next summer. Then one day, while I was at the teller's window at the bank, it fell out as I was fumbling with my driver's license.

I hadn't thought about the ticket, or JD for that matter, in months. I looked at the ticket and was struck by the irony. Today's date was June 28, 1993. The same day as the ticket one year later.

There was no doubt in my mind what I'd do next. I went straight to the off-track betting shop.

I bet $6 to Win, #2 (a new designation that replaced Letter B) in the 4th Race at Belmont. And then I made the same bet for my dad.

I cashed these tickets when the horse won. It paid $19.80 or a total of $59.40 for each winning ticket.

I went to my dad's house and put the money on the table.

"What's this for?" asked my dad.

For the first time, I told him the whole deal. The first bet, the ticket in JD's pocket at the wake, the ticket in my wallet, the date, the $59 and everything else. All he said to me was, "JD tapped you on the shoulder."

I can't argue with that.

Basil V. DeVito Jr.

Unbelievable Kentucky Derby Tale

Sadie's right, that track is crooked! Lora May, it isn't the track, it's the horses. They fix things up amongst themselves.

Joseph L. Mankiewicz, *A Letter to Three Wives*

The first Saturday in May is almost here, which means a bunch of three-year-old horses with Onewordnamesaslong-astheirtails will be running for the roses.

Ah, the Kentucky Derby. The most exciting two minutes in sports and the only day of the year anyone drinks mint juleps.

Everyone has a favorite Kentucky Derby story, and this is mine. Actually, it is my great-uncle's.

It happened back in 1955, when Unc drove back east to the bluegrass of Kentucky in a brand-new red convertible. He'd made a $500 down payment and was dead set on paying off the balance with a winning ticket on Swaps with the great Bill Shoemaker aboard in the Derby.

As the car dealer had advised in order to break in the new engine, Unc drove fifty-five miles per hour on the freeway the whole way. It took him five long, hot days with no air conditioning except the gritty wind in his face to reach Louisville.

Along the way, somewhere in New Mexico between Albuquerque and hell, Unc got a flat tire. Fortunately, it was five o'clock so it had cooled off to around a hundred degrees. Cost him five bucks to get it fixed.

It was about then that Unc noticed something, something you probably noticed a while ago. Fives. Everywhere Unc looked, the number five kept popping up.

It was a sure omen, Unc reasoned. After all, he had been born on May 5 in "none of your dang business what year!" as he always said. May, of course, is the fifth month.

Speaking of fifths, Unc was known to imbibe now and again later in the day, so maybe it wasn't an omen he had seen after all.

Anyway. On the morning of the Kentucky Derby on the first Saturday in May in 1955, Unc awoke with a jolt. He looked at the alarm clock. You guessed it. Five-till-six: 5:55.

"Did I mention I was staying at a Motel 5?" Unc would say, obviously embellishing his tale.

He raced down to the corner liquor store, still in his pajamas, and got the *Daily Racing Form*. He looked down to the fifth race. A horse named Five On Me was entered. In the Number 5 post position. At 5 to 1 odds.

That was the instant Unc realized what he must do. Forget Swaps in the Derby. Fate demanded he bet his bankroll on Five On Me in the fifth race. Back in his motel room, Unc pulled his suitcase out from under his bed and dug out his stash of cash from one of his dirty socks. He counted it. One hundred, two hundred . . . five hundred dollars.

He added the money from his wallet. Twenty, forty, fifty . . . fifty-five.

As if that wasn't eerie enough, he had two quarters and a nickel in his pants pocket.

Unc took a taxi to Churchill Downs. Yellow Cab number 5, by the way. The fare was five bucks. He tipped the cabbie the fifty-five cents change from his pocket. Superstitiously, Unc went to the fifth window and bet his last nickel, all $550, on Five On Me.

And they were off. Five On Me got a slow break from the gate and was dead last in the twelve-horse field as they headed around the first turn.

Then Five On Me started to make up ground. He was eleventh. Then tenth. The reddish chestnut moved up to eighth heading down the backstretch.

Unc cheered him on until his lungs hurt.

Turning toward home, Five On Me was seventh and still gaining. At the one-eighth pole, he closed in on the leaders.

Roaring down the homestretch, it was a five-horse race, and Five On Me was one of them.

Unc roared. He yelled. He shook his fist and cursed, "Come on, you sonufagun! You can do it!"

A photo finish.

Unc held his breath and waited for the results.

The omen came true. Five On Me was—what else—fifth!

Woody Woodburn

The Funny Cide of Life

A New York-bred gelding and six lifelong friends renewed the spirits of America during a history-making campaign for the Triple Crown in 2003. This average and unassuming group and their horse became a testament to the old adage that "good things happen to good people."

Funny Cide and the Sackets Six, as the buddies were dubbed, brought America to its feet, cheering on the underdog and drawing more people into horse racing than have watched in years.

Funny Cide thrust his owners, which includes the Sackets Six and four other partners, into the coveted winners' circle in no uncertain terms after stalking the pacesetter and winning the Kentucky Derby by one and three-quarter lengths. His run in the Preakness left everyone but the horse breathless, winning by an astounding nine and three-quarter lengths, a showing that came close to breaking the long-standing record of ten lengths set in the first Preakness run in 1873 by Survivor.

As I reminisced with one of the Six about our high-school years, the enthusiasm about recent wins and a date with destiny on June 7, a mere fourteen days away, was kept to a dull roar.

These friends from Sackets Harbor, a small village in upstate New York, had children in college, businesses to run, retirements to fund and mortgages to pay. They were an unlikely group to be investing in racehorses, but doing so gave the close-knit group another way to enjoy the camaraderie the friends had always shared.

Brothers Mark and Pete were good students and active in the local sports programs. JP (Jon) was the life of everyone's party, while Harold came from a large family and never caused any trouble, preferring to stay out of the limelight. We expected Larry to do well someday; he was a popular kid and knew how to throw a party. Jackie loved sports and excelled at anything he tried, always ready with a smile on his face—win or lose.

Their personalities haven't changed, and if the town wasn't decked out in Funny Cide memorabilia and reporters weren't hovering around, you wouldn't know this group of middle-aged men was at the heart of Thoroughbred racing history. Moreover, at times it seems neither do they.

They were your average kids, growing up on Lake Ontario, close to the Canadian border. Summers were spent cruising around the Village, hanging out on the corner, playing baseball or football, or swimming at the "Jump-Off" and daring each other to dive off the bridge. Fall brought pep rallies with the student body, athletes and cheerleaders marching from the school, through town to the cliffs along the lake, where the bonfire was set and school spirit was ignited along with the blaze. The Six were usually at the head of the pack. Maroon and gray were the school colors, colors worn by Funny Cide today.

Upon graduation the boys scattered to make their mark on the world. Some went to college, some went into business; all married and started families. Everyone stayed in contact.

Before I talked to any of these men about their experiences with Funny Cide I knew what they would say. I knew they would be humble and in awe of their success. I knew they would say it was the horse that was the hero and not them. I wasn't disappointed.

When I talked to Mark it felt like we had just had coffee at the local diner. Characteristically warm and friendly and happy to share his feelings, I could "hear" the big grin on his face and the pride in his voice.

He began the conversation about Funny Cide by telling me, "There were 34,000 or so racehorses born three years ago and I am still in awe that we were lucky enough to find Funny Cide. It just blows my mind. How did *we* ever end up with the *one* horse that could do it? We've always bought New York-bred horses, that's all part of it—a horse born right here at home."

Mark continued. "The first race Funny Cide ever ran, the jockey told us that he had 'potential' and that he might be a winner. The second race he ran, the same jockey told us that 'the lightbulb went on. *This* horse could win the Kentucky Derby.' I said, 'Yeah, sure, okay,' but didn't quite believe him. When we bought Funny Cide we thought he had potential for smaller races and we would be happy if he consistently placed."

In relating their purchase of Funny Cide, Mark said, "When we bought Funny Cide, things were tight and we didn't have much money to invest in anything. Something told us to take a chance—to go for it. All we expected was to *maybe* get our investment back, definitely have some fun following him to races and hopefully make a little profit. We never in our wildest dreams thought that Funny Cide would take us to the Kentucky Derby."

In a moment he will never forget, Mark recalls, "I was walking from the barn to the track with Funny Cide the day of the Derby and looked up at the stands full of thousands of people. All I could think was, *I still don't believe this is happening. How did we get this lucky? What did we ever do to deserve this?*"

Thoughtfully Mark said, "We own part of America's horse. He's the horse for the people, for the little guy."

As we finished talking, Mark summed it up by saying, "It's all about Funny Cide, not us. We haven't done anything special; we just invested in a dream. He's helped us promote our town and showed the world that there *is* life above Albany, that the North Country exists.

"We've been able to show the world what a wonderful town we live in and what great people are here. We didn't take a chance on Funny Cide when we bought him; he took a chance on us. This little horse has helped us show the world that sometimes the dreams of the little guy *do* come true; that what goes around, comes around. If you try to be a good person and give back to your community somehow, someday it will come back to you. Funny Cide rewarded us all in far greater ways than we ever deserved."

As I said, this is an unassuming group of men. They all share a sense of humility, loyalty to their community and love for their family. A family that has grown by thousands since that unforgettable Saturday in May.

They take no credit for their fame; they give all the glory to this little New York-bred horse that has more heart than the whole town of Sackets Harbor put together.

When Funny Cide can't race anymore, they will still be there for him. No matter what happens on June 7 at Belmont Park, Funny Cide's home track where he is undefeated, they will be grateful every day of their lives for the chance to be included in his success and to have owned a piece of America's horse.

Chris Russell-Grabb

[EDITORS' NOTE: *On May 28, Funny Cide turned in a sharp workout, his first since the Kentucky Derby and the Preakness. Trainer Barclay Tagg proclaimed him to be "sound, healthy and happy." As we went to press with this book, anticipation of a twelfth Triple Crown champion was reaching a fever pitch. The last horse to win all three races was Affirmed in 1978. Success at Belmont on June 7 will bring a $5 million bonus to the owners of Funny Cide. Regardless of the outcome, there is no doubt June 8 will find the Sackets Six enjoying a cup of coffee or a cold beer on the porch talking about the ride of their lives, having lived the American dream.*]

$\overline{7}$

HORSE . . . CETERA

*I have pulled your plows to feed your families.
I have carried your flag in parades to
   celebrate your independence.
I have run with all my heart for that buckle
   hanging on your belt.
I have shown you the world from my back,
And now we'll show the world together,
You are America, and I am your horse—
   America's Horse.*

Reprinted with permission of
American Quarter Horse Association©

They Neigh, I Pay

Although I'm a veterinarian, I don't proclaim to be an expert on horses.

I'm just the guy who brings home the bacon to a household consisting of my knowledgeable, horse-obsessed wife Teresa and daughter Mikkel. However, I do know something that they don't seem to understand or care about. After years of following their footprints and accompanying hoofprints, I've come to the startling conclusion about the essence of having horses in your life: They neigh, I pay!

I used to hear the adage that the best way to make a lot of money with horses is to start out with a lot more money. Trust me, that statement's more fact than fiction.

The purchase of your first horse is a harbinger of what's to come. You buy horses from people who make used car salesmen seem like choirboys and pay only about twice as much as you should. Every horse offered for sale is one of a kind, a special bargain just for you, a horse that never has been and never will be lame, is as gentle as a baby, loads easily into a trailer, is the one that the owners will sacrifice only to a good home. Yours, sucker.

You buy the horse. So far, so bad. Although your bank account has been lanced and has started bleeding, you don't feel the pain at first.

Next stop, the local tack store, where you test-ride a handmade one-of-a-kind saddle with a special seat. They always throw in the part about the seat being special, both for comfort and style, making it even more difficult to pass up a saddle that they say will almost certainly appreciate in value. Throw in blankets, halters, reins, brushes, combs, clippers, helmets, gloves, clothing and jewelry, and you've got yourself a small fortune invested already. Ka-Ching!

Then comes hay, sweet feed, high-priced nutritional supplements, feeders, buckets and, yes, even toys for horses. Ka-Ching!

But wait, your anemic bank account has just been minimally hemorrhaging until now. When the need arises to transport the horses from point A to point B in style, you just hit an economic artery. After becoming the proud owners of a new Ford F-250 V-10, crew-cab pickup, pulling a four-horse, slant-load Featherlite horse trailer with custom graphics, it's time to call the bank for a major transfusion. Ka-Ching! Ka-Ching!

Your yearly salary will show signs of needing a transfusion when your wife and daughter decide to show horses. It starts out low-key with local 4-H shows and competitions but rapidly escalates into big regional shows and eventually, huge national shows. At every step, I hear the words of my late father Bob, "The price of playing poker just went up," as we climb the ladder of financial brinkmanship to the top of the horse world.

Now your family surfs the Web and subscribes to a dozen horse magazines, looking for "the" winning horse to add to the collection. In a game that makes human personal ads seem both understated and true by comparison, the ads about horses claim that each is a national champion of some sort, a sure winner, sacrificed only for, you guessed it, a good home. Yours.

Everybody wants to see a video of the horse that they may want to buy, and soon your mailbox is stuffed with videos coming from the four corners of the United States and Canada. Your VCR is white-hot from watching them over and over, and your eyes squint from viewing grainy videos, shot in low light. Everybody says, "The pictures lie, he really is a lot better than what you see on the video." Yeah, right. False deadlines come and go, and you continue your frantic search.

Then—eureka!—you find him. The horse that has all the coveted abilities to win: head held low enough to scrape the ground with his forehead, trotting so slowly you'd swear you're watching a slow-motion replay, able to be steered by just the trainer in the stands moving her legs.

As you arrange for your panel of horse experts to view the video, someone always finds something about the horse that nobody else noticed and that kicks the prospect out of the running. At that point, like lemmings, everybody agrees, "Yeah. It's there. I didn't see that until you pointed it out. You don't want him."

Me? I see nothing, but I nod my head in agreement so that everybody thinks I'm one of them and certainly not a veterinarian who can't see something so apparently obvious about the health or stealth of a horse.

Now it's Christmastime, and even though you still don't have a horse for next year's shows, that doesn't stop you from going ahead and buying your daughter a custom show saddle with more silver than a Navajo gift shop, a hand-tooled belt buckle with her name in big letters, show clothes, new boots and much, much more. All dressed up for Christmas photos, she looks silly, kind of like Hollywood meets north Idaho. Ka-Ching!

Finally, after months of searching for the equine version of Mr. Right, you're so thoroughly exhausted and dizzy that you just buy the next horse that comes along. That way, you can tell everybody, and especially yourself, that after much consideration, you have indeed, found the perfect horse. But this horse needs a special trainer to reach his potential and, of course, it's best for the horse to live at the trainer's whose housing is better than yours. Ka-Ching! Ka-Ching! Ka-Ching!

Your IRA now eats hay and you need to call the Loan Arranger!

Well now, as much as I hate to admit it, as far as investments go, the ROI (return on investment) is actually great when you buy a horse. You have a wife and teenage daughter who obsess together, train together and travel to shows together. They draw close as they share the thrill of victory and the agony of defeat.

You sit in the stands, jostling elbow to elbow with the other dads, eagerly taking the twentieth video of the season as your daughter and her horse enter the arena. You marvel at the symphony of a 125-pound girl riding a 1,300-pound one-horsepower sports car. Your heart races and your palms sweat as the judges line up the entries to announce the awards.

When your daughter takes a blue ribbon, your wife and daughter hug at the arena gate and you get choked up with pride and joy. It's one of the greatest feelings in the world. But it's short lived.

For tomorrow, you're up at the stalls, manure fork in hand, tossing into the cart what remains of your retirement. Ahhh, I love the smell of horse manure in the morning!

Marty Becker, DVM

Of Great Horses and Men

Spending that many hours in the saddle gave a man plenty of time to think. That's why so many cowboys fancied themselves philosophers.

C.M. Russell

That's the ugliest horse I've ever seen. Now wait a minute, let me think on that. Yep, that's the ugliest horse I've ever seen.

I was only eight years old the first time I laid eyes on that horse. Up until that time in my life, I had not even considered the fact that there might be an ugly horse anywhere. Even the mules on the ranch where my dad worked weren't that ugly and they're ugly by design. It turns out that this horse's looks were also by design. It seems this horse's owner, plus the horse's purpose, had a lot to do with how he looked.

Picture this: a beautiful black stallion prancing on a hilltop, his mane flowing and tail shimmering in the sun as he rears up to fight the wind in a mock battle. Then he charges off down the slope to his perfect little band of mares and foals, protecting them from harm. How many times have you seen that on TV or in the movies? Isn't this how we visualize the perfect stallion?

Now picture this: a roman-nosed black stallion with a

white patch between his eyes that looks more like a scar than a patch. His mane has been roached low on each side, then grown out to about five or six inches, giving his neck the appearance of being deep and wide. His forelock is long and matted with burrs. His tail has been roached like that of a mule then grown out to where it looks like a fan. His fetlocks, too, have been clipped and grown back long enough to touch the ground. It's obvious that he has been kept in a small lot that has a mud hole in it because he has dried mud and dirt caked all over him.

You'd have thought that his owner had never seen a brush or a currycomb and you would never have guessed that he was an AAA running Quarter Horse. In reality, he was very pampered back at the ranch. He had his own barn, paddock and a personal groom. But it was to his owner's advantage that the horse looked scruffy sometimes. He was run only in matched races because there were no recognized tracks in Oklahoma at the time. The dirt and mud made it easier to match and raise the stakes on what appeared to be an ugly ranch horse.

I had just arrived in Pawhuska, Oklahoma, the day before to spend the summer of 1943 with my favorite aunt and uncle, who managed a stud farm just out of town. My uncle had been quite a racehorse man in his younger years, winning some pretty big races, but health problems had kept him close to home the last few years. His name was Albert Reynolds and he was known as a starter at all the local race, meets and matched races. He was a man you could depend on to give you a fair shake at the gate. If your horse lost the race, it wasn't because he didn't get a fair start. However, there's one little thing about Uncle Albert that I feel compelled to reveal and it's something that too many other people found out the hard way. You should never match him in a horse race. In all the years I knew him, he never lost.

On this day, he was about to start this high-stakes match race of 350 yards. It was between a good-lookin' sorrel blaze-faced horse owned by an Osage Indian family and Ol' Ugly.

I'm sure this horse had a more respectable name, but in the years I knew him I can never remember anyone calling him anything you could print except "that old ugly stud." He belonged to a local rancher by the name of Ben Johnson.

It seems that Ben also had quite a reputation around this neck of the woods for matching horse races. But Ben's reputation went far beyond ranching and racing horses. He was also a world champion steer roper and later Pawhuska, Oklahoma, would dedicate an annual memorial steer-roping event to their favorite son. This soft-spoken cowboy produced a son, Ben Johnson Jr., who also won a world champion title in team roping before going to Hollywood, becoming an actor and winning an academy award for his role in *The Last Picture Show.*

Now, Ol' Ugly was coming down the track toward the starting gates in a slow lope, ponied by a nice-looking bay horse ridden by a man named Dee Garrett. Dee also owned a ranch west of Pawhuska and dabbled in runnin' horses himself. He later owned a running Quarter Horse mare named Miss Pawhuska and a stallion named Vandy. The colts from these two horses produced a lot of changes in the record-book standings for sires.

Well, it was post time. Both horses were at the gate; nothing left to do but run 'em. "Who you ridin'?" Ben asked the Indian.

"My youngest," he said, pointing to a little kid about six years old. "And you?" the man asked Ben.

"I'll ride this boy," Ben said as he put his hand on my shoulder. " This your boy, Albert?"

"He's my nephew," my uncle replied.

"Good enough for me," exclaimed Ben. "Let's saddle 'em and run 'em!"

Before I even had time to react or understand what had just been said, Ben picked me up by the seat of the pants and the back of the collar and set me up on the big stallion. I had never ridden a stallion before and now I was piloting one in a match race! His neck alone was thicker than the horses and mules I had been riding at home. To say I was scared was an understatement.

Don't I get a say in this? What am I supposed to do? Am I going to die if I don't do it right? Why me? The only reason I wasn't throwing up was because there was something lodged in my throat. I think it was my heart, trying to pound its way out through my ears.

"Lift your legs," Uncle Albert said, as he was tossing an elastic overcinch across them to Ben on the other side. "This will keep you from falling off," he explained as they cinched it tight under the big horse. At this point, the horse and I were one. I could feel every ripple of every muscle in his back. I just couldn't feel my legs.

"Listen to me," Uncle Albert commanded. "If you get in trouble, like he falls down or somethin', you just straighten out your legs and the cinch will pop right off." Uncle Albert seemed to think that being up here on this horse wasn't trouble enough.

Ben led the big horse into the gate and then crawled up by his head to steady him while the other horse was being loaded.

"Here," he said, as he crossed the reins. "Hold these like this in one hand."

He then took off his belt, put it around the horse's neck, through the throatlatch of the bridle, and buckled it. I remember the sun glistening off the big gold and silver buckle.

"Get a death grip on this belt with your other hand and don't let go. Now listen to me. Here's what I want you to do," he instructed as I looked up at him. "When the gate opens you just try to shove the bit out of his mouth and scream!"

"Not a problem about the screamin' part," I tried to say, but nothing came out. As I looked back down the long straightaway toward the grandstand and all the people, to my surprise the starting gate and the horse's head were both gone! Just as the sound of the steel gates banging open came to me, I felt my arms being jerked out of their sockets and my head was suddenly snapped back. The big horse had dropped out of the starting gate a-runnin'! The death grip I had on the reins and belt, along with the overcinch, made sure that I went with him.

Never before had I felt such a force of power. The surprise of the start must have cleared my throat as I found myself screaming, first from shock, then sheer fright, then excitement. My eyes were filled with tears from the force of the wind and from the dirty mane, where my face was now buried. I took a short breath and screamed again as we blew by the eighth pole.

I was suddenly becoming aware of my situation. I was still alive, I was in a horse race and I was winning! I looked back and could see the blaze face of a sorrel horse in the distance. As I turned back to the task at hand, we were going by the grandstand and the finish line.

The big horse's ears were up and flicking back and forth. I had just ridden and won my first race! Now what? I pulled back on the reins, but he took the bit in his mouth like a vice, laid his ears back down and picked up speed. By the time I realized I was in a dilemma, another problem appeared. We were running out of track. The straightaway ended and we were at the turn. The big horse changed leads and ducked into the turn with such force that it was all the overcinch and my new grip on the reins could do to stay on top.

When we hit the backstretch, his ears came up again, but he didn't turn loose of the bit. Just as I realized that my peril wasn't improving and I still might die, I caught a glimpse of Dee Garret on the pony horse next to the outside rail. He swooped in and picked up the outside rein and pulled the big horse up. I was really lucky that Mr. Garrett had been there in the backstretch to save me. Years later, it occurred to me that he probably was more concerned about Ol' Ugly's safety than about saving me from certain death.

As we slowed down and were turning around to head back to the grandstand, he proclaimed, "Well, kid, you won that one pretty handy." Then he took the cigar out of his mouth and added, "You can stop screaming now."

Boots Reynolds

Of Great Horses and Men

Are You a Real Horse Mom?

Blind with love, my daughter has cried nightly for horses, those long-necked marchers and churners that she has mastered, any and all, reining them in like a circus hand.

Anne Sexton, "Pain for a Daughter"

You know you're a Horse Mom when:

1. You spend three days and nights in a cramped trailer in a dusty (or muddy) lot behind the horse barns for your vacation.

2. Your colleagues at work ask how your weekend was, you exclaim, "Great!" and then wonder how to explain exactly what was so great about sitting around a cold and drafty or hot and muggy (choose one) barn, getting dust in your eyes and hay in your teeth while your child alternated between giddy euphoria and sullen despair (depending on the judge, the horse's behavior and other factors imperceptible to a mere parent).

3. You realize you have graduated from nights spent walking a fussy or colicky infant around the bedroom

to nights spent walking a fussy or colicking horse around the barn.

4. You find horse-treat nuggets at the bottom of your daughter's clothes hamper and are inordinately pleased that at least you didn't find horse-treat mush at the bottom of the washer when you took her wet clothes out (this time).

5. You are glad to see your child eating vegetables as she takes turns biting from the same carrot with her horse.

6. One of your greatest life achievements is learning to back a trailer around a corner into a parking space without denting either of the much fancier trailers on either side.

7. Raking a brush through your hair and slapping on a hat qualifies as putting on your makeup.

8. Your daughter asks to borrow your hairbrush and you retrieve it later from her tack box, full of long, coarse hair (not yours or your daughter's).

9. The friendly farm veterinarian asks you to "Come here and hold this," and without gloves—you obediently grab the horse's tongue to hold it aside while his teeth get worked on.

10. You can hem a pair of show pants with safety pins and duct tape in thirty seconds flat.

11. The equine feed bill is a bigger portion of your family budget than the human feed bill.

12. Ditto the medical bills.

13. And shoes.

14. You wish your child would spend more time hanging around the mall. It would be cheaper than what's required for all the time she spends hanging around that horse.

15. You cry when your child comes in dead last in her show class. You also cry when she comes in first.

Barbara Greenstreet

Horse Lovers Are
Really Sick People

Did you ever stop to wonder what exactly it is about horses that makes so many people fall obsessively in love with them?

One contributing factor is the number of horse-related stories so many of us read as kids. *Black Beauty*, *The Black Stallion*, *My Friend Flicka*, CW Anderson's *Billy and Blaze* stories, *Misty of Chincoteague*, *King of the Wind* . . . the list goes on and on. And, of course, every horse-mad girl (and boy) that I've ever known has a collection of Breyer horse models. But what exactly is the unknown thing that pushes a normal kid to ask, over and over again, "Mommy, Daddy, when can I have a pony?"

I have long believed that it is very easy to fall in love with horses. Why shouldn't it be? They are beautiful, powerful animals; the stuff of fantasy and legend. They are an integral part of our country's history and the rest of the world's as well. The very fact that a mere person can bond to and form a part-nership with such a large and intelligent creature has inspired art, literature and myth throughout the ages. But how . . . why . . . what makes it happen?

I have a theory about that. I believe that the love of all things equine, the true love, is a virus. Most people are carriers of the infection. Many will suffer the symptoms at some point in their lives, usually late childhood to mid-teens. Then there are those who are terminal, destined to exist in the grip of the horse-love virus for their entire life span.

What other rational explanation could there be to explain the intense emotional, physical and financial sacrifices we make for our horses? Why on earth would a normal, sane person dedicate all of his or her time to grooming a very big animal that is going to roll in the mud as soon as he gets back outside? It certainly can't be considered typical behavior to spend the better part of the day picking bits of poop out of a stall with a pitchfork, or spending all of one's free hours in a barn. And why would anyone even want to be at the barn when the weather is soggy, freezing or hot enough to melt your eyeballs? The concept of horse ownership seems to defy all logic.

It starts innocently enough. The average young girl rides a carousel horse for the first time. Not long after, she graduates to pony rides. One Christmas morning, she receives a toy horse or her first copy of *Black Beauty*. Her parents notice their little darling clipping pictures of horses out of magazines and making a scrapbook. Her weekly allowance is deposited into an elaborately decorated, equine-themed coffee can for the future horse-purchasing fund. The Barbie dolls are shoved into the closet and replaced with Barbie's horse, Breyer models, Grand Champions, or whatever other brand the local toy shop carries. Christmas rolls around again, and the obligatory letter to Santa simply begs, "Please bring me a pony."

Her parents chuckle to themselves, "Oh, she'll grow out of it," and in some instances, they could be right. There are those who escape the clutches of the virus. Puberty hits and the rush of hormones occasionally is strong enough to extinguish the infection. But not always.

If the virus persists, the requests for driving lessons are now accompanied by those for riding lessons. The coffee-can fund is in the bank and the horse-crazy teenager is looking for a part-time job to raise additional cash. Instead of rock stars and athletes, posters of galloping horses cover the bedroom walls. Books on stable management and horse care join the well-read storybooks on the shelf. Horses are scribbled on the covers of notebooks. Book reports and class projects consistently revolve around an equine subject. Shopping expeditions always include a quick side trip to the local saddlery. No, she may not own a horse, but she already has riding boots, a hoof pick, brushes and a halter, all displayed in a place of honor in her bedroom.

If the parents are willing to treat the symptoms, the victim may get riding lessons. If she is truly fortunate (and her folks have the cash), she might actually get a horse. Then there are those poor, sad souls, the riders without horses. Perhaps college got in the way, or marriage and motherhood. The virus is still there; nighttime finds the subject tossing and turning, dreaming of a morning gallop across verdant fields. Oftentimes, these folks may have to wait until the mortgage is paid and the kids have moved away before being able to satisfy the needs of the disease.

I am not trying to scare you by telling you all of this. I only seek to warn you, to let you know what to expect in yourself or younger members of your family. You see, I speak from experience. I am a terminal horse-love virus patient. It hit me early, when I was about three and had received my first Breyer model horse. It stayed with me through my childhood, up to college and into adulthood. My parents were very understanding, and provided therapy during my teen years in the form of riding lessons and a big, black gelding named Shadow.

I'm in my late thirties now. My family still loves and supports me. They never fuss when I miss weekend gatherings because I need equine treatment. They don't comment when I can't spend money on them, because I've already spent it all on my horse. If the basement in my house is full of tack, horse blankets and other equipment, they just smile and walk around it. And at Christmas, there are as many gifts for my horse under the tree as there are for me. They know the virus can't be fought, only accommodated.

One of my best friends recently had a baby. I went to visit them both and brought a stuffed pony for the new little girl. In a crib full of toys, it was the only thing she would hold on to. The contagion has been passed again.

Cristina Scalise

Me and Minnie Pearl

The American male, at the peak of his physical powers and appetites, driving 160 big white horses across the scenery of an increasingly hopeless society, with weekend money in his pocket and with little prior exposure to trouble and tragedy, personifies "an accident going to happen."

John Sloan Dickey

I stood on my knees in the back seat of the 1942, black, four-door Ford and put my elbows on the headrest of the front seats where my mother and daddy were sitting. I was going to ride in my first horse show.

Bubbling with an unfounded childlike confidence fueled by my excitement, I had no doubt that I would win my class. I had only one question. "Daddy, what am I supposed to do when the man tells me to canter?"

My daddy, a six-foot tall, 230-pound bear of a man with a Tampa Nugget cigar stuck in one corner of his mouth, replied, "When the man says canter, you trot your horse."

My mother, a short, stocky but pretty woman with black hair, turned toward the back seat, faced me and added, "Don't worry about it, Tommy. You're only four years old. No one expects you to canter the horse." Although her words were supportive, I sensed my mother's nervousness. I knew she didn't want me riding in the show, but as usual, my father had the deciding vote on what happened around our house.

I had grown up around horses. My daddy, whose main business was a grocery store, ran a riding stable on the side. I had been sitting on a horse from the time I could sit up. Our trainer would put me on a horse, hook a lead line to the animal, and I would follow him wherever he went. Recently, I had graduated to riding on my own without the lead line.

My horse was Minnie Pearl, a big, ugly, full-grown, dark bay mare with a head that looked like a mule's. My father trusted Minnie Pearl, and I had learned to ride on her rather than on a pony, which would have been more my size. Minnie was gentle and considerate as she proved the day I fell off and got my foot tangled in the stirrup. I was so short I couldn't even touch the ground with my hands as I hung from the side of the horse. Minnie just stopped and started grazing, waiting until the trainer came to liberate me. At four, I had no fear. I remounted and was off again.

When we got to the show at the Burlington City Park, I walked around the grounds, feeling grown up in my white, short-sleeved shirt, tan riding britches—the kind that flared out on the sides—and my brown riding boots that came up to my knees. I strutted around, aware of the "isn't he cute" glances I was getting from the adults in the crowd.

I walked to the ring, where classes already were underway. Bleachers were set up on one straightaway of the ring and they were about half full of people. Most people seemed to prefer to watch from along the rail, propping their arms and elbows on the top rail. I noticed the grandstands on one side of the ring, nearly full with people. I was too short to see over the top rail, but I got a good view of the action by peering between the top and lower rails. Several times, I got pelted with dirt clods flying from the horses' hooves as they moved around the ring. Worried that I would get my riding outfit dirty, I moved away from the ring. I found a big rock several yards away and climbed up on it. From this perch, I watched the bustle of horses and people.

When it was time for my class, I found my daddy and our trainer, who were at our trailer with Minnie Pearl. Back at our barn, I had a mounting box for getting on Minnie, but we hadn't brought it along to the show. So my daddy lifted me on to Minnie's back while the trainer held her reins. The trainer led Minnie, with me on her back, to the ring to wait for our class.

I don't remember what kind of class it was—probably a pleasure class. It was not a class for kids. Everyone else in the class was an adult. I sat on Minnie at the gate to the ring, surrounded by adult riders, waiting for the preceding class to end.

As the gate opened and I started in the gate, a man I didn't know thrust a stick at me and said, "Here, boy. Use this on that old horse."

I took the stick and entered the ring.

Remembering my daddy's instructions, I turned Minnie to the right and urged her into a trot, keeping to the rail, trying to stay out of the traffic. After a minute, the announcer said, "Walk your horses. Please walk your horses."

I reined in Minnie to a walk. After a few seconds of walking, the announcer said, "Canter. Canter your horses."

The class was crowded with at least fifteen horses. Horses started passing me one after the other. I had never cantered a horse before, but something possessed me to whack Minnie across the rump with that stick. She took off, much too fast for good form. We were passing every other horse in the class as she carried me pell-mell around the ring.

Suddenly, I was Roy Rogers, Minnie was Trigger and we were heading off a cattle stampede. I was having the time of my short, but reckless, life. The wind cooled my face and flapped my shirttail as Minnie and I circled the track.

The crowd went crazy, laughing and cheering. Above it

all, I could my mother yelling, "Herman, Herman. Get him, Herman. He's cantering. He can't canter."

The announcer said, "Walk your horses. Please walk your horses." I pulled Minnie to a walk. The crowd and my mother stopped yelling, but there was soft laughter and a buzz in the crowd.

The next direction from the announcer was, "Reverse. Reverse and trot your horses." I turned Minnie's nose to the outside rail of the ring until she was headed in the opposite direction, kicked her in her flanks and started posting to her trot.

After we had trotted for a couple of laps, the announcer again slowed us to a walk and followed with the canter command. Once again, I whacked Minnie on the flank and sped around the ring. The crowd came alive again, yelling and screaming, but they couldn't outyell my mother, who again yelled for my father to do something.

After the last canter, the announcer had us line up on the infield grass, following the directions of the ringmaster. We sat still on our horses while the judge walked from one end of the line to the other, looking over horses and riders. He wrote his selections on a piece of paper and gave them to the announcer, who called out the winners.

With each named called, my excitement waned. I wasn't among the winners and I was embarrassed as I walked Minnie Pearl out the exit gate with the other losers. As I neared the gate, I saw my father waiting for me there, a big grin on his face, the ever-present cigar in the corner of his mouth. I felt better. My daddy was proud of me and all around me adults were congratulating me, telling me how well I had done.

That confused me. I couldn't understand why I didn't get a ribbon if I had done so well. One thing I wasn't confused about, I'd just had the most fun I'd ever had on the back of a horse and I wanted to do it again, and next time I'd win a ribbon.

I spent the rest of the day exploring the creek and the big

rocks of the city park. Minnie Pearl grazed contently waiting to be trailered home. Finally, as we climbed into the car for the trip back home, my father said, "I have a surprise for you. After your class, the judges got together and decided you deserved a special prize for your showing today. They've asked me to give you this."

He pulled out a purple ribbon and handed it to me. I didn't know what place purple represented, but I didn't care. I proudly pinned the ribbon to the pocket of my white shirt and fell asleep before we got home, dreaming of my next adventure on horseback.

Tom Truitt

"Hey, mister, when you finish her horse,
would you build me one, too?"

Attitude

My friend Janet Dean ran her horse Shanghai through the gate. She was riding well, leaning for leverage as they circled the first orange barrel. She could feel her chaps flapping against her leg and knew the barrel was teetering but would stay up. She rode Shanghai all out for the second barrel. This was a good ride. She knew it.

The angle was perfect on the third barrel and Janet's heart raced as she yelled, "Go, go!" and dirt flew from the horse's hooves.

They raced back through the outdoor arena gate where her dad stood with a stopwatch.

"Yeah," Janet screamed. "Yeah!"

She let Shanghai take a wide circle back toward her father. "Well?"

Mr. Dean had on jeans, a checkered shirt and a Jayhawk's cap. He shook his head. "Not as good as last year," he said.

"But it felt so right."

"Maybe you're a better rider this year. Maybe you're helping the horse rather than the horse helping you. It might be time to start a new horse. Old Shanghai has to retire sometime. If not this year, the next, or the year after."

Dust blew across their arena. Janet patted Shanghai on the

shoulder. "Darn good horse, though," she said, shaking her head.

The hottest horse she could find and afford was an unbroken two-year-old, a little mare named Bistro. Her friend Angie had bred her just south of the Kansas border, in Oklahoma.

"She's a brat," Angie said.

Janet and her father stood leaning on a gate across the eight-stall barn. Angie was inside with a plastic bag tied to a whip.

"What do you mean, 'brat'?"

"You'll see." Angie let the little red mare out of her stall. Bistro's trot was light and she appeared to float across the barn. Angie waved the plastic bag.

Bistro had a white stocking on her right hind leg. Pop! She nailed Angie's bag with one kick.

"Dang!" Janet's father said. "I don't know about this."

"Let's see her outside," Janet said.

They took the mare out into the pasture. Bistro was quick, running toward the fence at full speed and spinning around after a sliding stop. She'd dig her hooves into the ground and throw dirt. She kicked up spray as if the dirt were water and she loved coming as close to the fence as she could without crashing into it at full speed.

Janet's eyes got big. "She's athletic."

"Yeah, but 'brat' could mean killer," her father said.

"Let me see her in the stall," Janet said.

Angie led the horse back to her stall and Janet spent several minutes nose to nose with Bistro. It looked like a case of pure love.

"Oh boy. Here we go," her father said.

The first problem came when Angie delivered the mare to Mr. Dean's ranch. Bistro wouldn't unload. She locked all four legs and it took thirty minutes and five men before they got her out.

"I've never seen a horse that wouldn't *unload*," her father said. "Won't go in a trailer . . . sure. That I've seen, but not this!"

Bistro was a sweetheart in the stall with Janet, but outside . . . well, outside, she was a brat.

Janet's father hired a cowboy to break her so that she could be ridden. He quit after the mare rose up on her hind legs and walked him into the corner. Bistro didn't just rear up, she walked on two legs like a man.

The cowboy scooted out of the stall on his belly and said, "I quit."

Janet wasn't allowed to watch the next cowboy. Her father hired tough Bill Hooley and told him to use the whip if he had to.

All Bill remembered was a white hoof in his flak jacket and looking up from the ground to see Bistro bucking through the barn. Bistro crashed through the metal fence across the door and would have ended up in Colorado if she hadn't been bucking with her head down. She ran into a stock trailer and knocked herself out just for a moment.

They were able to lead the stunned horse back to her stall without anymore trouble. Everybody looked at the broken metal fence and scratched their heads.

Bill Hooley handed the whip back to Janet's father and kept on walking. "Getting tough ain't gonna work," he said as he climbed into a black Ford 150. "That horse doesn't *want* to be broke."

The next morning they found Bistro running free in the barn. Mr. Dean looked at the stall. "Too smart," he said. "Now she's letting herself out. That's what's wrong. She's too smart for her own good."

Bistro nuzzled Janet. Her head was over Janet's shoulder. Janet looked at her dad.

"Don't even think about it," her father said. "Someone else has to break her."

"Well who? I'm fifteen."

"I dunno, but not you."

They found a young ex-marine, raised on a ranch in Utah. Rode broncs for a while until it hurt too much. His name was David and he was tall and taut like a rodeo man.

"I'll try it," he said. "But nobody goes near her for one month. Not even Janet. No visits to the stall, no hugging, no nothing. Bistro has to be totally dependant on me. I feed her. I water her."

Janet said, "I love that horse, David. We've got a bond."

"My way or not at all," he responded.

Janet looked at her father and he nodded.

So, Janet began spying on them from the side door. She didn't let Bistro see her.

David spent the first day just standing in Bistro's stall with his back turned to the horse. By day two, Bistro would throw her head over his shoulder, begging for attention, but David ignored her.

David did the feeding. David did the watering. David cleaned the stall.

On day three, David led Bistro out into the barn. He put a rope on her and worked her in a circle for a while. Then Janet was surprised to see him give Bistro a Mountain Dew. The horse grabbed the plastic bottle in her teeth, threw her head back and downed it in quick gulps.

By day six, Bistro was saddled. "You can watch," David told Janet. "Besides, I might need you to call the hospital."

Janet's grin was weak.

David put one foot in the stirrup. Bistro bounced a little. "Whoa. Whoa!"

David put a little weight in the stirrup and finally raised himself off the ground. The horse edged sideways. "Stop it." David got down.

He tried again. Bistro stood still.

David took off the saddle and gave the horse a Mountain Dew.

"What are you stopping for?" Janet asked.

"You think I didn't want to throw my leg over? Oh yeah, I did." He patted Bistro's neck. "But this horse needs patience."

The next day, he was riding Bistro at a walk. The day after, they loped.

At the end of the month, David handed Janet the reins. "You're going to have to ride sometime," he said. "This horse will always be a one-person horse and she needs to know she's yours."

Janet smiled. She hopped on Bistro and they walked around and around the barn.

"Good thing she's got a couple of years," her father said.

David just nodded and opened a Mountain Dew for himself. "They'll be something special by then. They're both smart. Which one you gonna send to college?"

Mr. Dean just blinked.

Gary Cadwallader

"Broke? Yeh, he's broke the corral,
the stall and the wagon!"

A Frosty Georgia Morning

On a frosty Georgia morning, in our old Ford truck, Dad and I drove down the dirt road to the barn on the way to check on our horses. We made an odd, silent pair. I was an awkward twelve-year-old on the brink of womanhood, suspended in the ugly-duckling stage. Dad seemed to have pulled back lately, and I was unsure of his love now that I was no longer little or cute. One thing was certain, though, we both shared a passion for our horses.

A cold snap had swept into the valley overnight. Peanut, my favorite of our seven horses, had given birth to her first colt the day before, and although we had seen the foal right after she delivered, I was eager to get back to the farm and run my hands through the colt's thick chocolate coat, softer than any stuffed animal.

We were excited about this colt, the son of Sunny, our proud Arabian stallion with a wild streak, and Peanut, who was plump and white with brown markings and a scooped nose. Although my uncle argued that Peanut was really a very large pony, she was my favorite mare. Dark brown with black mane and tail, our new colt promised to offer the best of both his parents: gentleness and strength. Daddy let me name him and I called him Pride.

Dad drove our pickup to the pasture gate and we climbed

out in the crisp air. As I pulled on my gloves, I saw Daddy glance in the direction of the iced-over pond. Peanut stood alone at the pond's edge. Her ears perked up when she saw us and she ambled over. Dad spoke to her.

"Hey, girl. Where's your baby?" Peanut answered by simply moving closer to Dad, searching for a treat. She was a big baby herself.

"Get her some oats. I'll find the colt," he said. I ducked into the tack room where the feed was stored, scooped up some of the sweet-smelling feed and came back out to the barn's main aisle to see Peanut staring into one of our open stalls. I found Dad in the stall, down on his hands and knees, patting Pride, who was lying on his side.

"Come on, boy, stand up," he urged, but Pride didn't respond. Dad put his hands near the colt's muzzle, over the nostrils. He turned to me with a grim expression. "I think he's frozen." I couldn't believe it.

"Are you sure?" I asked. "Maybe he's asleep." I moved around by Pride's head, gently stroked his neck and ran my fingers through his cool, soft coat. "Wake up, Pride." I wanted to see a quiver, but there was nothing.

"Peanut must have left him alone and when the temperature dropped last night, he fell asleep and froze," he said. I looked over at Peanut stuffing herself with oats, oblivious to the plight of her new colt. At that moment, I hated my favorite mare.

"Why did she leave him?" I asked, choking back tears as I continued to stroke Pride's fine coat. Daddy stroked alongside me.

"It's not her fault. She's a new mama, she didn't know any better," he said. I tried not to cry, but a tear escaped, slipped down my cheek and landed on the motionless colt. Dad must have seen. Suddenly, he put his strong arms under the colt's limp body and scooped him up into his arms.

"Open the tailgate," he ordered. I ran ahead of him to the truck and pulled down the tailgate. Dad lumbered along awkwardly under the weight of the limp colt. I scrambled up in the truck bed just before he gently laid the foal next to me.

"Hold onto him," he said. I wrapped my arms tightly around Pride's downy neck and we pulled off, headed toward our old farmhouse, now vacant for the winter. There, I held open the back-porch door while my father carried the colt in his arms, up the stairs. What was he doing?

"Open the door," he said. I reached up for the hidden key and unlocked the door. He struggled through the doorway, angling the colt several ways before finally passing into the kitchen. "Open the oven," he instructed. I hesitated. He was scaring me, but I obeyed. Gently, he lifted the colt onto the open oven door, turned the oven on low and began rubbing his hands back and forth across the colt's body. With heat and love, my dad was trying to coax the colt back to life. I joined him.

"Come on, boy, come on," I said, rubbing the colt's neck and sweet face. Dad and I worked together for some time but we didn't say much. I felt miserable that I hadn't been there when Peanut had abandoned him, but as I worked along with Dad to try to save Pride, waves of sadness were replaced with a sense of purpose.

The room grew uncomfortably warm and we stopped working for a moment to slip out of our jackets, then we continued our efforts for another twenty minutes. The colt still didn't move. Dad gave a final pat to Pride's neck and spoke.

"Do you think he's going to come around?" he asked. I ran my hand along Pride's neck one last time and felt the fluffy, cold coat pass under my fingertips. I answered Dad with a somber shake of my head. Despite our efforts, we had lost the fight.

We stopped at my uncle's house down the lane to see if he could help Dad bury Pride in the back pasture. Dad explained what had happened and our efforts to revive the colt in the warm kitchen.

"Now why'd you do a stupid thing like that?" my uncle asked. He had been around farm animals his entire life.

"You know you can't bring somethin' frozen back to life. Didn't you learn that in college?" Dad gave me a sidelong glance.

"We needed to try," he said. My uncle shook his head in dismay.

"Craziest thing I ever heard," he said. But I knew my dad wasn't crazy. He had attempted the impossible for me. I knew then how much Dad loved me.

A few weeks later, our prissy Welsh pony Flicka was due to foal. Against Mama's strong objections, Dad loaded her into the trailer and brought her to our city home. Together, we broke up a bale of hay and spread it all around the concrete floor of our garage, which was attached to our house. He unloaded Flicka, took her inside the garage and shut the door against the cold. A few days later, Flicka gave birth to a healthy colt, whom I named Banner. For the next few weeks, until the cold passed, our entire house had an overpowering smell, but Dad and I were happy. Mama? She counted the days until spring!

Janie Dempsey Watts

The Waltz

You can tell a gelding, ask a mare, but you must discuss it with a stallion.

Author Unknown

As I once told my daughter Suzy and grandaughter Kaitlyn, the waltz is a beautiful dance, but you should choose your partner carefully. I know that seems to be a curious remark, but perhaps you will allow me to explain.

Every day, before and after school, I had a part-time job working on a farm that had fifteen Thoroughbred horses. In addition to mucking out their stalls, I had to enter each one and pour six to eight quarts of oats into the feeding pan, which hung on the back wall. Hay came from the loft above and water from a hose that we pushed through the bars, thereby saving time.

These expensive, high-spirited animals weighed approximately a thousand pounds, so we all wore steel-toed boots for protection. On this particular day, I had stayed after school to play basketball, and I still wore my sneakers because I intended to return to the game after finishing my chores. The horses, whinnying loudly, didn't appreciate my tardiness.

One of the horses had the show name of Bismarck, however, we quickly gave him the nickname Woodhead because he possessed a serious personality disorder. Whatever he thought was in his best interest usually collided head-on with the comfort and safety of the person unfortunate enough to be in proximity to where he intended to go.

Each stall was made of wood on the bottom and steel bars on the top. A large Dutch door provided entry. By opening only the bottom part and ducking down, I could quickly deliver the oats to the bucket located in the rear corner. Getting the oats there reminded me of driving toward the basket when I played basketball. The hungry horses challenged me by trying to get at the oats in the same way that a good guard tried to stop me from advancing on his basket. Bismarck, I mean Woodhead, rarely failed to get his oats before anyone ever got near his bucket. Eating was his goal and he never minded being called for fouling.

Less hearty employees feared Woodhead's combative charge, so they would open the bottom part of the door and pour the oats on the floor. Straw came up to the horse's knees, so this cowardly behavior encouraged him to eat his bedding, thereby increasing his chances of getting sick. In Woodhead's case, the caretakers just didn't care. He'd put fear into anyone daring to enter his stall.

Hazardous duty, like good basketball, requires intuitive action. I'd pretend to swing a punch at his head and he would back off, but only for a second. His retreat made it possible for me to swiftly cross the stall floor and slam dunk the oats into his bucket. He always managed to eat half of them before I got out the door. This time, as he stretched his neck for the oats, I swiped at him with my left fist, instead of my right, and connected. Ouch! He truly deserved his stable name. Babying my hand slowed my slam dunk, giving Woodhead time to attack again. He stepped on my foot.

Horses do not like to step on foreign objects—Woodhead included. He immediately lifted up his hoof. Of course, he continued consuming his oats without regard for my

suffering—none of this would interrupt his meal. My shouting into his ear set the stage for the dance of death. Having
a sneaker on instead of my steel-toed boots resulted in
increasing the decibels of my painful cry. Woodhead had
just experienced one of the few times I had hit him.
Screaming next to his ear persuaded him not only to lift his
foot off my foot, but to shy to the right.

At this point, I became conscious of another problem
beyond my immediate pain. My sneaker lace had somehow
gotten caught between his shoe and his hoof. When
Woodhead shied right, my foot followed. He literally tried
to sweep me off my feet. How could I refuse him? In desperation, I grabbed for his neck and clung for dear life.

The waltz began.

Keeping step with my partner made me cry out each time
that his left front foot hit the floor. Each cry into my partner's ear encouraged him to dip and twirl faster. Holding on
to his neck became less a matter of good form and more a
matter of survival. If I'd fallen, I was sure that he would have
kicked me to death.

The word waltz comes from German and means to roll,
turn about or tumble. These steps didn't appeal to me.
Bowing to my deteriorating interest, Woodhead accelerated
from the waltz to the jitterbug. I had no choice but to go
along. While I provided the music by screaming into his ear
in steadily increasing octaves, he turned and leapt. The pain
in my foot became unacceptable. My dance ticket had worn
out. No one was going to try to cut in on this made-for-each-
other couple.

Somehow, I had to reach down and dislodge the lace. I
tried this once. Fortunately, as I let my right arm slip off his
neck, Woodhead danced us into a corner. Instead of falling, I
hit the wall and ended right back cheek to cheek. If the wall
hadn't stopped me, I would have gone down, and our dance
would have quickly ended. He needed lessons, and I told
myself I would give him a free one with a shovel, as soon as
we broke up.

After a while my screams turned to moaning in his ear, "OH! OH! OH!" each time his hoof crushed my foot. Perhaps he thought I had gotten romantic because of my grasping and gasping. No one ever tried to embrace him before, so this physical closeness had to confuse him. A look into his big brown eye gave no indication he felt loved. In fact, he had a look of intense fear and hatred for his partner.

Round and round we went. Stomp your partner's foot. At this point, my foot felt like a soft banana. The pain had gone beyond feeling. It no longer hurt quite so much. I couldn't get the lace loose and didn't dare let go of his neck. Woodhead did not like his dance partner, and I'd had my fill of him, too. As we passed his oat bucket for the umpteenth time, he stopped to sup. The lace simply released. Thanking him for the dance, and not bothering to curtsy, I dove for the door and ended up in the aisle rolling around in pain.

At the emergency room, the doctor laughingly said, "Well, what have we here?" I wanted to kick him, but that would have added to my foot's discomfort. The nurse removed the sneaker in order to X-ray my foot. It immediately blew up like a football. I had left a basketball game to go dancing with a horse and ended up with a football shaped foot. Would you believe the X-rays showed not one single bone broken? Guess old Woodhead turned out to be light on his feet after all.

The very next morning, I entered the stall next to Woodhead's and stuck a long flexible funnel through the bars and into his bucket. Then I pored in eight quarts of oats.

I would later become a great engineer.

William Geen

Guard Duty

I was eleven when we arrived in the refugee camp in Austria, after having fled our war-torn country, Hungary, in 1947. The camp, located on the outskirts of a small town, was dismal, but at least all of our immediate needs were taken care of and we were grateful to the Lord for that.

The people who ran the camp set up a school for the children and organized a scout group. Soon I was a Girl Scout and even went to a scout camp that summer, held in the beautiful Tyrol region of Austria.

The scout camp, located in the wooded mountains of Alm, was quite a nice setup. On one side of a clear, rushing creek were the tents for the girls and our troop leader, Mrs. Kovacs. On the other side, the boys and Mr. Kovacs, the other troop leader, were camping out. But we went for our meals on the boy's side and the nightly campfire was held there as well.

These campfires were always the highlight at the end of the day. We girls, with Mrs. Kovacs, would cross the little bridge that went over the creek and join the boys around the fire, singing songs, telling stories and playing games. All of us had a wonderful time beneath those beautiful, tall, whispering pine trees that covered the entire area.

To teach us courage and responsibility, I guess, our two troop leaders soon devised a plan. Every night, while the rest of the troop trekked across the bridge to the boys' side for the campfire, one girl would stay behind as the sole guard. This girl was given a whistle in the event she became scared or needed help of any kind, but other than that, she would be alone in the big dark woods for a couple of hours. If she blew the whistle, she would be heard and help would arrive within a few minutes, the leaders told us.

Most of the girls, at eleven and twelve years old, were not happy with this arrangement, but complained only to each other about it. Nevertheless, the ones who got early turns seemed to do their job well, never once blowing the whistle while sitting in the dark for two hours. But the stories they told each other later, of strange noises coming from the pitch-black woods, frightened the dickens out of the girls who hadn't yet had a turn.

"I heard terrible grunting and I was sure a bear was coming to eat me," a girl named Anna told us as we lay in the tent that night.

"So why didn't you blow the whistle?" I asked, chills running up and down my spine.

"Because I didn't want everyone to call me a chicken," Anna replied. "And I'm glad I didn't. The bear went away after a while. I'm lucky he wasn't hungry."

"I heard strange noises when I was on guard," another girl piped up. "It sounded like a woman crying. I even called out to her, but there was no answer. I decided it must have been a ghost and that she finally went to haunt someone else. But Mrs. Kovacs said it was probably only an owl. I still think it was a ghost, though."

"I wonder if there are any wolves in these woods? My turn is coming up soon," still another girl asked.

"Mine, too," I said, "and I can tell you one thing: If I get scared, I will blow the whistle. I'd rather be called a chicken than be eaten by a bear!"

So the following night, my turn to be the guard arrived. Mrs. Kovacs placed the whistle, hung on a long string, around my neck and handed me a flashlight.

"Remember, we'll be just across the creek. If you get scared, blow this whistle," she said, smiling at me. The other girls glanced back at me as they walked away, glad it wasn't their turn. Then they were all gone.

I sat down on a campstool in front of my tent, my heart already pounding too fast, butterflies doing a jig in my stomach. I could see the campfire across the creek and hear the distant singing voices. Everything would be all right, I told myself, glancing uneasily around the now pitch-dark camp and woods. The other girls had survived their two hours as guards, and so would I.

I looked up above the towering pines, and saw the stars and a crescent moon in the sky. I inhaled the wonderful smell of the pines. I began to relax and feel quite good. This wasn't so bad. In fact, it was nice to be alone in the quiet woods, I decided, and I began humming a little tune to entertain myself.

Suddenly, I heard a noise. A very loud thump! Thump! Then it stopped. "Who's there?" I called out. No reply. Then I heard a rustle, followed by more thumps. The noise was getting louder and louder. Again I called out. For a moment there was stillness followed by more thumps. Was my imagination playing tricks on me? I stood up, peered into the woods toward the noise and called out once more. This time the rustling became more frantic and the thumps became louder. There was something or someone out there. It was real, not my imagination and it was heading my way!

What if my friends were playing a trick? Would I be the only one to call for help and forever be known as "the chicken"? Resisting the urge to blow my whistle, I tried to think quickly. It couldn't be a wolf, I thought right away. A wolf would sneak up without all that noise. It had to be a bear and it was getting too close for comfort. I hugged the wall of the cabin and stared deeply into the woods, the thump, thump, thump growing louder and coming closer. I could feel the vibration each thump commanded. Whatever was coming was large, larger than a little girl could handle.

It certainly wasn't a ghost, and must be bigger than a bear.

As I raised the whistle to my lips, the huge thumper of the night came crashing into view and stopped right in front of me. I shined my flashlight on him.

"Snort! Snort!" went the thumper, bobbing his head up and down.

"You're a horse!" I shrieked, spitting the whistle out of my mouth. "A big, giant horse! Hello there, boy. Where did you come from?" I held out my hand as I talked to him. The horse's muzzle touched my fingers gently. He snorted again. I boldly reached up and patted his head.

"There, there, boy. You must be lost or something. I'm sure they'll find your owner in the morning. Meanwhile, you can keep me company, because I don't like to be alone in the dark and maybe you don't either," I said as I continued patting him. "Maybe my guardian angel sent you my way, just so I wouldn't be scared."

The horse snorted again. I wondered if I had something in the tent I could give him as a treat.

"You wait here. I'll be right back," I told him, creeping into the tent and feeling around for the box of keks that I'd saved. "Here. I think you'll like these, boy." Keks were a kind of cookie-cracker combination that was very popular in Austria at the time, and we had each received a packet in case we got hungry between meals.

The horse did, indeed, like the keks, and wanted more and more. Soon my package was empty. I walked around the camp boldly now, my visitor behind me the entire time. Noises I heard no longer frightened me. I had a guardian with me. I was actually sorry to hear voices crossing the creek as the others were returning.

"Look, Mrs. Kovacs, I had company tonight," I called out to them. "So I wasn't alone at all."

"A horse! Look girls, Renie has a horse with her," one of the girls shrieked excitedly as a whole bunch of them gathered around my companion and me.

"Where did he come from?" "I wonder whose horse he is?"

"Weren't you frightened when he came?" And many other questions followed. Mrs. Kovacs then blew the whistle, and her husband, from the boy's side, came running across the creek.

"He probably belongs to the farm nearby. We'll check with the farmer in the morning," Mr. Kovacs said, going back to get a rope. "We'll tie him to a tree for tonight."

The following morning, some boys went to the farm, and it turned out that the horse had gotten out of the fenced pasture and galloped through the woods. Until he found me, that is!

"I had a horse just like this one in Hungary," I told the farmer when he came to get my companion. "I used to ride him all the time. Then we had to sell him because of the war."

"Well," he said, "you can come and ride Rudy while you're here. He is pretty gentle and he seems to have taken a real liking to you."

And that's what I did. I went to ride Rudy several times before we went back to the refugee camp and all of the other girls considered me the bravest of the guards for not blowing my whistle when I heard a thump in the pitch-dark night.

Renie Szilak Burghardt

Battle of the Titans

I have worked for years to establish a good reputation as a horse trainer. My horses are easy to catch, they stand tied, take their shots without theatrics and hold up their feet when asked. Even Gem.

Gem is 12 hands of unrepentant, buckskin-colored obnoxiousness. I tell her she's undisciplined, spoiled and the reason that ponies have such a bad reputation. She says she missed her calling in life. Despite four legs and a tail, she's an actress at heart. She thinks that Hollywood needs her. Sometimes I almost believe her.

She mastered the art of impersonation by watching TV through the living-room window. I changed all the door knobs so she can't join us inside anymore. In her Shirley Temple disguise, she's everybody's darling, so cute and sweet. When she's practicing her Dennis the Menace routine, even the chickens hide. But her most stunning achievement is her Alexis Colby impersonation. She can even copy those hard-eyed, conniving expressions, and she watched *Dynasty* just twice!

Recently, I needed two colts shod and Gem's feet trimmed, so I called my farrier. When he found my schedule wasn't going to match his, he said not to worry. Just put the horses in the corral. He had done them all before without a problem. He could turn them out when he was finished. I agreed and blithely went on my way. He was a big, good-natured fellow who had owned and trained horses all his life. Everything would be fine.

The farrier arrived. Gem was standing at the gate to meet him in her Shirley Temple disguise. He caught her and took her over to his pickup parked inside the gate to the pasture. He pulled out his wooden toolbox with the dowel handle. She rubbed his back while he trimmed her feet. She was cooperative if overly affectionate.

He rubbed her ears and turned her loose. She followed him back over to the corral while he caught one of the colts. He had to shoo her out of the way so he could lead the colt out. Back at the pickup, he picked up the young horse's left front foot. Gem stuck her nose over his shoulder to see what he was doing. He shoved her away, so she went around to the other side and stuck her head under the horse's belly to see what the shoer was doing. That made the colt nervous, so the farrier chased her away. Put out, she morphed into Dennis the Menace mode as she wandered back over to the pickup and began nosing through the tools. She dumped a box of horseshoe nails in the dirt.

"Go away," the farrier yelled, slapping her on the rump.

Satisfied now that she had his undivided attention again, Gem came to help, nosing through the dirt where our shoer was trying to pick up the nails. He swatted her hard and chased her off. Alexis Colby emerged.

Ears back, she stared at him. He ignored her and returned to the colt. He lifted a foot and tucked it between his knees. Seconds later, the colt jumped forward. The farrier held on and growled at the youngster. A few seconds later, the colt lunged harder.

The farrier stood, only to see Gem peering innocently at him from behind the colt. When the man turned his head toward the colt, Gem flattened her ears and threatened to bite the youngster who promptly jumped forward again.

This time the farrier chased her across the irrigation ditch.

"And stay there!" he growled, shaking his file at her.

They swapped glares as he returned to the colt. He was shaping a shoe on the anvil when something grabbed him by the belt and jerked him backward. He staggered, arms windmilling for balance. Gem bounced by, tail in the air and head waving. Score two for the pony.

He grabbed a halter. She couldn't be a pest if she was tied up. She teased him. He could scratch her rump or back but not her neck. Finally, he smacked her with the lead rope. She bolted back across the irrigation ditch.

But Alexis was just warming up. She sneaked up and grabbed the colt's halter rope and tried to lead him away. She stole the hammer off the anvil and dropped it in the dirt. She found the farrier's good hat in the back of the pickup, pulled it out and stomped on it. She dumped his water jug. Each time he tried to retaliate, she pranced back across the irrigation ditch out of reach.

It was into this battle of the titans that I arrived. Unobserved, I opened the gate and walked into the pasture in time to see Gem grab the dowel handle of the toolbox in her teeth and carry it across the irrigation ditch. Left with only a hammer and a mouthful of nails, the farrier erupted from under the colt, face mottled with rage. Whuffling through his moustache and the nails in his teeth, he brandished the hammer at his tormentor. Eyes glittering, Gem slung the box back and forth. Nippers, files, hoof knives, nails and other shoeing tools flew everywhere. When the box was empty she flung it away too, and stood glaring at him, head high, daring him to top that.

He roared.

"Gem!" I yelled, appalled.

She whipped her head around, eyes wide. A look that said "uh-oh" appeared on her face and she bolted into the pasture.

The farrier jerked his hammer down at the sound of my voice. He turned back to the colt and nailed on the shoe.

I picked up the tools Gem had scattered, dusted off the

farrier's hat, refilled his water jug and apologized repeatedly for my little darling's behavior. Monosyllables were the only reply. Gem watched from the far end of the pasture.

I held the other colt and paid the farrier when he finished. He loaded his tools and climbed into his pickup and started it.

"Thank you," I said hesitantly.

"Mmm," he replied.

He turned around and I opened the gate. Racing hooves sounded behind me as the farrier started through the opening. Gem thundered into the yard, head out, ears flat, eyes focused on the retreating pickup. I slammed the gate in her face and she bounced away, tail flagging. Alexis wins again.

So much for my reputation. Anybody know a good farrier?

Lynn Allen

Great-Grandma Hazel and the Sidesaddle

I remember finding great-grandma's sidesaddle in the barn in the late spring of 1971. It was covered with barn dust, the soft dark green fuzz that feels kind of silky between your fingers. You don't dare to blow it, though, because it always seems to end up in your nose.

I managed to find some saddle soap and a sponge and when the saddle was clean, I caught one of the ranch horses in the pasture to see if the saddle really would fit a horse. I caught the only one that was gullible and brought Acey Duce to the barn. I saddled him the best way that I could figure out because there were more straps to that saddle than I knew what to do with. It had two horns on it, and I knew that I had to put my right leg over and around the top one, then my left leg had to go under the bottom one that curved down.

I was quite curious about the sidesaddle. I knew that it was the only way for a lady to ride in times long past. There was only one stirrup to this saddle and it was covered with a very small piece of leather, I guessed to keep one's foot from sliding through. A little purse was sewn to the right side of the saddle, and there were latigo strings on the skirts at the cantle. I was very fascinated by the saddler's design, but wasn't sure how to ride in it or even if I had put the darn thing properly on the horse.

Grandma was in her kitchen with my mom, my great-aunt and a lady from town who worked for Grandma. They were very busy cooking lunch for the hay crew that was due in any minute to be fed. I tied Acey Duce to the orchard fence and then asked Grandma if she would show me how to ride in the sidesaddle. Her answer to me was "No." She didn't have time at the moment. I must have seemed pretty sad at her response because she looked at me and said, "Wait until the hay crew is fed and the kitchen is cleaned and I will show you."

Grandma was sly. She was hoping that I would get bored and tired of waiting for her, put the horse and the saddle away and that would be the end of it. Unfortunately for her, I was very determined to learn how to ride in this saddle. I was still sitting at the back-porch door waiting for her two hours later when she finally poked her head out and said, "I see that old horse is still standing there!" I jumped up and nodded.

Grandma was four feet, ten inches tall and maybe ninety-eight pounds when soaking wet. She was also a woman of very few words. She walked out to the apple orchard where Ace was standing patiently, waiting to see who was coming and what we were doing. Grandma looked over the saddle and the straps and checked the cinch. "My dear," was all she said while undoing one strap and rearranging a few buckles. She led Ace to a convenient spot and mounted him.

Now poor old Ace had no idea what was going to happen. When Grandma got herself settled comfortably in that saddle, she picked up the reins and took off flying across the pasture in front of the house. She jumped the big irrigation ditch and kept on running across the pasture. She then pulled a sliding stop, did the prettiest rollback to the right and ran that fat Quarter Horse right back the way he had come. She jumped the ditch again, slid to a stop in front of me, then very ladylike and daintily swung her legs to the side and slid down from the sidesaddle. She walked up to me, handed me the reins and said, "That, my dear, is how you ride sidesaddle."

My jaw was hanging down and I was shocked at seeing my eighty-year-old great-grandma ride like that. I asked her if she would teach me the art of riding aside that summer. Once again, she told me "No." For the second time that day, the look on my face must have softened her. She asked me, "Why in the world would you want to ride with both legs on one side when my generation fought to put our legs on each side?" I couldn't answer her. I only asked again if she would teach me to ride in that saddle.

Bless her heart, she did and we had a wonderful summer in 1971. I learned to ride and I liked it so much that I entered the local horse show in the fall. Unfortunately, Grandma had a stroke in late-summer and she passed away before she ever got to see me compete. Since that summer, I always ride in her honor and I know in my heart that she is watching from above and smiling every time I ride like a queen.

Dottie McDonald Linville

Trail Etiquette

There is a certain universally understood etiquette among trail riders. For instance, you don't run your horse up on another horse's rear end or gallop off without checking with the rest of the group first. And it is customary to shout out a warning to the riders behind you when you pass a potential hazard. By yelling "bottle!" or "wire!" or even "turtle!" you alert them to the obstacle in their path so that they can avoid it. The system usually works well, but not always.

I had been at the new barn only a summer, but had spent most of those weeks exploring the extensive trail system with new friends. Riding for hours on end in open spaces was a welcome change after years of being confined to a ring. I'd spent all that time showing and training, but now I felt that I finally was riding. My Appaloosa mare Geri had also settled into the new routine and was getting very trail-savvy.

One morning in early fall, a group of five of us headed out for a trail ride over terrain I was still unfamiliar with, but that the rest of the group knew well. At one point, the trail flattened and widened out, the perfect place for a gallop. The group started out at a good clip, with Geri and I bringing up the rear.

Then, ahead of me, I heard a cry of "hole!" I mentally thanked the rider for the warning and cast my eyes downward to watch out for the hole. Stepping into a hole while galloping could be disastrous for both horse and rider. A few seconds later, I heard another warning shout of "hole!" from a different rider, and I looked down with even more earnestness. Then, I heard a third shout of "hole!" this time from the rider just in front of me. Yet, as frantically as I scanned the ground, I still saw no signs of a hole.

I began to wonder, were they shouting "hole" or could it be something else? I looked up just in time to see a four-foot-tall metal *pole* rushing toward me. The pole marked a county-owned gas line and it had a huge sign on it, making it clearly visible to anyone who wasn't looking down for a hole. Had I not overreacted, I would have left Geri alone to take us safely past the pole. After all, she wisely had kept her eyes on where she was going and was on course to pass just to the left of the pole. But I panicked and tried to get a horse who was going at a full-out gallop to change direction in the space of four strides. All I succeeded in doing was to pull her off balance and even closer to the looming metal protrusion. As a last-ditch effort, I pulled my right foot out of the stirrup and bent my knee to draw my leg up, a move that can keep your knee from hitting the arena gate at the walk, but isn't nearly as easy at a gallop. As we flew past the pole, the center of my shin slammed into the metal bar.

My howl of pain brought the ride to a quick halt. I grabbed my throbbing, bleeding shin and muttered expletives punctuated with the word "pole," as the rest of the group looked on in confusion. "Didn't you hear me yell 'pole'?" someone asked. "Yes, but I thought you said 'hole.' I was looking for a hole, not a pole." I give the group credit for stifling their laughter until it was obvious I hadn't broken a bone.

Three years later, with the scar on my right shin fading, I tend to forget about my painful collision that fall morning. That is, until I'm out riding in a group with someone who does remember. On those days I hear the cries of "bottle!" and "wire!" and "large metal rod sticking straight up out of the ground, Christine!"

Christine Barakat

The Gift of a Dream

There was probably no greater horse lover on the planet. I subscribed to three horse magazines and my bedroom was wallpapered with photos, calendars, cutout pictures and paint-by-number artwork. A young teen, I lived, breathed and dreamed horses. I saved for weeks to buy a huge wall-sized poster of wild horses running through a river, their manes flowing and hooves flying—it was beautiful. I had found it on the back of my dad's *Enquirer* and had carried the ad around with me for ages until I had enough money to send away for it.

My obsession with horses was so great that I kept sugar cubes in my jacket pocket on the miraculous chance that I would somehow run into a horse I could befriend. More than anything, I wanted to ride. As consumed as I was with all things equine, I had never actually ridden a horse.

My parents had friends who owned horses, and although I was never allowed to ride them, we visited often and I always brought my sugar cubes and felt immense pride at my knowledge of the proper way to feed them: hand up, palm flat, trying not to squeal when the velvety, slobbery lips whisked them off my hand. It was the highlight of my week to visit them. I longed to throw my leg over the black one's back, sliding John Wayne style into place, winding my hands through the horse's mane and riding off into the sunset. Not that I even knew how to do it, but that didn't stop me from daydreaming.

My best friend Stacey was also a horse lover. Since the sixth grade, we had spent hours and days cutting out horse pictures for our walls, fantasizing of being grown, married and owning neighboring horse ranches, where we'd do nothing but ride to our hearts' content. No one but Stacey understood how much I longed to ride a real horse, (and a black one at that.) Stacey had been riding several times and I was green with envy as she described her days of riding with her family. I would have given anything to go with her even just one time. But we were poor and couldn't afford the rental fees, so I had to wait and dream.

The summer we were thirteen, Stacey and I made plans to go to Lake Comanche in northern California, an hour from where we lived. We were thrilled to be spending our first day on an outing without parents. We packed our bathing suits, lunches and hiking shoes and chattered every night about what we would do with the whole day to ourselves. The day finally came and Stacey's mother drove us to Lake Comanche. Stacey and her mother were both strangely quiet on the drive up and I caught them several times exchanging mysterious smiles and even giggling, as though there were some secret joke between them.

We finally arrived at the lake and Stacey's mother gave me a big hug. Then she said, "Have fun!" with twinkling eyes, and drove off, leaving us on the hot, dusty road that I knew didn't go to the swimming area.

"Where are we?" I looked at Stacey.

She just smiled and said, "C'mon." She walked down the dusty path and disappeared over a hill, leaving me wondering where on earth we were.

I ran to catch up to her and saw her standing next to a horse corral, her arms through the fence, happily petting a brown mare.

"Wow!" I scrambled down the hill and hopped onto the

fence rail, surveying the crowd of horses milling about in the shade of a great tree. It was an incredible scene for me. I had never seen so many horses in the flesh and I felt as if I were dreaming.

Stacey looked at me and just grinned. "Pick one," she told me.

"What?"

"Pick one. We're going to ride. I saved up so we could rent two horses all day!" She fairly exploded as she finally let her secret out.

I just stared. I couldn't believe that she was doing this for me. What kind of thirteen-year-old does this for a friend? It was an incredible gift. I couldn't believe that I was going to ride a horse. A real horse. Me. On a horse. All day. Wow.

I finally absorbed it all and threw my arms around her. We laughed and giggled and danced around. It was a golden moment that still brings tears to my eyes, twenty-five years later.

I looked carefully at the horses and spotted him. He was the horse of my dreams: black with gentle eyes and a flowing mane. I couldn't have wished for a more perfect horse. He was beautiful.

We told the man who ran the stable which horses we wanted, and even though my head was in the clouds, I listened to the rules and watched him saddle my dream horse. When he asked me if I knew how to ride, I nodded and hoped that what I'd read in magazines and books could be applied in real life. I was shaking.

The man gave me a leg up and told us where the horses could rest in the shade and drink at the river. I felt like I was in a movie. John Wayne, move over. The saddle creaked and I loved the sound. I loved it all: the horse smell, the dust we kicked up, the feel of the reins in my hands, even how sore my legs were getting. I was in heaven.

The day was a dreamy, sunny, perfect day. My horse was patient as I learned how to handle him and we got along from the start. I learned to canter and Stacey and I even raced through the hills, laughing blissfully and living out our dream. The day drew to an end and the sun splashed a brilliant wash over a golden day that I've never forgotten. In the years that have passed since that magical summer day, I've ridden many more times. But never has any gift meant more to me than that of a thirteen-year-old girl to her best friend. It was the gift of heart, of soul—the gift of a dream.

Susan Farr Fahncke

Confessions of a Horse-Show Father

It can be set down in four words the best of everything. The best hay, oats and water.

Sunny Jim Fitzsimmons

"For sale: Registered QH gelding. Shown by thirteen-year-old girl. To good home only."

I'd just walked in the door when Andrea, my eleven-year-old daughter, waved a newspaper in my face, the ad circled in bright red. With dramatic sighs, she announced that she absolutely could not face life anymore without a horse of her own. I thought we had solved the life-with-horse-crazy-daughter problem when I agreed to riding lessons at the local stable. But we both knew I would give in to Andrea eventually. I always did. I never could resist those golden ringlets circling her head like angel fluff, or her husky little voice telling me I was absolutely the best Daddy in the whole world.

And so I agreed, somewhat naively, that if we could find "something nice" in the neighborhood of $300, I'd pop for a horse.

The following Saturday, we drove out to see the QH gelding listed in the ad. Susan, Andrea's riding instructor, came along to make sure he would be a suitable mount for her student.

"Smooth-gaited and very responsive," she said after trying him out. "Yes, he is a suitable mount for a starter horse."

For Andrea, it was love at first sight.

"Oh, Daddy," she cried. "I just love Pancho. He is absolutely the one I want."

I reached for my checkbook, congratulating myself that we'd found a suitable mount, and I still had enough of my weekend left for a round of golf. I looked expectantly at the horse's owner. After all, how much could a starter horse cost?

"Thirty-five hundred dollars," he said, not even cracking a smile.

I gulped. Whatever happened to the "something nice for three hundred dollars" I thought we were pursuing?

"What's your best offer?" I asked. "This is more than I planned to spend on a starter horse."

"This is a registered Quarter Horse," he replied, his voice dripping with indignation.

Aha, so that's what QH meant.

"I'll think about it," I said.

The ride home was agonizing. In the back seat, Andrea shed elephant-sized tears as she waved a mournful good-bye to her suddenly beloved Pancho. But I remained stead-fast. We'd find a horse all right. But not for that kind of money.

Golf dates evaporated as we ran down every promising horse-for-sale ad. We drove fifty miles to follow up on the ad stating, "super disposition." We found a gentle-natured plow horse with a head a yard long and feet like dinner plates. The "green-broke but gentle" horse, we vetoed immediately when he knocked down his handler while trying to get out the barn door.

We ended up back at the home of Pancho, and I wrote out a check for 3,500 bucks. There went my new golf clubs. But my angel showered me with kisses. "You're the absolutely *best daddy* in the whole world."

Heck. Who needed new clubs? I could play another year with the old ones.

Like every father suddenly thrust into horse ownership, I learned that buying the horse was only the beginning. I hadn't even recovered from the $3,500 hit, when Andrea informed me that Pancho needed saddle, bridle, halters, brushes. At the saddle shop I discovered the prices of "proper" horse equipment to be on par with a trip to Disney World. Seven hundred, fifty dollars for a skimpy little saddle that looked like an oversized pancake.

"But it's a Stubben," Andrea sighed wistfully. "They're totally the best."

Well, if a horse of her own could keep my daughter's attention on four-legged creatures, rather than two-legged ones with raging hormones and body piercing, I was all for it. We emerged from the saddle shop loaded down with, among other things, the Stubben saddle and a checkbook now even lighter.

I admit, when watching Andrea ride her new horse for her lessons, I puffed up like a peacock, even though I didn't have a clue what she was doing. One day, the instructor mentioned a fun show at the stable, and would I like to enter Andrea and Pancho? One look at my daughter's face and, of course, I wanted to.

"I need a proper outfit now that I'm going to show," she announced. Back to the saddle shop. You guessed it. You don't find a proper outfit without another hefty swipe at the checkbook.

At the fun show, I stood at the rail watching horses rumble by, sending clouds of dust into my face, which was becoming the same color as the ring. Andrea emerged from her class, all smiles, clutching a dinky scrap of yellow ribbon. It seemed she had placed third in horsemanship (third out of four, but who's counting?). The radiant look on her face almost made me forget that I had turned down a complimentary round of golf at The Wilds to be there for her triumph.

More shows followed and, believe it or not, I was getting into this horse-showing stuff. In one class, Pancho suddenly broke into a gallop, lapping the field.

"That's my daughter on the brunette horse," I bragged to the woman next to me. "She's beating everybody."

"Way to go Andrea,'" I yelled as she flew by.

"She's supposed to be trotting," the woman sniffed and moved away.

My darling came out of that class ribbonless. One look at her tear-stained face and I knew I was in trouble big time. How could I have embarrassed her by yelling at her in front of the whole world? She could die, absolutely die. But there were other shows where she came home with ribbons and radiant smiles. Hugs for Pancho. Hugs for Daddy, too.

One day, Andrea told me about a Quarter Horse show in Hutchinson. One small problem. We needed a trailer. Back to the want ads. I found a used two-horse trailer and plunked down another 2,500 bucks.

"How do you plan to haul it?" the trailer seller asked.

It just happened he had a truck for sale. There went my plans for the new runabout for the lake cottage I had hoped to buy. But I had a show horse now and a daughter who thought I was wonderful.

The season progressed. I dropped more money and we accumulated more equipment and more ribbons. Andrea now competed in Western classes, as well as English, requiring a whole new complement of saddles, bridles and show outfits. And I was hooked, a helpless victim of the lure of the show ring: beautiful daughters, beautiful horses; every weekend a total commitment in time, money and energy. There were no more weekends at the lake or golf tournaments with the pros, and I didn't even care. When my daughter came out of the ring with a blue ribbon, I could hardly wait to sign up for another show. The scraps of colored ribbons hanging from the mantel came to about $500 per inch, I figured, but what the heck. We were going after that high-point trophy!

My addiction pumped along at an alarming speed as I made plans for the next year's season . . . a new trailer perhaps, with attached living quarters for the out-of-state shows . . . a better truck to pull the new trailer . . . possibly a new horse. As the riding instructor had said, Pancho was a suitable starter horse, but if we were serious about showing, we needed a better one (another unwritten rule in the horse business: the present horse is never good enough).

After two years of this crazy lifestyle, I came home one evening to see one of those two-legged boy creatures I had worried about, sprawled in my recliner watching the latest episode of *Star Trek*.

"I'm not going to the stables tonight," Andrea announced with one of her dazzling smiles. "Kevin and I have something else planned."

"What about Pancho? What about your lesson?"

"Janie's taking my lesson tonight. She's riding Pancho this weekend because Kevin asked me to the school dance."

It was then I noticed the dazzling smile was aimed at Kevin, not me. In spite of my efforts and the enormous holes in my bank account, my Andrea had sailed into the uncharted waters of puberty, deciding boys were more fun than horses and they smelled better. I wouldn't be watching my beautiful daughter in the ring anymore. No more bragging rights about owning an almost-champion show horse.

Gradually, I have conquered my addiction. I'm selling the equipment and recouping some of my losses. Part of me even looks forward to getting my own life back: the golf games and the cool runabout for the hoped-for lake cottage.

But what about Pancho? I'm still attached to that little brunette horse who totally took over my life for two years. With a lump in my throat, I placed the ad in the newspaper:

"For Sale: Registered QH gelding. Shown by thirteen-year-old girl. To good home only."

J.L. Lindstrom

More Chicken Soup?

We would love to hear your reactions to the stories in this book. Please let us know what your favorite stories were and how they affected you.

Many of the stories and poems you have read in this book were submitted by readers like you who had read earlier *Chicken Soup for the Soul* books. We publish at least five or six *Chicken Soup for the Soul* books every year. We invite you to contribute a story to one of these future volumes.

Stories may be up to 1,200 words and must uplift or inspire. You may submit an original piece, something you have read or your favorite quotation on your refrigerator door.

To obtain a copy of our submission guidelines and a listing of upcoming *Chicken Soup* books, please write, fax or check our Web sites.

Please send your submissions to:

Chicken Soup for the Soul
P.O. Box 30880, Santa Barbara, CA 93130
fax: 805-563-2945
Web site: *www.chickensoupforthesoul.com*

Just send a copy of your stories and other pieces to the above address.

We will be sure that both you and the author are credited for your submission.

For information about speaking engagements, other books, audiotapes, workshops and training programs, please contact any of our authors directly.

A Helping Hand

A portion of the proceeds from the sale of each copy of *Chicken Soup for the Horse Lover's Soul* will be donated to the Equine Rescue League, Inc. in Leesburg, Virginia. The Equine Rescue League (ERL) is a nonprofit organization that supports the responsible use of working, sport and pleasure horses, ponies, donkeys and mules. Their goals are to prevent the neglect or abuse of any equine, to offer educational programs to the community, and to provide shelter, rehabilitation and adoption for those animals in need of their services. You can contact ERL by calling (703) 771-1240, by visiting their Web site, *www.equinerescueleague.org*, or write to them at P.O. Box 4366, Leesburg, VA 20177.

For anyone wishing to volunteer, make a financial donation or use the services of a horse-adoption, equine-therapy, or rescue-and-rehabilitation program, as well as for those who have fallen on hard times and need a hand caring for their equine partners, we would like to direct you to our Web site, *www.horseloverssoul.com*.

Want to get more connected to horses? AQHA can help.

If the stories in this book have inspired you to take the next step and become more involved with horses, the American Quarter Horse Association (AQHA) can help through their 4aHORSE referral service. AQHA has several programs and offers real options for the horse-loving public, especially the casual horse lover who is thinking of taking the next step.

Whether you are planning a vacation and would like to include horses, or you need information on how to purchase a horse, find a trainer or vet, The American Quarter Horse Association is ready to help you discover how special horses can be. Call 1-877-4-A-HORSE or visit *www.4ahorse.com*.

Who Is Jack Canfield?

Jack Canfield is one of America's leading experts in the development of human potential and personal effectiveness. He is both a dynamic, entertaining speaker and a highly sought-after trainer. Jack has a wonderful ability to inform and inspire audiences toward increased levels of self-esteem and peak performance.

Jack currently has three wonderful horses living in his stable and rides with his wife Inga, his son Christopher, and his step-daughter Riley.

He is the author and narrator of several bestselling audio- and videocassette programs, including *Self-Esteem and Peak Performance, How to Build High Self-Esteem, Self-Esteem in the Classroom* and *Chicken Soup for the Soul—Live.* He is regularly seen on television shows such as *Good Morning America, 20/20* and *NBC Nightly News.* Jack has co-authored numerous books, including the *Chicken Soup for the Soul* series, *Dare to Win* and *The Aladdin Factor* (all with Mark Victor Hansen), *100 Ways to Build Self-Concept in the Classroom* (with Harold C. Wells), *Heart at Work* (with Jacqueline Miller) and *The Power of Focus* (with Les Hewitt and Mark Victor Hansen).

Jack is a regularly featured speaker for professional associations, school districts, government agencies, churches, hospitals, sales organizations and corporations. His clients have included the American Dental Association, the American Management Association, AT&T, Campbell's Soup, Clairol, Domino's Pizza, GE, ITT, Hartford Insurance, Johnson & Johnson, the Million Dollar Roundtable, NCR, New England Telephone, Re/Max, Scott Paper, TRW and Virgin Records. Jack is also on the faculty of Income Builders International, a school for entrepreneurs.

Jack conducts an annual eight-day Training of Trainers program in the areas of self-esteem and peak performance. It attracts educators, counselors, parenting trainers, corporate trainers, professional speakers, ministers and others interested in developing their speaking and seminar-leading skills.

For further information about Jack's books, tapes and training programs, or to schedule him for a presentation, please contact:

Self-Esteem Seminars
P.O. Box 30880
Santa Barbara, CA 93130
phone: 805-563-2935 • fax: 805-563-2945
Web site: *www.chickensoupforthesoul.com*

Who Is Mark Victor Hansen?

In the area of human potential, no one is better known and more respected than Mark Victor Hansen. For more than thirty years, Mark has focused solely on helping people from all walks of life reshape their personal vision of what's possible. His powerful messages of possibility, opportunity and action have helped create startling and powerful change in thousands of organizations and millions of individuals worldwide.

He is a sought-after keynote speaker, bestselling author and marketing maven. Mark's credentials include a lifetime of entrepreneurial success, in addition to an extensive academic background. He is a prolific writer with many bestselling books such as *The One Minute Millionaire, The Power of Focus, The Aladdin Factor* and *Dare to Win,* in addition to the *Chicken Soup for the Soul* series. Mark has also made a profound influence through his extensive library of audio programs, video programs and enriching articles in the areas of big thinking, sales achievement, wealth building, publishing success, and personal and professional development.

Mark is also the founder of MEGA Book Marketing University and Building Your MEGA Speaking Empire. Both are annual conferences where Mark coaches and teaches new and aspiring authors, speakers and experts on building lucrative publishing and speaking careers.

His energy and exuberance travel still further through mediums such as television (*Oprah,* CNN and *The Today Show*), print (*Time, U.S. News & World Report, USA Today, New York Times* and *Entrepreneur*) and countless radio and newspaper interviews as he assures our planet's people that *"you can easily create the life you deserve."*

As a passionate philanthropist and humanitarian, he's been the recipient of numerous awards that honor his entrepreneurial spirit, philanthropic heart and business acumen, including the prestigious Horatio Alger Award for his extraordinary life achievements, which stand as a powerful example that the free enterprise system still offers opportunity to all.

Mark Victor Hansen is an enthusiastic crusader of what's possible and is *driven* to make the world a better place.

Mark Victor Hansen & Associates, Inc.
P.O. Box 7665 • Newport Beach, CA 92658
phone: 949-764-2640 • fax: 949-722-6912
FREE resources online at: *www.markvictorhansen.com*

Who Are the Coauthors?

DR. MARTY BECKER is passionate about his work fostering the affection and connection between animals and people we call, "The Bond." Marty coauthored; *Chicken Soup for the Cat & Dog Lover's Soul, Chicken Soup for the Pet Lover's Soul* and *The Healing Power Of Pets,* which was awarded a prestigious silver award in the National Health Information Awards for 2002.

Dr. Becker is featured on ABC-TV's, *Good Morning America,* writes a weekly column for over 350 Knight Ridder newspapers and hosts two new nationally syndicated radio programs, *Pets Unleased* a two-hour live talk radio program and a two-minute pet vignette, *The Pet Update.*

A contributing editor for *Dog Fancy* and *Cat Fancy,* the world's most popular pet magazines and a frequent contributor to *Reader's Digest,* Marty is the Chief Veterinary Correspondent for *Amazon.com* and has been featured on ABC, NBC, CBS, CNN, PBS, and in *USA Today, USA Weekend, The New York Times, The New York Daily News* and *Washington Post.*

Marty and his family enjoy life in Northern Idaho and share Almost Heaven Ranch with two dogs, six barn cats and five Quarter Horses; Chex, Gabriel, Glo Lopin, Pegasus and Sugar Babe.

Contact Marty Becker at:
P.O. Box 2775 • Twin Falls, ID 83303
Phone: 208-734-8174 • Fax: 208-733-5405
Web site: *www.drmartybecker.com*

GARY SEIDLER founded U.S. Journal and Health Communications with his coauthor and former partner, Peter Vegso, over twenty-five years ago. Retiring in 1999 and relocating to Los Angeles, Gary is a Thoroughbred owner and breeder who enjoys the energy and enthusiasm of racing. Gary devotes his time to expanding his nonprofit foundation, which sponsors a summer camp for at-risk kids and to producing documentaries which promote health, wellness and recovery.

Contact Gary Seidler at:
1450 Bella Drive • Beverly Hills, CA 90210
Phone: 310-246-1639• Fax: 310-246-1797
e-mail: *gary@horseloverssoul.com*

PETER VEGSO continues to grow the businesses he and Gary founded over 25 years ago. Health Communications' first *New York Times* bestseller appeared on the list in 1985. Recognized by *Publishers Weekly* as the #1 Self-Help Publisher, HCI is guided by their mission statement "Making a difference in the lives of our readers and the people they come in contact with."

Diversification within Peter's businesses includes; a professional publishing and conference division, U.S. Journal Training, which serves the mental health community, and Reading, Etc., a custom design and architectural elements company which includes two retail stores.

Peter enjoys his 140-acre Thoroughbred breeding and training facility in Ocala, Florida, where the hardest working manager in the world, Chuck Patton, handles daily operations. It is their intention to not only win the Kentucky Derby but also the Triple Crown before their spirits leave this planet.

Contact Peter Vegso at:
3201 SW 15th Street • Deerfield Beach, FL 33442
Phone: 954-360-0909• Fax: 954-360-0034
e-mail: *peter@horseloverssoul.com*

THERESA PELUSO met Peter Vegso and Gary Seidler in 1981 and got acquainted with horses through the partner's interest in Thoroughbreds soon after. Prior to that, her only connection to horses was her Irish grandmother, who loved the ponies and jumped at the chance to move to Florida in the early 1960s to be near Hialeah Park.

While working on this book, Theresa was introduced to these intuitive animals through the eyes of the writers. Through their stories she came to understand what a powerful bond we all share with horses, and developed a spiritual connection to the community of warm, generous people who graciously shared their world—and the incomparable world of horses—with her.

Contact Theresa Peluso at:
3201 SW 15th Street • Deerfield Beach, FL 33442
Phone: 954-360-0909 • Fax: 954-418-0844
e-mail: *theresa@horseloverssoul.com*

Contributors

The stories in this book are orginal pieces or taken from previously published sources, such as books, magazines and newspapers. If you would like to contact any of the contributors for information about their writing or would like to invite them to speak in your community, look for their contact information included in their biography.

Lynn Allen says it's her mother's fault that she's horse crazy. As a toddler, she threw Lynn on a horse instead of carrying her around the barnyard while she did chores. Since then horses, cows and agriculture have been Lynn's passions. A free-lance writing career helps support those expensive habits.

Judy Pioli Askins grew up behind Belmont Racetrack where she developed her lifelong love for horses. She has enjoyed twenty-seven years in television: writing, producing, directing, acting, teaching and coaching. Her devotion to Parelli Natural Horsemanship, and her special brand of humor keep her workshops and coaching sessions in great demand.

Christine Barakat is a lifelong rider who gave up hunter equitation for combined training. She later gave that up for trail riding with friends. She has worked in both the United States and Europe as a riding instructor, stall mucker and groom. She is currently an editor with *Equus* magazine.

Teresa Becker resides in Bonners Ferry, Idaho with her veterinarian husband Marty and two beautiful children, Mikkel, age seventeen and Lex, age thirteen. A physical education teacher with a master's degree in athletic administration, Teresa now dedicates her time exclusively to enjoying life with her family which includes cats, dogs, fish and horses.

Denise Bell-Evans and her husband Dave raise horses for English disciplines on their Amarugia Horse Farm. The horses include stallions, brood mares, youngstock and riding horses. Denise, whose active lifestyle was curtailed when diagnosed with MS, concentrates on enjoying farm life and family, which includes her five children and her grandson.

Francis Brummer was born on a farm west of Dunlap, Iowa. After nine years sailing in the Navy, he became a professional cartoonist in 1954. Having sold over 35,000 cartoons worldwide in his career, Francis is semi-retired and draws about six hours per week. We appreciate his collaboration with Steve Sommer on the cartoons in this book.

Sissy Burggraf was born in a small town in southern Ohio. After working for eight years as a vetinary assistant she opened Lost Acres Horse Rescue and Rehabilitation. LAHRR was established in 1994 as an alternative to euthanasia, slaughter or abandonment for abused, neglected or injured horses. Visit LAHRR at *www.geocities.com/sblahrr*.

Renie Szilak Burghardt was born in Hungary, and came to the U.S. at the age of fourteen. A free-lance writer, her works has appeared in *Chicken Soup for the Christian Family Soul* and many other anthologies. She lives in the country and loves nature, animals, gardening, reading and spending time with family and friends.

Sharon Byford-Ruth is the author of, *The Arabian: A Guide for Owners*. With her business partner, Betsy Teeter, Sharon operates Legendary Arabians, home of the champion Arabian stallion, Aul Magic+/, at Caliente, California. Sharon is the proprietor of Book Stall, an Internet store for books about Arabian horses, new and out-of-print *www.horsebooks.com*

Gary Cadwallader lives in Kansas City, Missouri. He raises American Saddlebreds. His stories have appeared in *Canter* magazine, *Literary Potpourri* and *The Phone Book.*

Patricia Carter is a forty-nine-year-old horse lover from Toronto, and mother of a now eleven-year-old horse-crazy daughter. Sharing their love of horses has been an incredible experience for her family, one which has given them countless hours of laughter and pleasure.

Jennifer Chong and Donovan, a young Hanoverian, have been partners since he turned three. Donovan is making a name for himself in dressage, but he also enjoys jumping and hacking out. Jennifer is a student at Harvard Law School and her first book, *To the Nines: A Practical Guide to Turnout and Competition Preparation*, will be available in 2003.

Diana Christensen is the owner of Shalimar Farm in Louisiana where she enjoys the company of four Andalusians, one Welsh pony and one Peruvian Passo. Her moniker, "Diana Dancing Horses," gives you an indication of what she enjoys most about her equine dressage partners—they're great dancers!

Diane M. Ciarloni has served as editor for *Speedhorse/The Racing Report* for the past eighteen years. She has written *Legends I*, which focuses on legendary horses of the past, and contributed to *Legends II* and *III*. She's a consistent contributor to *Guideposts* and its series of animal anthologies. Her work has been cited in *Best American Sportswriting*.

Michael Compton is the editor of *The Florida Horse* magazine, published by the *Florida Thoroughbred Breeders' and Owners' Association* in Ocala, Florida. Michael serves on the Board of Directors of the Public Education Foundation of Marion County and is married with two children. Some of his earliest memories were of attending the races and watching Affirmed in 1978–79 with his late father and grandfather.

Mary Gail Cooper is a school librarian who lives in North Carolina with her husband of twenty-seven years. Two of their children have started college; one daughter lives at home. They still have three horses and an assortment of cats and dogs.

Jan Jaison Cross has enjoyed her career as a jockey, riding in several hundred races at tracks in New Jersey, Pennsylvania and Florida, as well as her time as a trainer and bloodstock agent. In 1999 she began teaching high school in the horse country of Marion County, Florida. Today Jan rides the trails on her 17 hand ex-race horse Cookies.

Barbara A. Davey and her husband live in Verona, New Jersey. She works in public relations and fund-raising and is the author of *Does God Have E-mail?* a collection of inspirational short stories. Barbara's story "A Legacy in a Soup Pot," appears in *Chicken Soup for the Woman's Soul*. Her e-mail address is *wisewords2@aol.com*.

Kris DeMond lives in Pennsylvania with five Percherons, two Appaloosas, an American bulldog, an ornery kitten and a thirty-nine-year-old pony who is still used in the lesson ring-when *she* "feels like it." Kris runs a small riding/driving lesson business and offers the carriage for weddings and other fun affairs.

Basil V. DeVito Jr. has more than twenty years experience in the sports business. He has held positions in the NBA, The National Thoroughbred Racing Association, the WWE and the XFL. He also authored the *New York Times* bestseller, *WrestleMania: The Official Insider's Story*.

Christina Donahue and her husband Don own Stonecrest Farm, located just outside of Charlotte, North Carolina. They raise rare Egyptian Arabian horses, which are renowned for their beauty, intelligence and loving dispositions. Chris is in the process of writing a series of children's books about the adventures of an Arabian filly.

Susan Farr Fahncke is the author of *Angel's Legacy* and has stories in many *Chicken Soup* and other inspirational books. She is the founder of 2TheHeart.com and teaches online writing workshops. Susan can be reached through her Web site or at *editor@2theheart.com*.

Lisa B. Friel is a free-lance writer and photographer based in Alexandria, Virginia. Her work appears in popular publications including *USA Equestrian, Virginia Horse Journal* and *Horse & Hound*. Lisa is an amateur rider and competes in the Ladies Sidesaddle Division.

Kimberly Gatto is a professional writer and lifelong horse owner. She is the author of *Michelle Kwan: Champion on Ice* and *An Apple A Day*, with two additional sports titles currently in publication. Kim enjoys dressage and eventing with her two horses Chutney and Grace.

Bill Geen, a retired executive, lives with his wife Barbara in upstate New York. Bill's love of horses started sixty years ago. He shares his experiences with horses and lessons he's learned along the way in letters to his grandchildren which will be featured in a new book entitled *Letters from Grandpa*.

Debra Ginsburg, a staff writer for *California Thoroughbred* since 1985, is a member of the National Turf Writers Association. Her work has appeared in *The Chronicle of the Horse, Backstretch* magazine and *Winning Connection*. She is working on a mystery novel involving horse racing and a book about California's equine millionaires. Contact Debra at *debieg@ctba.com* or (800) 573-2822.

Bill Goss appears monthly on Animal Planet and his stories have been published in *Reader's*

Digest, Maxim, Daily Word, Chicago Tribune. He wrote *The Luckiest Unlucky Man Alive* and *There's a Flying Squirrel in My Coffee: Overcoming Cancer with the Help of My Pet.* Contact him at P.O. Box 7060, Orange Park, FL 32073 or *www.BillGoss.com.*

Barbara Greenstreet is a writer, educator and "horse mom" living in western Washington state with a menagerie of children and pets ranging from honeybees to horses. She has been published in *Northwest Baby & Child, WritersLounge.com, WeeOnesMagazine.com, In the Family, Big Apple Parent, Wildland Firefighter, Massage,* and *Horse & Rider.*

Starr Lee Cotton Heady, granddaughter of homesteaders, now lives in Florida. She is a Certified Horsemanship Association (CHA) instructor in English and Western riding and a licensed mental health counselor. In addition to sharing her private life with horses, StarrLee uses horses in private practice and provides equine assisted psychotherapy for a nonprofit organization (*www.traversekids.org*).

Laurie Henry, a former "Dove Girl" for Dove Soap, shares life in Aqua Dulce with her husband of twenty-six years. They have four children and two grandchildren. As the kids have grown and moved on with other interests, horses remained in Laurie's life and especially in her heart. Her best friend for the past eight years has been Sonny Boy.

Kimberly Graetz Herbert is the editor of *The Horse: Your Guide to Equine Health Care,* a monthly not-for-profit magazine focusing on the health, care and management of horses. A contributing editor to *The Blood-Horse,* the Thoroughbred industry's oldest weekly news magazine, she is the mother of two and lives on a small farm in Central Kentucky.

Debbie Hollandsworth's close-knit family consists of her husband, two teenagers and three brothers. They live adjacent to her parents' 240-acre family farm, where they raise miniature horses and background cattle, and stable the horses and teams the family enjoys riding. Debbie owns a restaurant at the local sale barn.

Paula Hunsicker is a horse breeder and a free-lance writer. Her work has appeared in the National Reined Cow Horse Association's publication, *The Stock Horse News,* and *Performance Horse* magazine.

Jennie Ivey lives in Cookeville, Tennessee, and owns and rides both Quarter Horses and Tennessee Walking Horses. She is a columnist for the Cookeville *Herald-Citizen* newspaper and the coauthor of *Tennessee Tales the Textbooks Don't Tell,* a collection of stories from Tennessee history. She can be contacted at *jivey@multipro.com.*

Dr. Michael Johnson is an author, national columnist and cowboy. His latest release, *Cowboys and Angels,* was named Best Non-Fiction Book of 2002 by the Oklahoma Writers' Federation. Michael lives on a horse farm in Idabel, Oklahoma.

Carol Wade Kelly, her husband Jeff and son Taylor manage a small ranch that consists primarily of retired racehorses. Starflite retired from the track as a four-year-old and after a very successful breeding career, died peacefully in his stall of heart failure in 2000 at the age of twenty-nine.

Roger Dean Kiser lives in Brunswick, Georgia, with his wife Judy, also a writer. Roger is the author of *Orphan, a True Story of Abandonment, Abuse and Redemption.* He has authored and/or coauthored twelve books in four countries. Visit Roger and enjoy his work at: *www.rogerdeankiser.com/index.htm.*

Jeanette Larson was born with the "horse-lovers virus." After spending years starting colts, training dressage horses, galloping race horses and then retraining dressage and race horses for new careers, Jeannette retrained herself and is now a magazine editor. She enjoys her four remaining horses while trail riding on the weekends.

Edwina Lewis is a nonfiction writer and a writing instructor at the University of Houston-Clear Lake. Her inspiration is her family—husband, children, grandchildren, dogs, rabbits and chickens—and her large extended family. She is currently working on *For My Father's Love,* a book about father/daughter relationships.

J.L. Lindstrom realized a lifelong dream when the family moved to a ten-acre "ranchette" where they have raised and shown horses for over twenty years. Now a golden-ager, the ground is too hard and the bones too brittle for riding, so the love for horses is expressed through writing and painting.

Dottie McDonald Linville lives with her husband and two sons in Indiana where she raises Blue Black Arabian horses. You can meet Dottie and her Arabians at *www. juniperdesertarabians.com*. Dottie is a certified instructor and judge with the World Sidesaddle Federation, Inc. and president of the Hoosier Ladies Aside. For more information on riding sidesaddle visit *www.hoosierladiesaside.com*.

Vikki Marshall owns Destiny Farms Sporthorses, breeder of Thoroughbred performance horses. She successfully competes in hunter and dressage, breeds and trains her own horses and retrains horses who have been neglected. Currently writing a novel about experiences in the equestrian sports industry, Vikki has received honorable mention in the 2002 *Olympiad of the Arts* short-story competition.

Tom Maupin, Stacy's dad, is forty-three years old and was introduced to the wonderful world of horses by his wife Crystal. Horses have introduced them to a wonderful network of friends, and have given them the opportunity to continually improve their marriage, lives and health. They trail ride as often as they can.

Tiernan McKay is a free-lance writer based in Scottsdale, Arizona. Her magazine articles focus mainly on health, travel, Christianity, sports, and of course, horses. She continues to ride and show hunter/jumpers.

Jennilyn McKinnon grew up loving horses in the small town of Mendon, Utah, and the love affair hasn't ended. A wife, busy mother of five children, registered nurse and author, Jennilyn has had several stories and poems published. She is currently working on her first book.

Nancy Minor lives with her husband David in the Texas Hill Country.

John L. Moore is an award-winning journalist and novelist who ranches north of Miles City, Montana, with his wife Debra. They are ordained ministers and the parents of two grown children, Jess and Andrea.

Sandra Moore is a mother, pastor's wife and writer—in that order. She is a contributor to *Living Miracles: Stories of Hope from Parents of Premature Babies* from St. Martins Press. If you have a premature child, she'd love to hear from you. E-mail her at *smoore@innernet.net*.

Ky Mortensen was raised on a small alfalfa farm and now lives in Lexington, Kentucky with his wife and son. After serving a two-year Mormon mission in Spain, he returned to the U.S. to complete studies in equine science at Colorado State University. Currently he is Director of Industry Relations for the American Association of Equine Practitioners.

Jeff C. Nauman, Edgar Brown's grandson, is a rangeland management specialist and logistical officer for wildland fire suppression efforts in Idaho. He and his family raise Quarter Horses and compete locally in reined cow-horse, team penning and 4-H events, while promoting AJKyle's Meat Co. (*ajkylenauman@orofino-id.com*), their grass-based, meat-protein business.

Marla Oldenburg lives in Seattle with her daughters Jackie and Chelsea. Their horses Rosie, Mona and Mesa live on a friend's farm, where they all ride and operate a horse camp in the summer. Marla spent many years competing on the West Coast hunter/jumper "A" circuit. Her favorite horsey times are now spent bringing kids and horses together.

Pat Parelli's career is highlighted with diversity, from rodeoing to teaching Olympic competitors. Pat is applauded worldwide for his system of natural horsemanship that uses psychology, love, language and leadership. When not traveling the globe teaching people to teach horses, Pat is at home in Colorado or Florida with his wife Linda.

Mark Parisi's *Off the Mark* comic panel has been syndicated since 1987 and is distributed by United Media. His *Rim Shot* comic panel appears weekly in *Billboard* magazine. Mark's humor also graces greeting cards, T-shirts, calendars, magazines, newsletters and books. Lynn is his wife/business partner and their daughter Jenny contributes with inspiration (as do three cats).

Thirza Peevey began writing two years ago after decades in the horse industry and four years as a teacher. She has been published in several *Guideposts* series, including *Listening to the Animals* and the upcoming *Be Not Afraid*. She is currently working on two novels and was a 2003 winner of the Guideposts Biennial Writer's Contest.

Thomas Peevey has worked in the Thoroughbred industry since leaving high school in England in 1971. While in England, he worked for his uncles, Fred and John Winter, to learn the Thoroughbred business. He moved to Kentucky in 1981 to continue his career. Tom has been published in the *Guidepost* series, *Listening to the Animals*.

Tom Persechino is Senior Director of Marketing for the American Quarter Horse Association, where his mission is to connect people to horses. Growing up in Oklahoma, Tom was an active 4-H show participant who later went on to work at Oklahoma City's Remington Park Racetrack before joining AQHA in 1993.

Rhonda Reese, a former schoolteacher, is a columnist and staff writer for her community newspaper in Jacksonville, Florida. Married to her minister husband for almost three decades, Rhonda can usually be found at home spoiling her nine rescued—once skinny—strays, now basking in luxury as happy fat cats.

Boots Reynolds has designed greeting cards for Leanin' Tree Publishing for over twenty years, and his cartoons are a monthly feature in *Western Horseman* magazine. Boots is a founding member of the Cowboy Cartoonists International, and is currently working on a series of humorous paintings depicting historical events and rodeos in the West, as well as a recipe book on beans at his studio near Hope, Idaho. Visit his Web site: *www.sagebrushes.com*.

Jane Douglass Rhodes grew up riding American Saddlebreds in Louisville, Kentucky. She now lives in rural San Diego on Janra Ranch with her true love, three dogs and—alas!—no horses. There, she writes personal narratives and cocreates Gourditos and other whimsical artwork. E-mail her at *janedogranch@mindspring.com*.

Jan Roat is a ranch wife, mother, grandmother, free-lance writer and photographer. She has written and published with *Pine Ridge Rambling* for five years, before that with *West Bench Meandering* for twenty years. Jan is also field editor for *Country* magazine and associate editor for *Taste of Home* magazine.

Monty Roberts travels the world demonstrating his nonviolent approach to starting horses. Monty is the author of three bestselling books: *The Man Who Listens to Horses, Shy Boy* and *Horse Sense for People*. His latest release, *From My Hands to Yours* is a training manual using Monty's methods. Visit his Web site: *www.montyroberts.com*.

Robin Roberts, who has been a horse-show mom for many years, is now entering the show ring herself in the APHA Novice Amateur Division. She spends much of her time riding and writing, and finds them both challenging and rewarding. Robin is currently writing stories for children.

Melody Rogers-Kelly began dancing professionally at age fifteen. She performed on Broadway in *A Chorus Line*, on CBS television's *Two On The Town*, traveled to over sixty countries, and has appeared in movies. Melody is a certified riding instructor for the North American Riding For the Handicapped Association (NARHA), and enjoys a successful real-estate career in Beverly Hills.

Chris Russell-Grabb is a registered maternity nurse, and has been involved with horses for over forty years. She currently owns and operates, VS Belgians in Sodus, New York, with her husband Dennis. They raise and show registered Belgian draft horses, mini donkeys and Spotted Drafts.

Mitzi Santana and her two daughters live in Virginia. Mitzi was raised around horses, riding before she could walk. Mitzi has enjoyed many disciplines in riding, but admits her favorite is a trail ride with her family. She is an active 4-H volunteer for the Horse N Around Fluvanna 4-H. Contact her at *msantana@cstone.net*.

Cristina Scalise has volunteered with the Equine Rescue League of Leesburg, Virginia, for the past twelve years. Although she dearly loves all of the fifty or so hoofed residents of the League, Albert has a very special place in her affections. Ms. Scalise invites interested readers to visit the League in cyberspace at: *www.equinerescueleague.org*.

Jerri Simmons-Fletcher is an aspiring author and songwriter. She has two American Quarter Horses, Lily and Tucker, whom she loves very much. She is currently attending college and is directing a youth praise team.

Steve Sommer has been a cartoon gag writer for about twenty years. He currently writes and publishes an agricultural advertising cartoon calendar called *Country Chuckles*, and lives in

Merna, Nebraska. We appreciate Steve's collaboration with Francis Brummer on the cartoons in this book.

Carole Y. Stanforth is a freelance writer whose romance with horses began twenty-five years ago when her husband loaned money to a struggling local businessman. He defaulted and repaid the loan with four Quarter Horses, which ultimately became a herd of thirty, including miniature horses. Her husband says it was the most expensive business deal he ever made.

Joyce Stark was born and lives in Scotland. She has traveled widely throughout Europe and the U.S. and says her main hobby is "people." She has had her works published in the *Chicago Tribune, Saturday Evening Post, Rosebud, Highlander* and many publications in the U.K. Contact her via e-mail: *joric.stark@virgin.net.*

Stephanie Stephens is a print and broadcast journalist based in Laguna Niguel, California, is an expert in the equine and pet genres. She syndicates a radio show, *Animal Magnetism,* and hopes for an end to pet overpopulation. With a master's in journalism from New York University, Stephens's work has appeared in more than thirty magazines. You can visit Dan Shaw from "The Guiding Sight" at *www.danandcuddles.com.*

Gayle Stewart has seen her work published in *Equus, Horse Illustrated, Horse of Course, Oklahoma Today, Dallas Morning News, Kansas City Star, The Daily Oklahoman* and *The Denver Post.* In 2001, one of Gayle's pieces was honored with the USA Equestrian Media Award for best magazine article in an equestrian publication.

Dave Surico is a sports writer who lives in the northwest suburbs of Chicago with his wife Lynn and their two children.

Marguerite Suttmeier was a flight attendant for United Airlines for thirty-two years until she retired to a ranch in North Idaho with her husband of thirty-one years. Tom and Marguerite have four horses, one dog (a heeler named Josie Wales) and four cats. She enjoys cross-country skiing, walking, drawing, reading and quilting.

Sandra Tatara has two grown sons, and expects her first grandchild in August 2003. She paints in several mediums, raises registered Quarter Horses, which have competed in pole bending and barrel racing events, and enjoys trail riding. Sandra has had several short stories published and has a novel awaiting publication.

Tom Truitt was born in Burlington, North Carolina in June 1940. Tom has been a teacher, assistant principal, principal, assistant superintendent and superintendent of schools. Currently he is serving as executive director of the Pee Dee Education Center (a consortium of eighteen school districts) in Florence, South Carolina. Tom is married with one son and two grand-daughters.

Tracy Van Buskirk has been riding horses since she was small. She loves both horses and creative writing but has never done either professionally. Tracy describes the opportunity to bring both interests together for this book as "a wonderful experience." She can be reached at *kriksubnav@hotmail.com.*

Theresa (T.C.) Wadsworth-Peterson raises APHA and AQHA horses. Her father put her on her first horse and now, some forty years later, T.C. trains horses and raises her own foals, as well as mini-Schnauzers. She enjoys rodeos and cow horse competitions, and especially being in the middle of her remuda.

Janie Dempsey Watts has strong roots in northwest Georgia, where she and her family enjoyed their ponies and horses. She has been published in newspapers and magazines, and recently completed *Moon Over Taylor's Ridge,* a novel with elements of romance, mystery and Cherokee history. She holds two journalism degrees.

Janice Willard, DVM, MS, is married with two children and lives on a small farm in Idaho shared by horses, goats, sheep and llamas. The household also includes several dogs, cats and a very officious parrot. Janice and her husband are veterinarians and Janice studies animal behavior, is passionate about music and loves to sing. Contact *Janice at janwill@turbonet.com.*

Robin Traywick Williams is chairman of the Virginia Racing Commission and the author of *Chivalry, Thy Name Is Bubba,* a collection of humorous, general-interest newspaper columns. She lives on a farmette in Crozier, Virginia, with her husband Cricket, their daughter Katie, and a full complement of cats, dogs, horses, fish and groundhogs.

Craig Wilson's column, *The Final Word,* appears Wednesdays in *USA Today.* Random House published a compilation of his columns, *It's the Little Things: An Appreciation of Life's Simple Pleasures,* last year and he is at work on his second book. He lives in Washington, D.C., with his partner Jack, and their dog Murphy. Contact Craig at *cwilson@usatoday.com.*

Woody Woodburn is an national award-winning sports columnist for *The Daily Breeze,* in Torrance, California. Featured in *The Best American Sports Writing 2001* and *Chicken Soup For The Baseball Fan's Soul,* he is married with two teenagers and is currently working on breaking three hours in the marathon (even if he has to do so on horseback). E-mail him at *Woodycolum@aol.com.*

Laurie Wright is happily married to a Special Forces soldier and the mother of two beautiful girls. Owner of a small breeding and training operation in Colorado, Laurie's passion is Arabians because of their incredible generosity of spirit, extremely engaging personality, and how easy they are to train.

Gerald W. Young (1908–2001) wrote stories throughout his life. In public relations for over forty years, he lived out his retirement on the Ohio farm where he and his wife, Carrie, raised ponies. Gerald was a former director of the Welsh Pony Society of America. We thank Carrie for sharing his work with readers.

The President's Escort. Reprinted by permission of Gayle Stewart. ©2003 Gayle Stewart.

Fly, Misty, Fly! Reprinted by permission of Janice Willard, DVM, MS. ©2002 Janice Willard, DVM, MS.

Like Pegasus, Laughter Takes Flight. Reprinted by permission of Barbara A. Davey. ©2003 Barbara A. Davey.

At the End of His Rope . . . a Winner! Reprinted by permission of Stephanie Stephens. ©2002 Stephanie Stephens.

Don't Fence Him In. Reprinted by permission of Tom Persechino. ©2001 Tom Persechino.

Regalito. Reprinted by permission of Diana Christensen. ©1999 Diana Christensen.

Touched by an Equine. Reprinted by permission of Melody Rogers-Kelley. ©2002 Melody Rogers-Kelley.

Going Where No Horse Has Gone Before. Reprinted by permission of Carole Y. Stanforth. ©1993 Carole Y. Stanforth. This story is an adaptation of a story which first appeared in *The Western Horse* issue number 62 in June 1993.

Billie Girl. Reprinted by permission of Laurie Henry. ©2002 Laurie Henry.

Passages of Time. Reprinted by permission of Mary Gail Cooper. ©2002 Mary Gail Cooper.

Aul Magic. Reprinted by permission of Sharon Byford-Ruth. ©2002 Sharon Byford-Ruth.

A Horse in the House. Reprinted by permission of Diana Christensen. ©1999 Diana Christensen.

Side by Side. Reprinted by permission of Sissy Burggraf. ©2000 Sissy Burggraf.

My Friend Bob. Reprinted by permission of Diane M. Ciarloni. ©2001 Diane M. Ciarloni.

The Magic Carpet Pony. Reprinted by permission of Robin Traywick Williams. ©1999 Robin Traywick Williams.

Handled with Care. Reprinted by permission of Sandra Moore. ©2002 Sandra Moore.

To Chutney, with Love. Reprinted by permission of Half Halt Press, Inc. ©2000 Kimberly Gatto. Previously published in *An Apple A Day.*

New Life for Rosie. Reprinted by permission of Marla Oldenburg and Bill Goss. ©2002 Bill Goss.

Lessons from Lou. Reprinted by permission of Edwina Lewis. ©2002 Edwina Lewis.

Bit by the Bug Thanks to Finger Paint. Reprinted by permission of Tiernan McKay. ©2002 Tiernan McKay.

His Special Gifts. Reprinted by permission of Debbie Hollandsworth. ©2003 Debbie Hollandsworth.

Horse at Harvard. Reprinted by permission of Jennifer Chong. ©2002 Jennifer Chong.

Tall in Faith. Reprinted by permission of Mitzi Santana. ©2000 Mitzi Santana.

Ride the Yule Tide. Reprinted by permission of Jan Jaison Cross. ©1996 Jan Jaison Cross. Originally published as *Home for Christmas* in the December 1996 issue of EQUUS and subsequently in the EQUUS bestselling *TrueTale* book, *Straight from the Heart* ©1997.

Racehorse Poor. Reprinted by permission of Carol Wade Kelly. ©2003 Carol Wade Kelly.

Happy Horses. Reprinted by permission of Michael Compton. ©2002 Michael Compton.

Down the Stretch He Comes, Hanging on for Dear Life. ©2002 *USA Today.* Reprinted with permission.

Allez Mandarin. Reprinted by permission of Thomas Peevey. ©2003 Thomas Peevey.

The Fastest Mule in the West. Reprinted by permission of Debra Ginsburg. ©2002 Debra Ginsburg.

Da Hoss. Reprinted by permission of Ky Mortensen. ©2003 Ky Mortensen.

Girly's Gift. Reprinted by permission of Dave Surico. ©2003 Dave Surico.

The Destiny of Edgar Brown. Reprinted by permission of Jeff C. Nauman. ©2002 Jeff C. Nauman.

A Tap on the Shoulder. Reprinted by permission of Basil V. DeVito Jr. ©2002 Basil V. DeVito Jr.

Unbelievable Kentucky Derby Tale. Reprinted by permission of Woody Woodburn. ©2002 Woody Woodburn.

The Funny Cide of Life. Reprinted by permission of Chris Russell-Grabb. ©2003 Chris Russell-Grabb.

Of Great Horses and Men. Reprinted by permission of Boots Reynolds. ©2003 Boots Reynolds.